Acclaim for Jessica Warner's
The Incendiary

"Jessica Warner's *The Incendiary* shows you just how good history can get: a tour de force of original thinking; deep immersion in a lost world (or in this case, underworld); prodigious empathy with its hapless antihero; and exhilarating, knife-sharp writing that concedes nothing to fiction writers at the top of their game. Don't be fooled by its modest size and ostensibly eccentric subject; this is rich, ambitious history, executed in literary fireworks: a small glory and a joy to read."

—Simon Schama, author of *Citizens* and *A History of Britain*

"Magical . . . well-nigh perfect, almost clinically exact . . . the scale and scope of Jessica Warner's ceaseless fascination with human failings is prodigious and hugely impressive."

—Simon Winchester, *The Globe & Mail* (Toronto)

"[An] invaluable narrative . . . one of the pleasures of this book lies in the revelation of an almost forgotten world of landladies, spies, dockyard workers, tavern owners, and the rest of the then mundane world. It is a panorama of hidden eighteenth-century life, as fresh and as vivid as if it occurred yesterday."

—Peter Ackroyd, *The Times* (London)

"Excellent . . . precise, admirably researched, and written in an engagingly wry style."

—*Times Literary Supplement*

"[An] engrossing study . . . the real pleasure of this book comes from Warner's lively and fluid style. It is a mark of her considerable skill as a historian."

—*The Guardian*

"As an historian Jessica Warner has rare gifts—she makes the past come alive without the condescension of hindsight, and she writes beautifully. Her excavation of John the Painter from eighteenth-century documents shows that she also has an eye for a good story."

—Brenda Maddox, author of *Rosalind Franklin: The Dark Lady of DNA* and *Nora: The Real Life of Molly Bloom*

"This is a fascinating tale of a bizarre incident of the American Revolution. George the Third's England, it seems, was as susceptible to terror panic as George Bush's twenty-first-century America. Jessica Warner writes history carefully and well."

—Russell Baker, author of *Growing Up*

"[Warner] is a sure guide to the lower strata of Georgian society, and deftly conjures up the atmosphere and anxieties of late-eighteenth-century England. . . . This is a fascinating story, and Warner's telling of it is informative and stimulating."

—Noel Malcolm, *The Sunday Telegraph*

"Jessica Warner spins a riveting tale of the night side of the American Revolution: the story of the poor, ambitious, unscrupulous, unlucky man who tried to decapitate the British war machine."

—Richard Brookhiser,
author of *America's First Dynasty* and
Gentleman Revolutionary

Praise for Jessica Warner's
Craze: Gin and Debauchery in an Age of Reason

"One of the year's most entertaining and timely books."

—Paul Collins, *The Oregonian* (Portland)

"Social history at its gimlet-eyed best."

—*Kirkus Reviews* (starred review)

"[Jessica Warner's] prose is both lively and accessible, and she keeps the narrative moving along."

—Jonathan Yardley, *The Washington Post*

"Entertainingly told . . . Warner writes with great flair. . . . [She] is especially good at bringing to light the role of women in the gin craze."

—*Austin American-Statesman*

"Provocative . . . Warner has done impressive research. . . . *[Craze]* is a crisp, detailed review of the history of the place and period."

—*The Sun* (Baltimore)

"Fascinating . . . Warner evokes a vivid picture of eighteenth-century London, complete with its public hangings and slums that seemed to overflow with gin."

—*The Seattle Times*

"An intoxicating concoction . . . Warner has a particular genius for statistics and anecdotes that leave your jaw hanging."

—*The Globe & Mail* (Toronto)

THE INCENDIARY

ALSO BY JESSICA WARNER

Craze: Gin and Debauchery in an Age of Reason

THE
INCENDIARY

The Misadventures of John the Painter, First Modern Terrorist

---

A brief account of his short life,

From his birth in Edinburgh, *anno* 1752,

To his death, by hanging, in Portsmouth, *anno* 1777.

To which was once appended

A meditation on the eternal foolishness of young men.

JESSICA WARNER

THUNDER'S MOUTH PRESS · NEW YORK

THE INCENDIARY

The Misadventures of John the Painter, First Modern Terrorist

AVALON
publishing group incorporated

Published by
Thunder's Mouth Press
An Imprint of Avalon Publishing Group
245 West 17th Street, 11th Floor
New York, NY 10011

Copyright © 2004 by Jessica Warner

This book was originally published in October 2004 under the title *John the Painter*.
First paperback printing October 2005.

LIBRARY OF CONGRESS CATALOGING-IN-PUBLICATION DATA IS AVAILABLE.

ISBN: 1-56025-733-4
ISBN13: 978-1-56025-733-2

10   9   8   7   6   5   4   3   2   1

Book design by Sara E. Stemen
Printed in the United States
Distributed by Publishers Group West

To Barbara S.F.
of course

"Do beating drums, and flying colours, purge a band of robbers and murderers of all guilt? Does it signify as to the nature of the crime, whether he who commits it wears a red coat or a brown? whether he holds a painter's brush in his hand, or a general's truncheon? . . . are we, because our armies are not so large nor so well armed or disciplined as the *English*, and their clean-handed friends the *Hessians*—are we, I say, to sit down, and suffer our throats to be cut tamely? Every American, who believes his cause to be a just one, ought to exert himself in whatever way he can be serviceable to his country. If in the field, let him carry arms; if not, let him light a torch."

> From *A Short Account of the Motives which Determined the Man, Called John the Painter; and a Justification of his Conduct; Written by himself, and Sent to his Friend, Mr. A. Tomkins, with a Request to Publish it after his Execution* (1777)

"It is evident from the accounts received from Portsmouth and Bristol, that there are in this kingdom some desperate partizans of the American rebels, who finding that Great-Britain is likely to gain a decisive victory in the field, are endeavouring, by the most hellish plots, to undermine her glory, and prevent her success. Of all bad characters, an incendiary is the foulest. He acts as an assassin armed with the most dreadful of mischiefs, and in executing his diabolical purposes, involves the innocent and the guilty in the same ruin. May every being so lost to humanity live an object of conscience-goading pain, and die an object of universal contempt!"

> From *The General Evening Post* (18–21 January 1777)

"The subtlety, and shrewdness of the offender, bespoke him the man of ability, while his conduct in other respects betrayed him a fool."

> From *The Life of James Aitken, Commonly Called John the Painter* (1777)

CONTENTS

A MANDA FOREMAN, in the introduction to her stunning bio-graphy of Georgiana, duchess of Devonshire, admits to being more than a little seduced by her subject.[1] I admit to no such thing. The subject of my biography was an ordinary man, and a poorly behaved one at that. He broke into people's houses and held up stagecoaches. When he worked—and this he did as little as possible—he showed up late and stole from his employers. Once he shot a dog. He even raped a woman who was innocently tending her sheep. Then, in the autumn of 1776, his behavior took a decided turn for the worse. He tried to burn down two English towns. The first was Portsmouth and the second was Bristol. Had he not been stopped, he would have burned down each of the dockyards that kept the Royal Navy afloat, and had he succeeded, the American Revolutionary War might very well have ended in 1777 and not in 1783. An American official, moreover, had given the plot his blessing. That man was Silas Deane, Congress's representative in France.

James Aitken, alias James Boswell, alias James Hill, alias James Hinde, is best remembered for the fires that he set. The men who tried and punished him for his crimes knew him only as John the Painter. He was a painter in the most ordinary sense of the word. He did not paint portraits. He did not dabble in watercolors. Instead, he painted houses and the occasional sign. This made him one of the "common people," and unlike the duchess of Devon-shire, he was destined to be ignored while alive, and forgotten once dead. John the Painter was determined not to let that happen to him. If someone had stopped to ask him what he was rebelling against, he would have said obscurity. He was, to quote from one of his confessions, bent on "accomplishing some great achievement."[2] He did this by setting fires in places where they would be noticed.

He succeeded by half. He was noticed, but in the end he was not remembered. For the briefest of time, for four heady months, he was on everyone's mind. George III received daily briefings from his ministers. Newspapers printed sensational stories, some true, some not. In Parliament, a bill was rushed through to suspend habeas corpus; such measures, it was argued, were justified when a nation was at war and when there were "traitors unknown to the public; perhaps ... incendiaries, the secret agents of America lurking in this kingdom...."[3] The Bow Street runners were sent after him. Citizens formed patrols, convinced that neither they nor their possessions were safe.

* * *

John the Painter was not quite twenty-five years old when he was hanged. In just four years, he saw more of his world than most people saw in an entire lifetime. Not including his time in Edinburgh, where he lived until the age of twenty, he spent perhaps a year all told in London, several months in Philadelphia, perhaps a month in Paris, and untold days in countless towns and villages all across England. By the end of his life, he had, by his own boast, committed a crime in almost every county in England.[4] He was forever in motion; he was young.

My pursuit of John the Painter took me on my own mad ramble across Britain, from Edinburgh to London, and from there to Portsmouth and Bristol. Everywhere I incurred debts. It was

Michael Gunton of the Portsmouth Museum and Records Service who gave me the idea to write about John the Painter. For this and much more I am eternally grateful. I bothered so many other people: Alison Brown of the Bristol Record Office, Margaret Cooke and Nicola Pink of the Hampshire Record Office, Sarah North of the National Archives of Scotland, Margaret Peat and Fraser Simm of George Heriot's School in Edinburgh, and, if truth be told, the entire staff of the National Maritime Museum. Not once did they laugh at me—not to my face at least. They should have. Each was competent and kind in equal measure.

And finally, this book got something that books rarely do these days: good old-fashioned editing. That unhappy task fell to not one but three people: Patricia Kennedy of McClelland & Stewart, Jofie Ferrari-Adler of Thunder's Mouth Press, and Andrew Franklin, the publisher of Profile Books. Each put up with a good deal of prattle, some spoken, most written. Without them, the book would be naked in places and overdressed in others, but without my agent, the deft and resourceful Katinka Matson, the book simply would not be.

B UT WHAT did he look like? He stood five feet seven inches tall, one inch shorter than the typical soldier in George Washington's army, but exactly the same height as the typical British recruit of the time.[1] Silas Deane, the American envoy to France, described him as "a diminutive looking man...of near middle size for height." But then again, Deane was judging him by the well-fed standards of colonial America.[2] William Baldy, a rope-maker at the royal dockyard in Portsmouth, said only that the man he had seen was five feet seven inches tall, and let it go at that.

The man's face was covered with red freckles, and his eyelids were "whitish," a feature sufficiently distinctive to merit mention in advertisements that offered a reward for his capture. His face was thin, his complexion fair, and his hair of a reddish or "light sandy colour."[3]

There was some disagreement about his build. Most of the people whom he met in his mad rambles across the English countryside described him as "thinnish," but one, a Mr. White, described him as "rather lusty than slender," *lusty* being defined in Johnson's *Dictionary* as "stout; vigorous; healthy; able of body."[4] But White had met him back in 1775, shortly after the young Scot had returned from America, and before he embarked on a journey that would take him to almost every major town in southern England, and from there to France and back again. When his journey finally came to an end, in the tiny Hampshire village of

Odiham, James Aitken (for that was his real name) was weary, thin, and, in the words of one witness, "altered to a great deal."[5]

Somewhere in his many journeys he met with a terrible accident. On his chest, just below his right shoulder, was a large scar where a bullet had pierced his flesh. He could not resist showing people this scar and making up a story about it. He had been wounded "in the wars," he said.[6] This was rubbish. James Aitken had never seen combat. It is true that he joined the British army on at least three separate occasions, but each time he deserted. What he did not tell his listeners was the truth: that he was a thief and a highwayman, and that someone had shot him in the course of a robbery gone wrong. The story provides us with an important clue: in his own mind's eye, he was neither a thief nor a painter. He was a man of proven courage.

That he even survived this wound tells us that he was a very healthy man. Time and time again he cheated death. Back in Edinburgh, where he was born, a fifth to a quarter of all infants never lived to see their first birthday.[7] In London, where he committed his first crimes, countless immigrants sickened and died within a few years of moving to the capital. In the ships that carried men and women to the New World, passengers and crews dropped like flies from typhus, typhoid, dysentery, and yellow fever.[8] And in the various prisons and lockups where he spent the last six weeks of his life, inmates "who went in healthy" were "in a few months changed to emaciated dejected objects."[9] Not James Aitken. He survived even in prison, fending off typhus (otherwise known as "jail fever"), only to die at the end of a rope. Perhaps Mr. White was right after all. James Aitken was decidedly "lusty."

In England, where he spent most of his adult life, people laughed at him, sometimes behind his back, sometimes to his face. His problems began the moment he opened his mouth. Almost everyone immediately took him for a Scot, although one witness, a man with no ear for accents, pegged him as an "Irishman."[10] Scot or "Irishman," it was all the same: he was distinctly unwelcome in England. If William Baldy, the ropemaker, was right, Aitken also had "a little stammering in his speech," or what Silas Deane described as "a faltering and tremulous tone."[11]

He was very particular about his appearance, and this invariably aroused suspicion. A Captain King, who employed him in January or February of 1776, described him as a "macaroni painter," which is to say that he dressed like a dandy and "appeared, for his occupation, above the common degree."[12] Mrs. Boxell, his first landlady in Portsmouth, found it odd that he "changed his clothes every day." So, too, did the publishers of *The General Evening Post* and *The St. James's Chronicle*, both of whom reported on Aitken's sartorial eccentricities.[13] William Baldy could scarcely believe his eyes. First he saw Aitken wearing "worsted stockings, speckled or mixed, which were very dirty as were his shoes"; then, just four hours later, he saw him wearing clean white stockings and clean shoes.[14]

People also found it odd that Aitken wore his own hair. Men of all classes commonly wore wigs, and yet Aitken, who was otherwise very fussy about his appearance, did not. "I had to look around a long time in a church or other gathering of people before I saw anyone with his own hair," wrote Pehr Kalm, a Swedish botanist who visited England in 1748. Even "clodhoppers," he added, "go through their usual everyday duties all with perukes on the head."[15] Not James Aitken. In the winter of 1776, when he was working in a small town just outside Portsmouth, he wore his hair clubbed, that is, tied up in a queue and stiffened with tallow and perhaps with powder as well.[16] By November, he had abandoned this style in favor of a more natural look. The queue was gone, and his hair, to quote Silas Deane, "hung loose on his shoulders, and down his neck."[17] The

JAMES AITKEN.
Alias, John *the* Painter.

John the Painter at the time of his trial, as pictured in The London Magazine, 1777. *It is tempting to think that this is an exact likeness of Aitken. Certainly it matches the description posted by the Navy Board. The face is thin (some might say haggard), his hair hangs freely, and his clothes are those of a working man.* COURTESY OF THE PORTSMOUTH MUSEUM AND RECORDS SERVICE.

The MACARONI PAINTER, or BILLY DIMPLE sitting for his PICTURE.

The Macaroni Painter, or Billy Dimple Sitting for his Picture, *1772, by Richard Earlom (1743–1822), after Robert Dighton (circa 1752–1814). A former employer, picking up on Aitken's numerous affectations, described him as a "macaroni painter." In this spoof, the macaroni painter is of course the painter himself (Dighton), but in the sitter we can see Aitken's fantasy self. Note in particular the exaggerated fan-tailed hat that identifies its wearer as a fop.* COURTESY OF THE LEWIS WALPOLE LIBRARY, YALE UNIVERSITY.

change was radical, deliberate, and highly significant. It marked Aitken as a new type of man: the Romantic revolutionary. The young men who enlisted in Washington's army wore their hair this way.[18] So, too, did the Jacobins, although they went one step further and wore their hair short. "This coiffure," Jacques-Pierre Brissot wrote in 1790, "is the only one which is suited to republicans: being simple, economical and requiring little time, it is care-free and so assures the independence of a person; it bears witness to a mind given to reflection, courageous enough to defy fashion."[19]

Aitken had one other affectation: he liked to wear a decidedly foppish hat. The hat that he chose was fan-tailed, so-called because its back flap, which was semicircular in shape, stood up straight; the crown, in turn, was all but hidden by two side flaps.[20] The effect was very flashy and was made flashier still by Aitken's habit of wearing his hat at a jaunty angle, or, as William Baldy put it, "cocked genteelly."[21]

The overall effect, however, was anything but genteel. He was working-class and he looked it. Deane was unimpressed: "His dress no way recommended him at Paris, nor would in the lower stations of life prejudice him anywhere." Deane's valet was unimpressed: "You never saw a worse looking fellow in your life." Edward Evans, a humble soldier, was unimpressed. How was the defendant dressed? the Crown's prosecutor wanted to know. "In a brown duffel surtout coat, rather shabbily," Evans answered.[22]

Everyone, starting with Deane's valet, remembered the musty brown coat. The other thing they remembered was the bundle that he toted wherever he went. In it were all his worldly belongings, starting with the socks and shoes that had attracted William Baldy's attention. Several times, fearing that he might be caught, he was forced to abandon his bundle. Each time, he left behind clues. There were shirts and shoes and dirty socks, and there were the items that he used to set fires—matches, gunpowder, nitre, and turpentine.

And there were books. He was forever reading—pamphlets, books, newspapers, anything that fell into his hands. Some he stole and some he bought. In Portsmouth, he left behind three books: *The Art of War and Making Fireworks, as Practised by the Army of the King of France*, an "English *Justin*," and Ovid's *Metamorphoses*.[23] After fleeing Bristol, he managed to amass yet another bundle, and in it, yet another "little library," this time consisting of Voltaire's *Henriade* and an unspecified number of pamphlets, all pro-American.[24] It was an odd assortment, one that identified its owner as a man whose ambitions and intellectual curiosity vastly exceeded his social horizons. The assortment says something else, something just as important: James Aitken, the man in the musty brown coat, drank from the same waters as the great figures of the Enlightenment. He stood, it is true, downstream from Voltaire, Montesquieu and Diderot, from the *philosophes* and the odd ways in which they read their own ambitions and political agendas into the texts of classical antiquity. But he stood there nonetheless.

The same man who was forever reading was also forever losing his temper. He was prickly, got into fights, and in general did the sorts of things that the *Diagnostic and Statistical Manual of Mental Disorders* (DSM), the standard diagnostic reference of the American Psychiatric Association, now associates with "intermittent explosive disorder." This particular condition, the DSM tells us, is characterized by "several discrete episodes of failure to resist aggressive impulses that result in serious assaultive acts or destruction of property"; such outbursts, moreover, are "grossly out of proportion to any precipitating psychosocial stressors." Hence Aitken's many tantrums and outbursts.

But is it so simple? A person with a mental disorder is assumed to be acting in a way that is at odds with other people's behavior, but was Aitken? By eighteenth-century standards, his outbursts are not all that unusual; nor do they necessarily offer any real insights into his personality.[25] This is illustrated by an incident that very nearly occurred just after Aitken had set fire to the rope house at Portsmouth. This was in 1776. He had bought some matches from a chandler (her name was Elizabeth Gentell), and almost all of them turned out to be defective. He was furious, and for a fleeting instant, he contemplated returning to her shop and avenging himself by firing into her windows.[26] Such things happened all the time in eighteenth-century Portsmouth. Sailors rioted; feuding neighbors took justice into their own hands; and homeowners woke up to find that all of their windows had been smashed in. There had already been five such incidents in 1776, the most recent having occurred in the middle of October. The plaintiff was Elizabeth Hall, and the defendants were Anne Robinson and her daughter Elizabeth. First they had beaten up Hall, and then they had broken the windows to her house.[27]

Aitken also drank a great deal, sometimes starting early in the morning, and often keeping at it throughout the day. Does this mean that he was an alcoholic, or that his judgment was impaired by alcohol? Not necessarily. By eighteenth-century standards, his drinking was unexceptional, and if he went about his day in a slight alcoholic haze, so did a good number of other men, women, and children.[28]

Only occasionally do we hear Aitken's own voice—in the transcripts of his trial and in the recollections of the various people he ran into in the last five months of his life. We know a fair amount about James Aitken, but that does not mean we know him. And what we do know is riddled with gaps. There are whole years lost to view, followed by days in which every detail comes into sharp focus—what he drank, what he wore, what he said, and so forth. Such days repay the telling, but the years in which his life was hopelessly ordinary are no less important. When he vanishes from sight, I have filled in the gaps as best I can, drawing on the work of social historians, and on the words and records of contemporaries whose lives at different points paralleled his. Some are common criminals; some are travelers setting out for the New World; and still others are felons waiting to hang—ordinary men and women whose lives and experiences were harrowing beyond our imagining. Always the goal has been the same: to place him in his world as he found it, with its many limits and few possibilities.

* * *

There were two constants in his life: war and overpopulation. His own short life was bracketed by two wars: the Seven Years' War, which ended in 1763, and the American Revolutionary War, which began just twelve years later, in 1775. The Seven Years' War is important because Britain emerged from it the undisputed power of its day. Britain did not have the largest or the best army. And it had less than half the population of its nearest rival, France. But it had two things that its rivals did not. The first was the Royal Navy, and the second was a vast infrastructure dedicated to keeping its ships fit for service. It was the Royal Navy that had carried armies to Louisbourg, to Quebec City, to Havana, to Madras, and to Manila; and it was the Royal Navy that had prevented the French from supplying their own remote outposts with men, ammunition, and food. After two French fleets, one from Toulon and the other from Brest, had been defeated in rapid succession, nobody dared to attack the Royal Navy on the high seas; still less did anyone dream of idling its ships by destroying the dockyards that kept them afloat.

Other powers had navies and the facilities to support them. But none could match the efficiency of the royal dockyards at Portsmouth, Plymouth, Chatham, Woolwich, and Deptford. Without these, the Royal Navy would not have been the military wonder of its day.

It could not last. No sooner had Britain humiliated its rivals than it became the empire that everyone loved to hate. Its enemies took heart when relations between Britain and its American colonies started to deteriorate, and they cheered when America at long last declared its independence from Europe's mightiest empire.[29] Unemployed aristocrats from across Europe besieged the American delegation to Paris, assuring them, in the stilted

words of one, of their wish to go "to your country, in hopes of finding an opportunity to use my sword in the cause of the liberty
against the oppressors."[30]

The American Revolution appealed to many people on both
sides of the Atlantic, but it appealed to bored young men most of
all. It was a cause that excited Nathan Hale, Alexander Hamilton,
and the Marquis de Lafayette, and it was a cause that attracted thousands of young men to Washington's army, while keeping thousands more from joining the British army.[31] And it was a cause that
excited young James Aitken, giving his life meaning and his youth-
ful energies a purpose. Each of these young revolutionaries had
been influenced by the great ideas of the Enlightenment, and
each, in the way of the Romantics, was intent on remaking those
ideas in his own image. They read and they dreamed and they read
some more, ceaselessly comparing themselves to the heroes of classical antiquity. "The great acquisitions of Rome, Greece, and
Athens, had their place in my mind," Aitken was later quoted as saying. "I can't say but I felt from thence the desire of accomplishing
some great achievement."[32] It is a pretty picture: a generation of
young heroes in the making, each going off to war, and each thinking noble thoughts, mostly about himself.

But when they took the time to look around, they saw that
there were hundreds of thousands of other young men just like
themselves. That brings us to the second grim constant in Aitken's
life. The population was growing at an unprecedented rate, and as
it grew, real wages sank in some regions and stagnated in others.[33]
Everywhere there were young people, and nowhere were there
enough jobs. In Scotland, the population grew from perhaps
1,265,000 in 1755 to just over 1,608,000 by 1801, this despite
extremely high levels of emigration. In England, the population
grew by nearly three million, from perhaps 5,943,000 in 1755 to

more than 8,664,000 by the turn of the century.[34] For those at the bottom of the ladder, the implications were dire. Fewer would be self-employed, and more would spend their lives as dependent wage-earners, never earning quite enough to support both themselves and a family.[35] And even as they scrambled to find work, the nature of work would be changing for the worse, requiring fewer skills and less education.[36] The cards were stacked against James Aitken even before he was born, and if he was to transcend his class and his destiny, he would need to be more than just smart: he would need to be very lucky.

CHAPTER ONE

His Boyhood

HE WAS not born John the Painter. He was born James Aitken, in Edinburgh, on the twenty-eighth of September 1752. A week later, on the fourth of October, he was still alive and his name was entered into the parish register.[1] For the first several weeks of his life, his parents, George and Magdalen, regarded his existence with a certain degree of skepticism, waiting to see whether he would in fact live. Their skepticism was justified. Anywhere from a fifth to a quarter of all infants born in Edinburgh died before reaching their first birthday, and nearly half of these died within four weeks of being born.[2] The Aitkens themselves had already had seven children, and after James they would have four more. The family was large even by the prolific standards of the time—in Edinburgh at least, the typical family numbered perhaps six in 1779—and with each addition the Aitkens became a little poorer.[3]

George worked as a smith. He did tolerably well, for somewhere along the line he managed to save enough money to become a burgess.[4] As a smith, he belonged to the Incorporation, or guild, of Hammermen, whose meeting place, in the chapel of St. Mary Magdalen, was just a few blocks away from the family's home in the Old Town.[5] Membership in an incorporation meant that the family could count on its members for disbursements of food and coal in hard times, and even more importantly, it meant that the Aitken boys could apply for admission to George Heriot's Hospital, a nearby orphanage school, in the event of their father's death.[6] George Aitken was no doubt literate, but not excessively so, and he was possessed of Vulcan-like strength. Smiths, it was observed in 1761, "require but little learning, for reading, writing, and common arithmetic are sufficient, but they should have great strength of body...."[7] Slight instead of burly, and enamored of books instead of work, James was in many ways his father's physical and intellectual opposite.

His mother, *née* Magdalen Boswell, was the daughter of a house painter, and she moved up just slightly in the world when she married George Aitken in 1741.[8] She was to outlive her husband by twenty-one years, and her son James by three, dying in 1780. In 1759, just two months after George's death, she gave birth to their twelfth and last child.

The family was large, its quarters were cramped, and precisely because of their uncomfortable proximity the children were probably never very close to each other. It was this way in most families. Children came one after the other, left home at an early age, and had little or no contact with the brothers and sisters whom they left behind.[9] Aitken himself would leave home in April of 1761, at which time he was taken in at Heriot's, and in 1767 he was farmed out as an apprentice to a local painter. He probably moved in with his new master, although the practice had ceased to be universal by the eighteenth century.[10]

Historians squabble endlessly over whether early modern mothers had any particular fondness for their children—after all, they had so many of them, and many of these were destined to leave home at an early age, never to return—but Aitken seems to have been fond enough of his mother.[11] This, at least, can be inferred from a note that he sent just before he was to be hanged, asking its recipient to "write to my sorrowful mother concerning my unhappy fate; but in the softest terms possible, as her grief I know will be very great on hearing of it."[12] This much we can say with confidence: if his mother had no time for him, and if his early years were unhappy and he spent most of them working instead of playing, he was no worse off than most.[13]

The family occupied a flat on Robertson's Close, just off the Cowgate. It was here that Aitken spent the first eight and a half years of his life. The building in which he grew up was probably six or more stories high, with a family living on each floor. (Today, most of the buildings in the area are nine stories high, the number that is typically given in eighteenth-century descriptions of the so-called "lands," or high houses, of the Old Town.) The ground floor was almost certainly occupied by a shop, with the better-off families in the building occupying its upper stories, above the noise and stench of the alleyway below. In its heyday, long since past, the Cowgate had been "the polite part of the town"; by Aitken's day, the nobles and government officials who had once built their houses there were long since gone, and the neighborhood was easily the poorest and most densely populated in Edinburgh.[14] Sir Walter Scott, who was born not far from the Aitkens's, provides this description: "The houses on each side of the lane were so close, that the neighbours might have shaken hands with each other from the different sides, and occasionally the space between was traversed by wooden galleries, and thus entirely closed up."[15]

Everywhere there were people, and there was not a moment in his childhood when he did not hear or see them. Robert Louis Stevenson, writing more than a century after Aitken's death, described the neighborhood as "some Black Hole of Calcutta." It was the sort of place where "houses sprang up story after story, neighbour mounting upon neighbour's shoulder," where it was "scarce possible to avoid observing your neighbours," where "high words are audible from dwelling to dwelling, and children have a strange experience from the first; only a robust soul, you would think, could grow up in such conditions without hurt."[16]

Mostly it was dirty. Excrement, most of it tossed from on high, clogged the narrow lanes, and pedestrians picked their way around it as best they could. It was this, more than anything else, that embarrassed Boswell when he set out to show Johnson his hometown. That was in 1773, by which time the problem was, to use Boswell's phrase, "much abated"; even so, "from the structure of the houses in the Old Town, which consist of many storeys, in each of which a different family lives, and there being no covered sewers, the odour still continues."[17] Edward Topham, who visited Edinburgh just one year later, had to agree. The stench was unbearable: "such a concatenation of smells I never before was sensible of; it has been sometimes so powerful as to wake me, and prevent my sleeping till it was somewhat lessened."[18]

At times it must have seemed to young Aitken that he lived in a falling world. Chamber pots were emptied into the streets below; refuse was hurled out windows; masonry became dislodged and fell on unwary pedestrians; and sometimes entire buildings—old, rickety, and weighted down with too many souls—came tumbling down. The year 1751 marked a turning point. That was the year when the entire wall of a house collapsed, killing young Edward Reynolds. This was too much for the town council. It ordered an inspection of the more perilous buildings in the Old Town, several of which were subsequently demolished.[19] A year later, just one month before Aitken was born, the council turned its back on the Old Town for good. It would henceforth put its energies into building a new town, one with "spacious streets and large buildings, which are thinly inhabited."[20]

But that part of Edinburgh, with its stately squares and orderly crescents, has nothing to do with our story. We mention the New

Town only because it—and not the Old Town—came to be associated with the Scottish Enlightenment.[21] To the extent that Aitken
imbibed the ideals of that glittering movement, he did so from
afar, from within the dark recesses of what was still very much a
medieval city.

* * *

He had a normal childhood. If he suffered, so, too, did everyone
around him. There were several years in which the Aitkens may
have had need of the primitive insurance scheme offered by the
Hammermen. In 1756, when Aitken was just four, Scotland was
wracked by dearth, and in 1762, 1763, 1765, and 1766, harvest
failures again forced up the price of food.[22] In 1763, there were
food riots in Edinburgh, although by this time Aitken was already
boarding at George Heriot's Hospital, where he was assured of
three meals a day.

His diversions were few, hard, and mirthless, starting with the
raucous celebration of the king's birthday. In Aitken's day, these
celebrations were still relatively tame, but even then they were
marked by heavy drinking, ostensibly to the king's health.[23] On
these occasions ordinary people reaffirmed a personal—if
improbable—relationship with their distant and not-very-person-
able monarch. These celebrations, with their pageantry, cannon-
ades, and colorful military displays, were young Aitken's first contact
with his king. He was eight when George III succeeded George II,
and he had no reason to hate either man. The Jacobite uprising of
'45 was a distant memory, and in any event, had never been popular
in Edinburgh.[24] The union with England, moreover, had been good
to the Scots. They earned, it is true, less than the English, but they
were earning more than their ancestors ever had; their sons were

finding their way into the government, into the officer corps of both the army and the navy, into the empire's many outposts; and their economy was growing faster than the English—as were their towns and cities.[25] If they did not love their king, they needed him, and that was reason enough to be loyal.

Public hangings were another source of grim entertainment, although they were far less common in Scotland than in England and Wales.[26] As a young boy, Aitken would almost certainly have witnessed the occasional execution; indeed, he could hardly have avoided them, as the Aitkens lived very near the Grassmarket, the open space where criminals were hanged and cattle bought and sold.[27]

At least once a week, along with the entire Aitken brood, he attended church at Greyfriars. Outside, in its famous churchyard, were reminders of Scotland's unhappy past. To the southwest

OPPOSITE, LEFT: *The Flodden Wall, with Heriot's in the background.* OPPOSITE, RIGHT: *Robertson's Close today. James Aitken was born in a tenement on or off this alley.* LEFT: *Greyfriars Churchyard. Aitken would have played among the tombstones as a boy. His father George was buried here in 1759.* PHOTOGRAPHS BY REESE WARNER.

stood the enclosure where some 1,200 Covenanters had been confined in 1679, while to the west stood the ruins of the Flodden Wall, which had been built in haste and panic after the Battle of Flodden in 1513. Beyond the old wall lay Heriot's. Its boys had their own pews in the church, and as a very young boy Aitken saw them on innumerable occasions, each dressed in a uniform of "sad russet cloth."[28]

In 1759, his father died and was himself buried in a remote corner of the Greyfriars churchyard. His death left Magdalen the head of a large and impoverished household. In many instances, widows were able to carry on in their husband's businesses, but in Magdalen's case this was clearly impossible.[29] As a result, both she and the children still under her care probably slipped still further into poverty. At some point, she may have moved in with one of her adult children, in which case she would have found herself looking after a whole new generation of infants and children.[30] The family became poorer, but it managed to cling to respectability nonetheless, with one daughter, also named Magdalen, marrying a goldsmith in 1767.[31] This, for the orphaned daughter of a smith, was a major step up in the world.

The loss of his father, aside from its obvious financial implications, probably had only a fleeting impact on Aitken's emotional development. There were countless children who had lost one parent or both—hence the establishment of institutions like Heriot's— and even in households untouched by death it was a common practice for boys, and to a lesser extent girls, to leave home at an early age, the poorer the earlier.[32] Once they did so their fathers and mothers ceased to play a central role in their lives. Losing his father placed young Aitken at an economic disadvantage, but it did not in and of itself mark him as a tragic figure. If anything, he may have viewed his father's early death as a mixed blessing, for without it he would not have been admitted to Heriot's.

This happened in April of 1761, just two years after his father's death. He was not yet nine years old. With Heriot's, his future suddenly seemed bright. His inevitable entry into the world of work was postponed (until 1767, when he started his apprenticeship), and he was to acquire a first-rate education, with the prospect, if he excelled, of ultimately going on to the University of Edinburgh. Heriot's owed its existence to a bequest left by George Heriot in 1624, and it had been housing and educating poor boys for just over a century. To be considered for admission, a boy had to be poor, seven years of age or older, and fatherless.[33] There was one other criterion: the boy's father had to have been a burgess. Aitken met all of these criteria, but so, too, did countless other unfortunate boys. There were always more applicants than places for them, and the few who were admitted could count themselves very lucky indeed.

His intellectual attainments were incidental to the admissions process. In the nineteenth century at least, the school's governor was asked only to give "his opinion of the boy's general attainments for his age," while his guardians were asked questions designed to see whether the candidate fell within the mandate of the founder's will.[34] Aitken was presented by Sarah Sandilands, the eldest daughter of a wealthy merchant and the wife of Thomas Durham of Boghead.[35] In 1695, the Sandilands had made a substantial donation to the school, in return for which the family was entitled to "name and present two male children" every year, provided that they conformed "to the statutes of the said hospital," were under "ten years and six months of age," and were otherwise "clean and wholesome." It is unknown how Aitken or the plight of his family came to the attention of Sarah Sandilands; at the very least, her intervention on behalf of young James tells us that the Aitkens had not fallen so low as to be without protectors and patrons. (Another of Sarah's protégés was the future artist Henry Raeburn.)

Aitken very nearly missed being admitted. In 1763, two years after he began at Heriot's, the school's finances were such that no boys were admitted; the year after that, only one boy was admitted. Aitken's younger brother, George, was also lucky. He was one of only seven boys admitted in 1766. He joined his brothers James and Nichol there, Nichol having been admitted in October of 1760. With three of their boys admitted to the school within a span of five years, the Aitken family must have had good connections and known how to use them.

Each of the boys was given a physical examination before being formally admitted to the school. This was standard practice at Heriot's, and it was almost certainly Aitken's first encounter with a physician. The boy was thin, but otherwise healthy. In any event, Heriot's afforded him ample opportunity to put on weight. The

Heriot's Hospital from the Grassmarket *by J. M. W. Turner (1775-1851).*
Heriot's rises in the distance, a beacon of hope and order amidst the squalor and crushing
poverty of Edinburgh's Old Town. COURTESY OF THE NATIONAL GALLERY OF SCOTLAND.

food, while monotonous and unappetizing, was plentiful. In 1795,
breakfast consisted of a mutchkin (just under a pint) of porridge,
along with a half-mutchkin of milk or buttermilk. Lunch consisted
of beef and broth on Sundays and Thursdays, and of mutton and
broth on Tuesdays; on Mondays, Wednesdays, and Fridays, the
boys had to settle for bread and milk, but on Saturdays, they were
treated to table beer, whose low alcohol content was no doubt a
source of chronic complaint. Supper was the same as breakfast,
with bread being substituted for porridge during the summer.[36]
Like sailors, Heriot's boys did without vegetables, and like sailors,
they were prone to scurvy. Few Lowland Scots ate as much meat or
drank as much milk as the boys at Heriot's, but at least they got
their vegetables, primarily in the form of kale or cabbage.[37]

Nothing could have prepared him for the experience of living at Heriot's. With its turrets, carvings, and breathtaking courtyard, the building, known then as the "Wark," resembled nothing so much as a palace, and the contrast between it and the Aitkens' cramped flat off the Cowgate could not have been greater. The building was enormous—in Aitken's day the students and staff occupied only a small part of it, leasing the remainder to booksellers and others— and it was magnificent, too magnificent, some uncharitable people said, for the paupers that it housed.[38] The historian William Maitland thought it "more proper for the residence of a great king than the habitation of a few poor and needy orphans. For, till this time, the vanity of man was not got to such a height of extravagance as to erect palaces for beggars."[39] Thomas Pennant, the naturalist and writer, thought it "a fine old building, much too magnificent for the end proposed, that of educating poor children."[40]

The school had a large staff, and for the first time in his life, Aitken found himself living a highly structured existence. In addition to the faculty, consisting of the schoolmaster, his two assistants, and the writing master, there was a staff of fifteen: a treasurer, a physician, a surgeon, a clerk, a steward, a cook, a gardener, a porter, a matron, and six women servants. The seven women, all confirmed spinsters and all forty-five years of age or older, were responsible for washing the linens, making the students' beds, sweeping their rooms, and tending to boys who fell sick. The schoolmaster and teachers were also supposed to be unmarried, as was the porter, whose duties included keeping beggars out and boys in during prayers and meals. Despite his best efforts, the boys were forever slipping out and getting into trouble. It was a constant struggle, one that was fought with stocks (the school had its own), chains, and whips. In 1731, two boys who had spent the night out were whipped and then expelled; in 1732, three more truants were whipped and placed in the school's stocks; and in Aitken's day, three boys, Charles and John Alexander and John Clark were forever leaving the school for a week or more at a time, despite their having "often received correction and been confined by chaining them together."[41]

The teachers never stayed for long. The two constants in his life at Heriot's were Mrs. Elizabeth Gillespie, whose tenure as matron of the housekeepers lasted from 1753 to 1776, and Alexander Peacock, who served as steward from 1737 to 1768. It was a grim and unaffectionate existence, but it was orderly, and that made it better than most.

As before, he was always surrounded by people, starting with the 140 or so other boys who attended the school. For the six years that he was there, he ate with them, took classes with them, and shared a common room with them at night. Adults—teachers, spinsters, and the porter—watched their every move, exiting only at night and only after they had taken one last head count.

His day started with yet another counting of heads. This took place just before dawn in the quadrangle, where a number for each boy had been chiseled into the paving stones. Aitken would take his place, his feet positioned below his own number, and wait to be counted. Everywhere he looked there were sculptures and medallions. Pride of place was given to a life-size statue of the school's founder, but there were also medallions of kings and queens: Henrietta Maria, Charles II, and James VI. There were also biblical figures and the figure of death adorning one of the windows. There were David and Solomon, Adam and Eve, along with mermaids and fanciful reliefs representing the four known continents: Europe, Asia, Africa, and America.

At seven, the boys were marched off to the chapel for prayers, and at eight into the refectory for breakfast. Classes started at nine in the winter and at ten in the summer, and were followed by lunch at noon. Classes resumed at two, lasting until five on Mondays, Wednesdays, and Fridays, and until four on Tuesdays and Thursdays.[42] Five times a day, the boys were called on to pray, in the mornings and evenings in the school's magnificent chapel, and at breakfast, lunch, and dinner. Sometimes mumbling and sometimes shouting, they gave "thanks unto God in express words, for the bountiful maintenance, which they, living there, receive from the charity of their pious founder."[43] At least once a day they prayed for the people who sat in authority over them, for the king and his privy council, and for the mayor and his council. Three times a week, on Tuesday, Thursday, and Sunday, a schoolmaster instructed the boys in their catechism, concluding each such session with a reading from an inoffensive sermon authorized by the Kirk. On Sundays, in addition to being catechized, the boys were lined up, two by two in order of seniority, and marched off to Greyfriars. There, in pews just ahead of the "back seats for the poor," they suffered through two sermons, one in the morning and one in the afternoon, after which they were once again assembled in twos and marched back to the school under the weary eyes of their masters.[44] It was in Greyfriars that Aitken and his brothers could catch a glimpse of their mother and such siblings as were still living under her roof.

At that time, Greyfriars was presided over by John Erskine, the leading figure in the evangelical wing of the Kirk and a respected classicist.[45] One of the many people who heard him preach was the future Sir Walter Scott. Scott liked him. Erskine himself may have been "a very ungainly person," and his sermons may have been lacking in "pulpit eloquence," but these deficiencies were more than compensated for by his "learning, metaphysical acuteness, and energy of argument."[46]

Erskine believed passionately in educating the children of the poor, and he made this one of his many worthy causes. In June of 1762, when Aitken was ten and had been at Heriot's for a year, Erskine delivered a sermon on the occasion of the founder's birthday, and in 1774, he delivered a sermon subsequently published under the title *The Education of Poor Children Recommended.*[47] Education, he argued, habituated poor children "to useful labour" and introduced discipline into their lives at an early age.[48] One thing led to another: children who had been taught to be "tractable, and obedient to the advice and authority of their teachers" inevitably grew up to be solid citizens who were submissive "to rulers, who in the just constitutional exercise of their power, are ministers of God for good, and terrors only to evildoers...." They were, Erskine confidently predicted, "in little danger of disturbing the quiet either of church or state."

The argument was not without its flaws. It did not occur to Erskine that education might plant doubts in the minds of its recipients, that instead of becoming happy workers they might instead become unhappy intellectuals. Nor did it occur to him that many men, no matter how much education and training they got, were destined to spend the rest of their lives not as prosperous tradesmen but as impoverished day laborers.

John Erskine matters because he was openly sympathetic to America and because Aitken heard him preach on a regular basis. Erskine was in close and constant contact with such American evangelicals as Jonathan Edwards, and in 1769, with war already looming, he wrote an impassioned plea for peace.[49] He blamed both sides for the impasse, but mostly he blamed Britain. The pamphlet, *Shall I Go to War with my American Brethren?*, was reasonableness itself, but in his attempts to dissuade Britain from military action Erskine came very close to justifying the use of unconventional warfare against superior military force. One line in particular stands out: "Despair sharpens the invention; and when it cannot find relief, suggests a thousand expedients of revenge."[50] In 1776, with the battles of Lexington, Concord, and Bunker Hill already fought, Erskine would write another pamphlet about America. Published under the bland title of *Reflections on the Rise, Progress, and Probable Consequences of the Present Contentions with the Colonies,* it, too, contained a line that could easily be construed as a justification for fighting a new kind of war. Americans, he observed, had been criticized for fighting from behind the cover of forests and thickets, and yet he himself could see no difference between raising "fortifications provided by God and nature" and "our army guarding against attacks by works of their own raising."[51] Erskine was a good and peaceable man, and he no doubt wrote these lines in complete innocence; others, however, read and heard something rather more sinister. We do not know if Aitken read Erskine's pamphlets, but this much is certain: he heard Erskine's sermons, and it was through them that he formed his first impressions of America and its impending struggles with Britain.

* * *

He got a good education. All of the boys at Heriot's were taught reading, writing, and basic arithmetic. This part of the curriculum was designed to prepare them for the trades, but two other components were not. The first was music—when Aitken was at Heriot's it was taught by Cornforth Gilson—and the second was Latin. The writer Joseph Collyer was against it, arguing that neither Greek nor Latin could be of "any real use to the generality of tradesmen and mechanics, even were they perfect masters of them."[52]

27

Aitken loved books and read indiscriminately. It was a passion that he shared with many other impoverished Scots. Their ranks included young Robert Burns, who was himself the son of a poor farmer, but they also included many lesser-known men and women, among them, an aged shepherd who possessed a library of 370 books. These, it was reported, were "upon many different subjects, as divinity, history, travels, voyages &c, besides magazines of different kinds, such as the *Scots*, the *Universal*, and the Christian magazines; a complete set of the *Spectator, Guardian, Tatler, Rambler* &c."[53] Alexander Somerville, a poor Scot who later became a journalist, was another such reader. When, for example, he read George Anson's *Voyage round the World*, "everything gave way to admit the new knowledge of the earth's geography, and the charms of human adventure which I found in those voyages. I had read nothing of the kind before...."[54] Aitken, too, was given to thinking about the world that lay beyond his own. At Heriot's, he had access to two globes, along with "proper books for giving the skills in geography and navigation." These items were purchased sometime in 1764, and they seem to have caught young Aitken's attention, for later in life he displayed an uncommon ability to find his way in unfamiliar settings, whether in southern England, France, or even in the wilds of America.[55]

He was an avid reader of newspapers, as were so many of his peers. Years later, when he was a wanted man, he would read about his various crimes in the newspapers, cringing whenever the advertisements offering rewards for his capture described him just a little too well. The newspapers, too, were the source of much of his information about America. Such news could be found in all the major London newspapers, and it could also be found closer to home in *The Scots Magazine*, which ran a regular feature under the heading "British North America."[56] If he was like most people, he did most of his reading in public houses and coffeehouses, which were always well stocked with newspapers.[57]

Many of the books that Aitken read as a boy probably came from the school's library, which was started in 1764. The original funds came from the Reverend John Erskine, who having delivered the school's commemorative sermon in 1762, had returned his stipend on the condition that it be used "for purchasing religious and moral treatises."[58] More varied—and more interesting—reading materials were to be found in the unused apartments that were at various times leased to printers, stationers, and booksellers; at the very least, these establishments would have piqued Aitken's curiosity, tempting him to read both broadly and eclectically.

It was a habit that would follow him into adulthood. Wherever he went, he toted books with him. One assortment, left behind in Portsmouth, contained two classics—an "English *Justin*" and Ovid's *Metamorphoses*—along with a book appropriate to his activities as an arsonist: *The Art of War and Making Fireworks, as Practised by the Army of the King of France.*[59] The "English *Justin*" was almost certainly the Marcus Junianus Justinus who abridged an earlier history of Philip of Macedon and Alexander the Great. The history was very popular in England, with separate translations appearing in 1663 and 1702. There was also a popular schoolboy's edition, first published in 1732 and already in its seventh edition by 1772. It was probably this version that Aitken owned.[60] His fondness for the *Metamorphoses* is equally unremarkable, as the text was hugely popular in the eighteenth century.[61]

Another assortment of texts, left behind in Bristol, contained various pamphlets (unspecified) by Franklin, a pro-American tract by Richard Price (we will return to him in due course), and "a volume of Voltaire's works, with the leaf turned down, in one of the pages of which the account of the massacre of Paris began."[62] This could only have been Voltaire's *Henriade*, which was available in English translation.[63] Aitken later bragged that Voltaire was his favorite modern author.[64] But it is hard to see exactly what attracted him to this particular book. Perhaps Aitken saw in Voltaire's fawning depiction of Henry IV the sort of hero he himself wished to be, or perhaps he simply happened upon the book, either buying it on the cheap or stealing it in the course of his many break-ins. Three facts are certain: he was interested in the classics, he could name Voltaire, and he wanted to be the sort of person who has a favorite author.

* * *

He probably made few friends at Heriot's. In his own cohort, there were the sons of respectable professionals, including two merchants, a vintner, and an armorer, and there were also the sons of decidedly more modest men, including a weaver and a shoemaker. The variety was a microcosm of the school itself. In Aitken's day, the student body was more or less evenly divided between middle-class and lower-middle-class boys. One, for example, was the son of a goldsmith (the occupation of the school's founder), and another was the son of a mere porter.[65] If the example of Alexander Somerville is at all representative, these distinctions meant a great deal to the boys themselves.[66] Somerville, a self-styled "working man" who grew up in the early 1800s, was constantly bullied by the oldest son "of the great farmer of the neighbourhood"; Somerville also ended up at the bottom of the heap in the boys' grim games. In one such game, the boys were divided into soldiers and radicals. "As the soldiers were the most respectable in the eyes of the better dressed sons of farmers and tradesmen, and as they took the lead in everything, they made themselves soldiers."[67] For his part,

Somerville was cast in the role of a radical, as befitted a boy who was as truculent as he was poor.

Fagging, which was already rife at Heriot's, was another source of misery. At the top of the hierarchy were the "garrers," the boys who were in their fifth year. The earliest mention of their existence dates from 1751, when it was reported that they were forcing all boys entering the school to take a pledge in which they agreed to say nothing about the system and its many abuses. In 1793, it was discovered that younger boys were routinely forced to clean the garrers' shoes; they were also forced to steal for them and beat up classmates who had run afoul of the so-called "garring law." It was a brutal system, and it survived each of the school's attempts to suppress it. Boys who had a little money might bribe the garrers; the rest, including Aitken, were left to suffer repeatedly and in silence.[68]

Aitken had another problem: he was a stammerer.[69] At the very least, a speech impediment, no matter how slight, would have poisoned his relations with both classmates and schoolmasters, causing the one to mock him and the other to underestimate his intellect.

Adolescence only added to his awkwardness. If he was like most boys of the time, its onset was late and its duration long, consistent with the stunting effects of a poor diet and hard physical labor (something that most Heriot's boys were exposed to once they started their apprenticeships at the age of fourteen or fifteen). By one estimate, the typical male did not reach physical maturity until his mid-twenties (today, by contrast, the average age is eighteen); by another, the typical adolescent male in late eighteenth-century London was five inches shorter than his counterpart today.[70]

* * *

The school divided its graduates into two tracks, and in both cases paid their way. The lucky few were marked for advancement to the University of Edinburgh, and the remainder were farmed out as apprentices. Boys in the first track were the rarest of creatures. They were the so-called "lads of parts," poor boys who were given the opportunity to rise through higher education. Few did.[71] The prospects of the boys in the second track were worse, and they found themselves going out into a world very different from that envisioned in the founder's will.

In April of 1767, the school's council, in conjunction with a visiting committee, met to decide which graduates would serve apprenticeships and which, if any, would be sent on to the university.[72] Aitken, in their opinion, had not distinguished himself, and when it came time to select a trade for him, the governors selected one that was singularly unpromising: house painter. He was fourteen years old.

It was a terrible choice. In the Middle Ages, only painters knew how to mix colors and apply them properly; by the eighteenth century, these skills had lost their specialist standing, and the trade faced competition from several directions. The biggest threat came from paint shops, which were starting to spring up in the larger towns. These shops were a threat because they could mix and sell paints at a fraction of the price charged by professional painters. One such shop was already operating in London by 1734, and its enterprising proprietor, Alexander Emerton, was only too happy to provide his customers with printed directions. With Emerton's paints and Emerton's little manual, homeowners were known to have "painted whole houses without the assistance or direction of a painter, which when examined by the best judges could not be distinguished from the work of a professed painter." Homeowners who did not wish to dirty their hands and clothes

Beer Street, *1751, by William Hogarth. The only person who is not fat and prosperous is the painter (upper left-hand corner).*

might hire common laborers to do the job instead. These, too, Emerton was only too happy to provide.[73]

Thanks to entrepreneurs like Emerton, there was already a glut of professional painters by 1747, the year when Robert Campbell published his career guide for boys and their parents. As far as Campbell was concerned, "no parent ought to be so mad as to bind his child apprentice for seven years, to a branch that may be learned almost in as many hours, in which he cannot earn a subsistence when he has got it, runs the risk of breaking his neck every day, and in the end turns out a mere blackguard."[74] "This branch," he added, "is now at a very low ebb, on account of the methods practised by some colour-shops, who have set up horse-mills to grind the colours, and sell them to noblemen and gentlemen ready mixed at a low price, and by the help of a few printed directions, a house may be painted by any common labourer at one third of the expence it would have cost before the mystery was made public." In 1761, the same year that Aitken was admitted to Heriot's, the trade was still hopelessly "overstocked," and parents were being discouraged from selecting it as a future occupation for their sons.[75]

The occupation was more than uncertain: it was dangerous even by the horrific standards of the eighteenth-century workplace. Tailors lost their eyesight after years of working in dimly lit shops. Shoemakers developed humpbacks after years of stooping. Porters were given to ruptures and hernias, as were sailors and just about anyone else whose job involved heavy lifting.[76] Construction workers fell off ladders and scaffolds and were paralyzed for life. But painters suffered even more, for over time they invariably succumbed to lead poisoning.[77] With mild exposure came fatigue, sleeplessness, pallor, loss of appetite, irritability, and sudden changes in mood. (One wonders if Aitken himself was so afflicted.) With prolonged exposure came weakness, abdominal pain, persistent vomiting, and clumsiness.[78] Contemporaries were not unaware of these effects. Franklin, writing in 1786, claimed that lead's effects had been understood "at least above sixty years." Painters' "constitutions ought to be hardy and sound," Robert Campbell had warned back in 1747. "They are," he added, "much exposed to heats and colds on the outside of buildings; and the strong smell of the colours, and the effluvia of the white lead they are among, is apt to affect their nerves and lungs, if they are not perfectly sound."[79] This was especially true of the laborers who mixed lead paints. They were "sure in a few years to become paralytic by the mercurial fumes of the lead."

Why, then, did Heriot's governors consign Aitken to an occupation that could promise little more than poverty, poor health, and an early death? One possibility is that the governors did so because the boy's grandfather, Alexander Boswell, was also a painter. But the likeliest explanation is that the school's governors had in some way found Aitken mentally or socially deficient, probably because of his stammering. Hence the selection of an occupation that required, in the words of one contemporary, "very small abilities."[80] It was an unfortunate choice, one that neither engaged Aitken's intellect nor did justice to it.

His master, John Bonnar, was a house painter in Edinburgh's Old Town.[81] Bonnar may have found work painting rooms in the houses then being built in the New Town (an English visitor, writing in 1774, gushed over "the present mode of colouring ceilings and rooms," insisting that "the paleness of the tints gives to their appearance much grace, ease, and modesty, blended with a certain degree of grandeur and dignity"), but it is likely that most of his business came from painting signs and storefronts in the Old Town. The English visitor did not like them. The merchants, he complained, "have the horrid custom of painting on the outside of their houses, the figure of the commodity which is to be sold within; which, in this place, makes the oddest appearance you can conceive; for each story, perhaps, from top to bottom, is chequered with ten thousand different forms and colours...."[82] Everyone, it seemed, was "remarkably fond of glaring colours," of red, yellow, and blue, which provided a bold background for advertising their wares and made a mockery of the understated refinement of the New Town.

Bonnar taught Aitken how to mix colors, paint figures, and draw.[83] He must have taught him well, for as a journeyman Aitken was able to find odd jobs wherever he went—in London, Birmingham, Exeter, Warrington, Havant, Titchfield, and even Philadelphia.[84]

In 1772, at the age of twenty, Aitken completed his apprenticeship and left Bonnar's employ with exactly five pounds in his pocket. The money came not from Bonnar but from Heriot's, with the understanding that it be spent on a new suit of clothes.[85] The sum fell far short of the thirty or more pounds required to set up shop as a master painter, and Aitken, like the vast majority of his peers, now entered the workforce as a mere journeyman.[86] His prospects were abysmal. In principle, a newly graduated apprentice spent several years as a journeyman, honing his skills and amassing a nest egg. After that, in his late twenties or early thirties, he set up shop as a master in his own right, married, fathered a new generation of workers, and became a pillar of the community. That was the theory and that was exactly what George Aitken had done. In practice, many journeymen never became masters.[87] They were not quite boys, but they would never be men—not as long as they were too poor to set up shops and households of their own.[88] Unable to go into business for themselves, they spent their lives in limbo, neither boys nor men, wandering, working for a succession of employers, and in most cases earning too little to support themselves, let alone a family. Because they were poor and despised, they were forever touchy on points of honor, and because they were considered to be little more than grown-up boys, they played the part, flying into rages at the slightest provocation. They stood for everything that John Erskine had warned against in *The Education of Poor Children Recommended*. In 1772, James Aitken entered their ever-growing ranks, a man in his eyes only.

In the meantime, he began working where and when he could. In most trades, work began at about six in the morning, and lasted until six or seven in the evening, with perhaps two hours off for meals.[89] Work was erratic, and on some days he worked to the point of exhaustion, and on others he mostly wandered and drank. He could count on being poorly paid, but he could not count on working.

He realized almost at once that there was no future in being a painter. He was young and ambitious, and the workaday world held absolutely no charm for him. He set his sights on becoming an officer. It was a quintessentially Scottish ambition. "I was born a Scotsman and a bare one," Sir Walter Scott once said. "Therefore I was born to fight my way in the world."[90] The same sentiment is to be found in *Scotch Modesty Displayed*, a pamphlet published in 1778:

> The army and the navy take away almost all our young gentlemen. The reason is plain, our gentry are both poor and proud...and we can neither submit to the putting our sons to trades, nor afford to place them in the genteeler walk of commerce, nor to buy them commissions, so we send them to fight for their bread.[91]

The claim was not wide of the mark. By the end of the Seven Years' War, as many as one in four Scots of military age were serving in the British forces.[92] Those who could purchase commissions did so, and those who could not served in the enlisted ranks. The one offered glory and advancement; the other most decidedly did not. Every once in a while, it is true, men were promoted out of the enlisted ranks, but such instances were few and far between, and such men as were promoted almost always had good connections and superior social skills.[93]

The idea of becoming an officer obsessed him. But it was not meant to be. His family was too poor to purchase a commission, and he continued to work odd jobs. But even these were becoming scarce. The local economy had been bad ever since Alexander Fordyce, a partner in the London banking house of Neale, James, Fordyce and Down, had absconded to France in June of 1772. The firm did much of its business in Scotland, and its subsequent collapse had an immediate and devastating impact on the Scottish economy. The firm's crash was followed by the failure of several other banks, including the Ayr Bank, which had been founded in 1769 to help finance the Scottish linen industry. This was by far the biggest financial crisis to hit eighteenth-century Scotland, and it occurred just as harvest failures were causing food prices to soar.[94] At the same time, the growing tensions with America were taking their toll on the Scottish textile industry, cutting it off from one of its most important markets. The result was a severe depression, lasting from 1772 to 1774. The "distress of the common people here is deeper and more general than you can imagine," a Glaswegian reported in 1774. "There is an almost total stagnation in our manufactures, and grain is dear; many hundreds of labourers and mechanics, especially weavers in this neighbourhood, have lately indented and gone to America. . . . "[95] Still others, hungry and unemployed, streamed south into England. Among their numbers was James Aitken. He was twenty years old, and he was never to see Edinburgh or his family again.

In 1772, then, Aitken's wanderings began. The fact that he left his home and family was unremarkable. Every year, tens of thousands of young men and women did just that, never to return.[96] In one eighteenth-century village not far from London, three-quarters of all boys and two-thirds of all girls ended up leaving, although few, if any, wandered as far as Aitken.[97] That distinction, to the extent that it was shared, goes to his fellow Scots, whose famous poverty forced them to wander ever farther afield. Those who remained in Scotland tended to travel shorter distances than their English counterparts, but those who left went everywhere—to Ireland, Poland, and Scandinavia in the seventeenth century, and to America, Canada, and the British Caribbean in the eighteenth.[98]

Again, his leaving was unremarkable. What was unusual was that, once he started his journeys, he could not stop. Everything about the man speaks to an overriding restlessness, and for the next four and a half years, from 1772 to 1777, he was in constant motion, never staying in one place for long.

CHAPTER TWO

His Adventures as a Highwayman

HIS LIFE changed completely when he left Edinburgh. This is not to say that his prospects improved. But from this point forward everything that he did, he did alone. He formed no close attachments and made no friends, and his social skills suffered for it, as did his attitude toward people in general. In 1772, however, he was still a hopelessly average young man. He was one of thousands of Scots who left their country for good that year, and even the age at which he set out for London—twenty—was dead average.[1] In England he found himself caught up in a sea of young people, each just as hungry and hopeful as he, and each inexorably drawn to London. They were all leaving home, tens upon tens of thousands every year.

London was just under four hundred miles to the south.[2] Young Boswell, traveling by coach and well into the night, made the journey in just four days in 1762, while the fictional Roderick Random, traveling sometimes on foot and sometimes by cart, meandered and dawdled, so much so that his trip took several weeks.[3] Random set out with one suit of clothes and six ruffled shirts, a modest wardrobe but one almost certainly better than Aitken's, and he spent much of the journey obsessing over highwaymen. So, too, did Boswell. "I was a good deal afraid of robbers," he confided in his journal. "A great many horrid ideas filled my mind."

There were further reminders of highwaymen just outside London. It was impossible to enter the capital without encountering

Crowd by a Gibbet *by Thomas Rowlandson (1756–1827). A crowd of respectable sightseers gawks at the moldering corpses of condemned felons.* COURTESY OF THE YALE CENTER FOR BRITISH ART.

their moldering bodies, hoisted high above the reach of curiosity-seekers and in varying stages of decomposition. To the north, on Finchley Common, there were five or six corpses on display at any one time; to the west, on Hounslow Heath, there were perhaps a hundred; and closer in, on the road that led past the gallows at Tyburn, there were yet further reminders of the awful punishments that awaited those who turned their backs on honest work.[4] Sixty years after the fact, Charles King could still remember being taken to see two gibbeted bodies on Hounslow Heath. The year was 1804, and he was just four years old. "The chains rattled," he wrote, "the iron plates scarcely held the gibbet together; the rags of the highwaymen displayed their horrible skeletons."[5]

All, however, was forgotten the moment he set foot in the capital. He was prepared for the crowding—some people said that Edinburgh's Old Town was the most crowded spot in Europe—but the sheer size and sprawl of the metropolis overwhelmed him.[6] With a population already in excess of 700,000, London was by far the largest city in Europe, larger even than Paris, and ten times larger than Edinburgh. He may have felt a surge of excitement when he first set eyes on the London skyline; certainly Boswell did when he first beheld it from Highgate Hill—"I was all life and joy... my soul bounded forth to a certain prospect of happy futurity. I sang all manner of songs"—but then again, Boswell was easily excited.[7]

Boswell, however, had something that Aitken did not have: people on whom he might call. His was a London in which everybody knew each other; Aitken's was not. Everywhere he went he was surrounded by strangers, and at times the loneliness must have been unbearable.[8] Even Boswell had his moments of doubt. A week after arriving in London, he was already having second thoughts. "I lay abed very gloomy. I thought London did me no good. I rather disliked it; and I thought of going back to Edinburgh immediately. In short, I was most miserable." Boswell was famously given to melancholia, but in those four lines he spoke for the experiences of thousands more.

* * *

It was a terrible place to be a Scot. By one count, Scots accounted for 6 percent of the metropolis's population, and everywhere they went they encountered hostility and prejudice.[9] No sooner does Roderick Random walk into a public house than its patrons start to insult him. What is in his knapsack? "Is it oatmeal or brimstone,

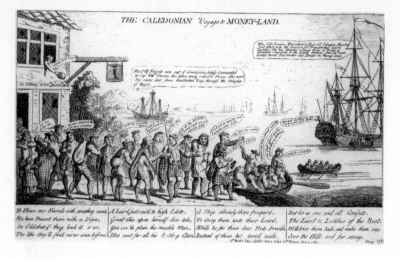

The Caledonian Voyage to Money-Land, 1763. After Irish Catholics, Scots were the most despised ethnic group in eighteenth-century England. Here they are shown wearing tartans and bonnets, even though most Scottish emigrants came from the Lowlands and dressed like everyone else. COURTESY OF THE BRITISH MUSEUM.

Sawney?"[10] No sooner do two Highland officers enter a London theater than the crowd turns on them. "No Scots! No Scots! Out with them!" These events are observed by another Scot, James Boswell, who is barely able to find the words to express his rage. "I hated the English; I wished from my soul that the Union was broke and that we might give them another battle of Bannockburn." "The rudeness of the English vulgar is terrible," he tells his journal.[11] Worse yet is in store when he meets Johnson for the first time. "Mr. Johnson," he blurts out, "I do indeed come from Scotland, but I cannot help it." Johnson's reply cuts him to the quick and he never forgets it. "That, Sir, I find, is what a very great many of your countrymen cannot help."[12]

We are all a comeing or Scotch coal for ever, 1763. English fears of being
overwhelmed by immigrants are writ large in this cartoon, one of dozens churned out by
the followers of John Wilkes in their campaign to oust the Scottish Lord Bute. The signpost
in the lower right-hand corner reads "From Edinb[urgh] to London." COURTESY OF THE
BRITISH MUSEUM.

English prejudice against the Scots was of long standing, but
with the accession of George III in 1760, it took a turn for the
worse. For two years, from 1761 to 1763, the king's former tutor,
the Scottish Lord Bute, was prime minister in the loosest sense of
the word. Bute's tenure, brief and misunderstood though it was,
gave rise to an outpouring of anti-Scots propaganda, most of it
orchestrated by the infamous John Wilkes.[13] Pamphlets, newspapers, and prints rolled off the presses, each saying the same thing:
that the Scots were overweening, oversexed (true enough in Boswell's case), and determined to make their fortunes in England—
and at the expense of the English.[14]

John Wilkes Esq., *1763, by William Hogarth. Wilkes did more than any other Englishman to stir up anti-Scots prejudice in the eighteenth century. He helped hound the Scottish Lord Bute from office in 1763, and in 1775 he blamed the Scots for the war with America.*

How sweet are the Banks upon Tweed,
Troth very sweet, it is agreed,
But England *has such Sweets in Store,*
As never bless'd our Scottish *Shore....*[15]

The prints are no better. Highlander or Lowlander, Scots are invariably depicted wearing tartans; some are shown wearing bonnets or swords; and all are scraggly, bony, and thin-faced, dull emblems of barbarism and poverty. Their destination is always the same: London.

In London we may thrive; I have been told,
That there the very streets are pav'd with gold.
London must surely be a conny town,

Where he takes gold in handfuls who stoops down;
Not Glasgow, tho' so rich in buildings rare,
Or Edinburgh, with London can compare;
Let us then hasten both to London town,
There fortune quickly will our labour crown.[16]

It was Aitken's bad luck to fit the stereotype in several important respects. Unable to make a living in his own country, he headed south, to London; his hair was a telltale red (as, for that matter, was Roderick Random's); and he was, in the words of his pursuers, "rather thin in person, and thin-visaged."[17] Above all, it was his accent that gave him away. Even Silas Deane, the American envoy in France, immediately took him for a Scot.[18] Deane said that Aitken spoke "in broad Scotch." Another man, upon hearing him speak, took him for "a Scotchman, and by his accent, from the northwest part."[19] He was right by half. Aitken was indeed from Scotland, but from the southeast and not the northwest. These differences mattered little: to English eyes and ears, Highlanders and Lowlanders were indistinguishable.[20] Both were foreigners. The reactions of one Englishman speak to the prejudices of a nation. The Highland troops of the Young Pretender had invaded England, and six of their officers and forty of their privates were billeted on him. He might as well have played host to a menagerie. "Their dialect (from the idea I had of it) seemed to me, as if an herd of Hottentots, wild monkeys in a desert, or vagrant gypsies, had been jabbering, screaming and howling together, and really this jargon of speech was very properly suited to such a set of banditti."[21]

The stereotype was wildly inconsistent. Images of wild Scots existed side by side with their exact opposite: that of the overeducated Scot.

The English in each science we outshine,
Surpass in knowledge human and divine,
And eke in oratory, all agree
They speak not English half so well as we.[22]

There was an element of truth to this. The Lowlanders (but
not the Highlanders) *were* better educated than most people in
England, and only in the north, in Cumberland, Westmorland,
and Yorkshire, did English literacy rates equal those found in the
Lowlands.[23] Again, it was Aitken's bad luck to fit the stereotype. He
was better educated than most people in England. He knew it and
he wanted them to know it.

At some point, probably during his first month in London, he
started to develop a chip on his shoulder. It was inevitable, given
the prejudice that he endured day after day. Even Boswell, a man
with every possible advantage over Aitken, was treated roughly.
Boswell was young and full of himself, and every slight, perceived
or real, made his blood boil. He went back and forth, sometimes
trying to assimilate, sometimes clinging to his heritage and identity.[24] He could never let down his guard. If it was bad for Boswell, it
was ten times worse for an immigrant like Aitken.

It would be a mistake, however, to assume that Aitken was a
Scottish patriot and that he later set fires in England because he
hated the English. There is nothing to suggest this. He expressed his
feelings about Scotland on only one occasion that we know of. A man,
anxious to win his trust, started talking about Scotland. In response,
Aitken gave only "a smile of approbation," and then asked questions
about a mutual acquaintance who happened to be Scottish.[25] That
was all. On another occasion, Aitken "refused to acknowledge where
he came from," saying only that he was "a native of Europe."[26] This is
not the boast of a Scottish nationalist, but a Romantic revolutionary.

*   *   *

He lost a great deal in London, starting with his pride and whatever savings he had brought with him. He also lost his virginity. We
know that he had "a connection with some women of the town"
during his second sojourn in London, between 1775 and 1776,
and it is almost certain that he enjoyed their company during his
first stay as well.[27] He is not to be faulted. Marriage was out of the
question—most men of his generation did not marry until they
were at least twenty-six, and many, having failed to acquire a nest
egg by that age, were destined to spend several more years or even
a lifetime as bachelors.[28]

His sexual encounters, such as they were, were perfunctory
and charmless, occurring sometimes in back alleys, sometimes in
public houses, and sometimes in rundown lodging houses.[29] Boswell's encounters were no more elegant. The aspiring writer was
twenty-two years old, he had been in London for less than a
week, and already he was complaining. "I was really unhappy for
want of women. I thought it hard to be in such a place without
them." His mood was much improved when he picked up a girl
later that same day. "I toyed with her. She wondered at my size,
and said if I ever took a girl's maidenhead, I would make her
squeak."[30] All of this happened in the most public of places: a
courtyard.

There is, however, one incident in Aitken's sexual history that
stands out. He raped a woman. This happened in 1776, outside
the tiny town of Basingstoke, in Hampshire. The victim was alone,
"watching some sheep."[31] The scenario was common enough—in
Yorkshire, at least, more than a fifth of all rapists singled out
women working alone in the fields—but the crime was not.[32]
Aitken himself mentions the incident only in passing, and we do

not know what he did, aside from using "threats and imprecations" to overpower the unfortunate shepherdess. It is perhaps significant that the rape occurred later in his career, just as his behavior was starting to become unhinged.

But again, in 1772 he was still an average young man. He did the sorts of things that other young men did in London: he found women and he found work.[33] He found both in the same place: a public house. Each of the trades, the painters included, had one or more "houses of call," or public houses where men went to find work, and Aitken seems to have had no difficulty in finding one that catered to painters.[34] Once there he had no difficulty finding work as a journeyman painter.

He was lucky to have found work at all, for London's job market was seasonal, fickle, and, as contemporaries liked to say, "overstocked." Moreover, he happened to come to London at a time when real wages were falling in all but the most skilled sectors.[35] And much to his horror, he quickly discovered that his prospects as a journeyman painter were no better in London than they had been in Edinburgh. The trade was nominally under the control of the Company of Painters, but its authority, like that of London's other guilds, was weak inside the City proper, and nonexistent outside of it.[36] London, moreover, was home to Britain's first paint shops, which allowed contractors and homeowners to dispense with professional painters for all but the most complex of jobs. So painters, like almost everyone else in the capital, engaged in moonlighting whenever they could.[37] In 1736, for example, two painters in Ratcliff sold gin as a sideline, as did a painter in Whitechapel.[38] Another painter, Richard Damsel of Shoreditch, found an even more lucrative sideline: informing on people who sold gin without a license.[39] The three neighborhoods—Ratcliff, Whitechapel, and Shoreditch—are another hint. These were three

of the poorest neighborhoods in East London, then as now housing recent immigrants to the city, and it is in such a neighborhood
that Aitken lived during his first several months in London.

Aitken, too, soon found a sideline: crime. Like so many other
people at the bottom of the social ladder, he was not a career
criminal so much as an occasional criminal, sometimes working
and sometimes stealing. Crime was to prove more lucrative than
working as a house painter, and more exciting as well. An editor's
hand, and a very heavy one at that, can be detected in the two
accounts of Aitken's descent into crime. They read suspiciously
like any other criminal biography: a promising youth is given
every possible advantage, in the form of schooling and vocational
training, only to fall in with the usual culprits: bad companions
and loose women:[40]

> On my arrival in the great metropolis, I applied to people in the
> painting way, and immediately got into employ. But business not
> long agreeing with my inclination, and having formed an acquain-
> tance with some extravagant young men, by whom I was led into
> all manner of vice and debauchery, I soon found the last farthing
> of my little pittance expended. In this condition, deserted by my
> companions, and in a strange country, I determined to relieve
> myself on the highway.[41]

It was the same old story. Bad company, Nathaniel Crouch
warned back in 1681, inevitably led apprentices astray, drawing
them into "drunkenness, whoredom, swearing, lying, cheating,
gaming, and what not...."[42] William Moraley had to agree.
Looking back on his misspent youth and trying to make sense of
everything that had happened to him since he had been forced to
immigrate to America in 1729, he blamed that old chestnut:

"company." "Company," he wrote, "was the thing I chiefly thought on...and how to support it...."[43] Even the famous highwayman Dick Turpin had once been an honest man, but that was before he fell in with "idle company" and "began to make unlawful measures to support his extravagances...." And it was "company" that brought down John Shepard, another felon who met his end at Tyburn. He had been a promising young apprentice—until he fell under the spell of the wicked Elizabeth Lyon.[44] These examples—and there are thousands more—were available to anyone who cared to read and heed. For those who could not or would not read, there were always the prints from *Industry and Idleness,* first published by Hogarth in 1747 and meant to be posted in the rooms and shops where apprentices toiled at their future trades.[45]

Every time he stole anything of value, he ran the risk of being caught and hanged. Steal five shillings in money or goods from a shop and hang; steal forty from a house and hang.[46] Each year brought new hanging offenses. Between the restoration of Charles II in 1660 and the death of George III in 1820, nearly two hundred new capital offenses were added to the criminal code, sixty-three of these between 1760 and 1820 alone.[47] In fairness, not everyone who robbed or stole was hanged. Sentences were commuted; pardons came down from Whitehall; and jurors balked. But enough men and women were hanged—perhaps seven thousand between 1770 and 1830—to make sure that potential malefactors always had examples dangling before their eyes.[48] Aitken had seen them time and time again—so many times, in fact, that they had lost their ability to shock or deter.

* * *

He bought a brace of pistols. He was doing nothing illegal. The Bill of Rights of 1689 guaranteed him and every other Protestant the right to own firearms, and he was to exercise it on several subsequent occasions.[49] Nor was there any law that prevented him from buying suspiciously large quantities of gunpowder, something that he would do soon enough.

As might be expected of someone who only a year earlier had dreamed of becoming an officer, he chose the one crime worthy of a gentleman: highway robbery. James Parquot, for one, refused to pick pockets, deeming it "a diminutive, low sort of thieving." Instead, he was "resolved to follow enterprizes more honourable, as he thought 'em, and daring," and it was for that reason that he turned to highway robbery.[50]

Did Aitken know that the typical highwayman had long since ceased to be a gentleman or an officer down on his luck? The truth, whether he knew it or not, was that by the late eighteenth century most highwaymen were men much like himself: tradesmen who had lost out in the new economic order.[51] The myth, however, was stubborn, and it persisted well into the eighteenth century, seducing new generations of young men and rendering them heedless to the gibbeted corpses of the many highwaymen who had tried and failed. Its siren song is hinted at in the *New Canting Dictionary* of 1725:

> I keep my horse; I keep my whore;
> I take no rents; yet am not poor;
> I travel all the land about,
> And yet was born to ne'er a foot.[52]

The image was incomplete without the occasional *beau geste*. This, too, served to set the highwayman apart from the common criminal. "I have been told that some highwaymen are quite polite and generous, begging to be excused for being forced to rob, and leaving passengers the wherewithal to continue their journey," a Swiss tourist had claimed in 1726.[53] "The gentleman...would have given me his gold-headed cane, but I refus'd it, by reason we had a good booty out of the coach, and I believ'd he might want his cane to support him, so we rode off." Or so William Hawkings, himself a highwayman, claimed shortly before he was hanged.[54] And when Aitken stopped a coach carrying a man and a woman, he returned two shillings, keeping the lion's share, seven shillings and six-pence, for himself.[55] Or so he claimed.

It was a career to which he was ill-suited. As far as we know, he had never ridden a horse in his life, and it was surely no accident that he committed all of his highway robberies on foot, brandishing his pistols at coachmen and hoping that they would be frightened enough to stop. The first robbery he committed was on Finchley Common, an area studded with the gibbeted corpses of failed highwaymen. Firing one of his pistols into the air, he succeeded in stopping a post chaise. He became greedy, stopping several more coaches that same night, along with various individuals riding on horseback.[56] They were easy pickings, for within a twenty-mile radius of London there were "always numbers of people passing and re-passing."[57]

His first foray as a highwayman was very nearly his last. Someone among his many victims that night had gotten a good look at him and had gone straight to Sir John Fielding. Sir John was London's most famous magistrate and he made it his business to go after criminals like Aitken. Sir John did not know it, but this was his first intersection with the man who would present him with one of his most difficult cases.

After Aitken, Fielding is the most important character in our story. The first thing that people noticed about him was that he was completely blind. He always insisted, just a little too adamantly, that his blindness was a blessing in disguise, allowing him to devote himself to "the rational delights of reflection, contemplation and conversation."[58] In his offices on Bow Street, he wore a large sash around his eyes, much to the amusement of the petty criminals who were forever being hauled before him. One of them was a boy by the name of Dick Ridgley:

> SIR JOHN: And how do you live?
> DICK: By my wits.
> SIR JOHN: That is odd indeed, considering your appearance.
> DICK: I'll tell you something more strange, if your worship won't be angry: It is that *two* of us should live upon so *scanty* a provision.[59]

He hated crime and he hated criminals. He said that he hated his job, but in fact he loved it. He made no attempt to hide his contempt for the people who besieged him in his offices. "Duty," he once wrote, "obliges me to live in a constant contention with the refuse of the creation; and to be so incessantly employed in this labour, as not to have leisure to converse with friends, or to enjoy, with any degree of comfort, the common necessaries of life—a station full of difficulties, full of perplexities, full of dissatisfactions."[60] His contempt for people less fortunate than himself is writ large in *Sir John Fielding's Jests*, a volume published shortly after his death and billed as "the smartest, wittiest, and drollest collection of original jests, jokes, repartees, &c. ever yet published." The collection does not flatter him. He tells mirthless jokes. He makes fun of immigrants, whether Jewish, Irish, or Scottish. He baits defendants, always laughing just a little too loudly at his own jokes and witticisms.

Sir John Fielding, 1762, by Nathaniel Hone (1718–1784). Boswell visited Sir John's offices in 1763, and wrote, "A more curious scene I never beheld: it brought fresh into my mind the ideas of London roguery and wickedness which I conceived in my younger days by reading The Lives of the Convicts, *and other such books. There were whores and chairmen and greasy blackguards of all denominations assembled together. The blind justice had his court in a back hall. His clerk, who officiates as a sort of chamber counsel, hears all the causes, and gives his opinion."* COURTESY OF THE NATIONAL GALLERY, LONDON.

The right words were forever eluding him. His failures as a writer can in part be explained by his subjects—crime and its prevention—but in this as in so many other things he was outdone by his famous half-brother, the novelist Henry Fielding. Henry could discourse on crime with elegance—his *Enquiry into the Causes of the Late Increase of Robbers* is proof of that—and at times, as in *The Covent Garden Journal*, with real wit.[61]

Sir John's real forte was fighting crime. In 1754, Henry died, and Sir John succeeded him as chief magistrate for Westminster. With the office he inherited two of Henry's pet projects, improving on each and using both to fight crime in and around the capital. The first was the creation of a body of professional constables to track down serious offenders. These constables operated out of the Fieldings' office on Bow Street, hence the name they later acquired: the Bow Street Runners. They were little more than glorified bounty hunters, but at the time they were the only professional police force in England. (Parish constables were unpaid, as were justices of the peace.)

It was the Fieldings' second reform that would ultimately prove Aitken's undoing. Again building on Henry's work, Sir John transformed the offices at Bow Street into a clearing house for receiving and disseminating information, not only on criminals at large, but also on unsolved crimes. Under this new arrangement, local magistrates reported both pieces of information to Sir John and his clerks. These reports were then gazetted and sent to local officials throughout England. This was done in *The Hue and Cry*, which Sir John distributed free of charge to mayors, justices of the peace, and jailers across England. These same notices were also published in various newspapers, which provided readers in both London and the provinces with physical descriptions of the criminals skulking in their midst.[62]

One of those readers was James Aitken, who loved to read newspapers. Shortly after committing his first crimes, he happened to see "an exact description" of his person and clothes. Immediately after this, he bought new clothes and made unspecified "alterations" to his appearance. He also gave up highway robbery for the time being and broadened his criminal repertoire to include shoplifting and breaking and entering.

He was not caught. But the prospect so unnerved him that he decided to decamp to America. He had probably been considering this for some time. He no longer felt safe in England, and he was also curious about the larger world. This is hinted at in one of his confessions. The phrasing is stiff and florid, but the sentiment rings true: "I had before made myself pretty conversant in the customs and government of most nations, but was at a loss which to make choice for my adventure. Among the rest, America presented itself to my imagination, and I readily believed it would turn out most to my advantage."[63]

That, however, was only part of the story. If Aitken was like everyone else, his primary reason for leaving was economic. In the stark words of John Harrower, a Scot who left for Virginia one year after Aitken, "This day, I, being reduced to the last shilling I had, was obliged to engage to go to Virginia for four years."[64] Once again, Aitken does not stand out. He was one of the forty-five thousand or more Scots who left for the New World between 1760 to 1775; the majority of these came from the Lowlands, and like Aitken, almost all of them were young, single, and poor.[65]

The pace of Scottish emigration to the colonies increased dramatically in the years just before the American Revolution, chiefly because of the economic collapse that had sent Aitken and thousands like him south in search of work.[66] By 1773, many in government were convinced that Britain would be depopulated if nothing was done to stem the seemingly inexorable tide of emigration to the colonies in North America.[67] Their fears were misplaced. Despite emigration, high infant mortality, and the constant specter of epidemic disease, Britons everywhere were reproducing themselves at prodigious rates, adding, in England alone, more than half a million new souls to the population between 1770 and 1779.[68] To its credit, the government seems to have realized that it did not have all the numbers that it needed to make an informed decision, and so at the end of 1773 it started making lists of all emigrants to America, a practice that continued until the war put an end to all emigration.

Aitken's name does not appear in the registry.[69] This is probably because he left before the registry went into effect, that is, before December of 1773. It is also possible that he was already using aliases, a practice that would become habitual upon his return from America in 1775. This, however, seems less likely, since we know that he was still carrying papers (specifically, the certificate issued to him upon completing his apprenticeship) that identified him by his real name.[70]

We do know that he was too poor to pay for his passage, and that because of this he was sold as an indentured servant when he arrived in America. He fit the profile to an astonishing extent. The typical indentured servant was young, male, unmarried, and trained in a trade that offered neither security nor the prospect of one day setting up on one's own. Many had already traveled great distances in search of work, most often from the provinces to London, making America the last leg in a journey that took them ever farther afield in search of work.[71] All of this was true of Aitken.

He wandered the dockside parishes of East London and spoke to several captains bound for America. One of them, a certain John Robertson, agreed to take him.[72] The usual arrangement was simple enough. An agent, typically a sea captain, agreed to provide a berth to America, along with food and clothing for the passage. Upon reaching America, he auctioned off those who survived to the highest bidder, invariably at an enormous profit. In return for their passage, most indentured servants committed themselves to working for four to five years without remuneration, during which time they would be provided with "all necessary clothes, meat, drink, washing, lodging, and all other necessaries."[73]

Strictly speaking, Aitken went to America as a redemptioner, agreeing to pay Robertson twenty-four pounds upon reaching America.[74] In theory, a redemptioner was given a certain number of days on arrival to find someone willing to assume and discharge his or her debt. When this search failed (as it invariably did), the redemptioner, sadder but wiser, was summarily auctioned off to the highest bidder.

Once he had signed his papers and sworn before a magistrate that he was single and under no obligation to any other employer, Aitken took up residence on Robertson's cramped ship, where he waited as it took on more supplies and more emigrants. The experience could only have been depressing. William Moraley, for one, found that his "brother adventurers" were "very dejected, from whence I guess'd they repented of their rashness."[75] This was even before his ship headed down the Thames and out into the North Atlantic.

The ship's last official stop in Britain was at Gravesend, twenty-six miles down the Thames. There it was boarded by a customs officer and a doctor. The one was looking for anyone who had been coerced into emigrating, and the other was looking for anyone who was too ill to make the journey. When John Harrower's ship was inspected, two men were taken ashore because they were suffering from the clap.[76]

Those who passed muster at Gravesend were issued new clothes, something that most desperately needed. When William Moraley first contemplated going to America, his beard was unshaven, his shirt was torn and "had not been wash'd for above a month," his shoes were "bad," and his stockings were "all full of holes." (His clothes were probably also infested with lice.) The passengers' clothes were also wholly impractical for a sea-crossing, and it was for this reason that Moraley was issued the coarse but functional "slops" of a sailor: a sea jacket, two crude checkered shirts, a woolen waistcoat, two cheap handkerchiefs, a pair of socks, "a pair of bad new shoes," and the obligatory wool cap.[77] The outfit may not have been fashionable, but it was functional, as even John Harrower, dressed in "a pair of long trousers down to my buckles," had to concede.[78] Aitken, too, probably spent his voyage dressed in sailor's slops.

From Gravesend, Robertson took his ship out to sea, keeping within sight of land as long as possible and making frequent stops to take on provisions and fresh water. Even so, these supplies never seemed to last the six to thirteen weeks that it took, on average, to cross the North Atlantic.[79] During that time, Aitken took his meals, such as they were, in a mess with several other men just as miserable as himself. The food was vile, and it only got worse over the course of the voyage. William Moraley complained of being "stinted in our allowance," with "three biscuits...given to each man for the day, and a small piece of salt beef, no bigger than a penny chop of mutton." Even the grog, "a thimbleful of bad brandy" twice a day, disappointed.[80] Two months into his own voyage, John Harrower was reduced to eating a dish called "scratch platters," made of biscuits "broke small and soaked in water until they are soft, and then vinegar, oil, salt, and onions cut small put to it, and supped with spoons."[81] Even Janet Schaw, a wealthy (and spoiled) young Scot who made the trip in 1774, was forced to go without when nine hogsheads of water were washed overboard, along with all of the chickens on deck and much of the remaining food for the voyage. She, however, was one of the lucky passengers. Below deck, conditions were much worse. For nine days, families of emigrants, most of them from the Highlands, were confined to the hold, unable to cook while a gale raged. They subsisted, as best they could, on raw potatoes and "a very small proportion of mouldy biscuit."[82]

Countless would-be emigrants died before they reached the New World. Most died of typhus, which was spread by the lice that infested their clothes and bedding. The fact that so many were half-starved made them all the more susceptible to disease. Gottlieb Mittelburger, a German who made the crossing in 1750, would never forget the "terrible misery, stench, fumes, horror, vomiting, many kinds of sea-sickness, fever, dysentery, headache, heat, constipation, boils, scurvy, cancer, mouth-rot, and the like." Most of all he remembered the lice. They fed on everybody, but especially on the sick, burrowing into their bodies and clothes and spreading disease as they moved from the dying to the living.[83]

Yet James Aitken survived. He was just twenty-one years old when Robertson's ship came in sight of the Virginia shore. He was skinny, covered with lice, and dressed in rags, and for the first time in his life he was wearing a beard. But he was alive and still hopeful of making a better life for himself.

CHAPTER THREE

His Adventures in Colonial America

A ITKEN'S ADVENTURES in America constitute the most obscure chapter in his short but eventful life. The job is made all the more difficult by the fact that he later gave two different versions of his movements in the New World. In one, he arrived in Virginia, only to run away to North Carolina, where he managed to find employment on a ship bound back to England. In the second and more elaborate version, he also arrived in Virginia, only to head north after running away from his employer. What ensues is a sort of poor man's grand tour of the eastern seaboard, with Aitken stopping briefly in a succession of cities and working as a painter before moving on. This version of events is plausible, as it is exactly what he was later wont to do in Britain; moreover, it shows him gravitating toward urban centers, much as we might expect of a person who had lived his entire life in cities. The best evidence comes from his subsequent conversations with John Baldwin, an American who lived in Philadelphia when Aitken is supposed to have been there. Like Aitken, Baldwin was a house painter, and when the two men met, they started dropping names. Aitken was able to name several Philadelphians, and this prompted Baldwin to say, "I see that you know the place very well."[1] In any event, in his two years in America Aitken had more than enough time to travel up and down the eastern seaboard. In 1690, for example, a certain Mr. Potter left his home in Virginia on the sixth of July, arriving in Boston a month later, and back home a month after that.[2] Potter enjoyed certain advantages over Aitken—since he sometimes traveled by horse and sometimes by water—but he was also traveling at a time when the roads were even more primitive than they were in the 1770s.[3]

This much is certain: in 1773, Aitken arrived in Virginia, in Jamestown, and unable to repay his debt to Captain Robertson, he was sold as an indentured servant. Two years later, in the spring of 1775, he left from North Carolina, probably from Wilmington and possibly from New Bern. What he did between arriving and leaving is largely a mystery, although this much can be said with certainty: his options were few and his disappointments were many.

His disappointments began the moment he first set eyes on America. As his ship approached Jamestown, all of the indentured servants on board were rousted from their cramped quarters and given a rough makeover. After several weeks at sea, their grooming and clothes left a great deal to be desired.[4] James Revel, who was transported to Virginia in the latter half of the seventeenth century, remembered being fussed over after weeks of neglect and abuse:

And after sailing seven weeks and more,
We at Virginia all were put on shore.
    Where, to refresh us, we were wash'd and cleaned,
That to our buyers we might the better seem;
Our things were gave to each they did belong,
And they that had clean linen put it on.
    Our faces shav'd, comb'd out our wigs and hair,
That we in decent order might appear.... [5]

Aitken himself was not immediately auctioned off (that would come soon enough), but what he saw next could only have alarmed him. Newly scrubbed and shaved, his fellow passengers (those who had survived the voyage), were forced to stand on deck as potential employers, most of them slave-owners, clambered on board to assess Robertson's newest offering of misfits and indigents, poking and prodding and asking leading questions. Poor Revel:

> The women separated from us stand,
> As well as we, by them for to be view'd;
> And in short time some men up to us came,
> Some ask'd our trades, and others ask'd our names.
>
> Some view'd our limbs, and others turn'd us round
> Examining like horses, if we're sound,
> "What trade are you, my lad?," says one to me,
> "A tin-man, sir." "That will not do," says he.
>
> Some felt our hands and view'd our legs and feet,
> And made us walk, to see we were complete;
> Some view'd our teeth, to see if they were good,
> Or fit to chew our hard and homely food.

Robertson's customers seldom liked what they saw. Most of them were looking for men who could work as farmhands, something that few indentured servants had ever done in their lives. When Charles Speckman, a career criminal, was asked what he could do, he quipped, "I could work, but not hard." Speckman then volunteered that he might be willing to work at "such trades as I worked at in London," at which his would-be master "turned his head and laughed."[6]

Aitken's turn came a few days later. Unable to find anyone willing to assume his debt to Captain Robertson, he, too, was put up for sale. He was not a towering physical specimen. But he was able to speak intelligently, and this mattered to employers intent on winnowing out the doltish and the intractable. He impressed one of them well enough, a certain Mr. Graham, who paid Robertson twenty-four pounds and took the unlikely young Scot home with him. All told, it had cost five or six pounds to transport Aitken to the New World, and for that paltry sum he was expected to work, without pay, for the next several years.[7]

Each day brought a new shock to the system, starting with the clothes that he was issued. The masters of indentured servants were contractually obligated to clothe them, and this they did with as little flair as possible. Mr. Graham's rustic offerings no doubt disappointed Aitken, who was very fussy about his clothes and appearance. Certainly James Revel was disappointed. "My European clothes were took from me," he complained,

> Which never after I again could see.
> A canvas shirt and trousers then they gave,
> With a hop-sack frock in which I was to slave:
> No shoes nor stockings had I for to wear,
> Nor hat, nor cap, both head and feet were bare.[8]

Revel was exaggerating, but not by much. The canvas shirt that he mentions was probably made of ozanburg, a coarse linen that was used to clothe slaves and indentured servants alike.[9] William Moraley also found himself clad in ozanburg. He hated the stuff. "The Negroes and bought servants are clad in coarse ozanburg," he complained, "both coat, waistcoat, breeches, and shirt, being of the same piece, and so rough, that the shirt occasions great uneasiness to the body."[10] Mentions of the hateful fabric can also be found in advertisements for runaway servants. James Patterson, for example, was wearing an ozanburg shirt when he ran away in December of 1772, and if Aitken was dressed anything like him, his sartorial plight was extreme. Patterson "had on, when he went away, a buff-coloured jeans coat, a blue broadcloth waistcoat, buck-skin breeches, an ozanburg shirt, *Virginia*-made shoes, and a very good hat." Mindful that he could be identified by this outfit, Patterson "took with him sundry other clothes," something that Aitken no doubt did when he, too, ran away.[11]

His shirt was a reminder that his status was little better than that of a slave. He had been sold once, to Mr. Graham, and he could be sold again. And perhaps most importantly, he was expected to stay put. This he could no more do in America than he had done in Britain. Other than that, his status was largely unchanged. In Britain, he had been too poor to marry; in Virginia, he was still too poor to marry, but now he faced the additional obstacle of having to get his master's consent in the unlikely event that he found a woman willing to have him.[12] As in Britain, he could not vote. He did, however, have one right in common with freeborn Britons everywhere: he could own property (not that this was a realistic option for a man too poor to pay his own way across the Atlantic).

The primary shock to his system was racial. Nothing could have prepared him for the experience of working side by side with Africans. They were everywhere. When he had left England in 1773, there were perhaps fourteen to fifteen thousand Africans in all of England; most of these lived in London, where at the very most they accounted for just 2 percent of the city's population.[13] Virginia, by contrast, was home to more than 40 percent of the colonies' growing population of slaves; by one estimate, its population of Africans numbered over 187,000 in 1770, climbing to over 220,000 just ten years later.[14]

On the Virginia plantations, slaves and indentured servants ordinarily lived apart, in huts or cabins of their own making, but other than that their lives were intertwined and in most respects indistinguishable. "We and the Negroes both alike did fare," James

Revel wrote. "Of work and food we had an equal share."[15] If any-thing, slaves received marginally better treatment. The reason for this is obvious: they represented a much larger financial invest-ment. William Eddis, an Englishman who lived in America in the years before the revolution, observed as much in 1770. "Negroes being a property for life, the death of slaves, in the prime of youth or strength, is a material loss to the proprietor; they are, therefore, almost in every instance, under more comfortable circumstances than the miserable European, over whom the rigid planter exer-cises an inflexible severity."[16]

Slaves had another advantage: they were more useful. Not only did they know a great deal more about farming than men like Aitken, they also possessed many of the same artisanal skills.[17] This was already the case in 1724, when it was observed that "several of them are taught to be *sawyers, carpenters, smiths, coopers,* &c. and though for the most part they be none of the aptest or nicest; yet they…will per-form tolerably well." Another visitor, a Scot who made a tour of the Chesapeake the same year that Aitken came to America, gave African artisans much higher marks. "There are Negroes here of all trades," he wrote, adding that "they are very true and come to be very good tradesmen."[18]

Aitken probably had very little opportunity—or call—to prac-tice his trade at Mr. Graham's. If he was like most other indentured servants who ended up in Virginia, he was probably marched out to a field and told to start working.[19] There, in his stiff ozanburg shirt and ill-fitting pants, he cut a very sorry figure. He was healthy enough, but he was by no means strong. And if he was like other indentured servants, he resented performing tasks that he consid-ered to be beneath him. Charles Speckman was mortified when he was given a hoe, and said so in no uncertain terms. He looked "very hard" at his master and "told him I was not used to that kind of work; he, however, took me to a field to shew me how to till up some corn; I told him the trade I was sent from London for, was much easier than this."[20] William Moraley, who was a watchmaker by training, was given the most menial of tasks. "Sometimes I have acted the blacksmith," he complained. "At other times, I have work'd in the water, stark naked, among water snakes. Sometimes I was a cow-hunter in the woods...."[21] At least Moraley did as he was told, albeit with a great deal of prodding. James Dalton, a convict twice transported to Virginia in the early eighteenth century, did not. He was already a hardened criminal by the time he reached Virginia, and no sooner was he sold than he made up his mind to run away. When he failed at this, he simply refused to work, stating that farming "was intended for horses and not for Christians."[22]

*   *   *

It was in America that Aitken first experienced moments of solitude. In his parents' home, in Edinburgh's Old Town, at Heriot's, in London, and on the voyage to America, he was forever surrounded by people; now, for the first time in his life, he could walk down a road and not once see a house or run into another human being. If he was like most Europeans, the experience unnerved him. It unnerved a compatriot of his named Janet Schaw, who in a journey of sixteen miles saw only one plantation.[23] The young Englishman Nicholas Cresswell described the road between Alexandria and Leesburg as "very thinly populated...almost all woods." "Only one public house between this place and Alexandria," he added gloomily.[24] And William Moraley walked for eight miles without once seeing a farm or house. He was convinced that had he continued down this road, "I should not have met with a house till I came to *Salem*...which was near two-hundred miles from me."[25]

Aitken was isolated in another and even more terrible way: he was without friends. And this, in a society in which contacts and reputation meant everything, marked him for failure.[26] Patrick M'Robert, a Scot who was in America at the same time as Aitken, put it very well. Poor immigrants, he wrote, could succeed in America, but it took time. "You have all to seek, and as it were, to begin the world anew; to acquire acquaintances; to struggle hard for a character, &c."[27] Pehr Kalm, who made the voyage in 1748, came prepared. Armed with three letters of introduction, he found it easy "to get acquainted."[28] He was the exception.

Aitken had few male friends and probably no female friends. The reason was simple enough: there were not enough women to go around—not, at least, among his fellow servants. This was a particular problem on the plantations, whose owners had very little use for female indentured servants. Women, moreover, were in a distinct minority among emigrants from Britain, accounting for only a quarter of the people known to have left between 1773 and 1776.[29]

For his first several weeks in America, he was too ill and too weak to think about women, let alone pursue them. Instead, he spent that time in silent battle with a succession of potentially deadly diseases. Some, like yellow fever and malaria, he had never been exposed to; others, like smallpox and measles, he had already weathered in the Old World. If he was like most other immigrants, he briefly succumbed to malaria or dysentery—or quite possibly both.[30] Malaria was especially deadly, as Pehr Kalm observed firsthand in 1748. "Strangers who arrive here are commonly attacked by this sickness the first or second year after their arrival, and it acts more violently upon them than upon the natives, so that they sometimes die of it."[31] Lesser afflictions were no less startling, if only because newcomers had no way of judging whether they were serious or not. Nicholas Cresswell, for one, probably thought that he was going to die when he discovered "small blisters...broke out all over my body, attended with an intolerable itching." These, it turned out, were nothing more than prickly heat.[32]

Those who managed to survive started complaining just as soon as they recovered their strength. Their letters and journals are sour with disappointments, each betraying just how naive and ill-prepared the typical immigrant was. First they complained about the weather. It was too hot. Or it was too cold. "The heat in summer is excessive and without intermission," wrote Pehr Kalm. "The winters are so severely cold as benumbs the inhabitants, and begins so early," wrote William Moraley.[33] The "excessive heat...caused me to faint twice," wrote Nicholas Cresswell.[34] Six months later, he was complaining that the winter was "more severe than ever I felt it in England." The heat "has ruined all vivacity...and renders us languid in thought, word and deed," wrote Janet Schaw.[35] Aitken, too, probably spent a great deal of time grumbling about the heat, and rightly so. Nothing could have prepared him for the stultifying heat of a Virginia summer. It was an inauspicious start for a man who would later come to romanticize America from afar.

As soon as he recovered his health and got his bearings, he ran away. Aitken gives us two versions of the circumstances under which he quit Mr. Graham's employ. In one, he behaves with a certain degree of honor, compensating his employer in part before decamping.[36] This payment could only have taken the form of labor. In the second version, he decamps almost immediately, having never intended to honor his side of the bargain.[37] The latter is probably closer to the truth, if only because it fits with everything else that we know about Aitken's work record.

The fact that he escaped at all is remarkable. Few did. Everything —from the strangeness of the land to the strangeness of the servants' manners and dialects—stood in their way. It is remarkable that so many even tried. William Eddis observed as much, and William Moraley, who had himself been caught and returned to his master, knew as much.[38]

The first obstacle was the requirement that servants carry passes when traveling.[39] Those without passes were, in Eddis's words, "committed to close confinement, advertised, and delivered to their respective masters."[40] Aitken, who was exceptionally literate, probably had no difficulty in forging such a document; in fact, it is almost certain that he did so, as he seems to have been able to travel at will after he was clear of Mr. Graham's estate. In any event, young men with foreign accents invariably stood out wherever they went. Even Charles Speckman, a smart and resourceful criminal, was easily caught. He had, he later confessed, failed to appreciate just how difficult it was to escape. "My servitude being very intolerable to me, I determined to make a trial of another escape . . . but not considering the expence, the danger in crossing the rivers, and having no pass from a magistrate, I was soon taken up. . . . "[41]

An obvious strategy was to avoid settled areas altogether, but this, too, had its drawbacks. Roads were bad and few, and bridges practically nonexistent. This was true everywhere in the colonies, but it was especially true in North Carolina, where Aitken eventually ended up. There the coastline was riddled with swamps and inlets, making it all but impossible to proceed on foot. The roads, such as they were, were "deep and difficult to be found."[42] They were also abandoned, and this was enough to reduce Janet Schaw to hysterics.[43] Those who headed inland, away from the swamps and estuaries, merely traded one form of misery for another. The swamps were gone, but the roads were just as scarce and even more awful. A Frenchman traveling through the Shenandoah Valley found himself on "a road that the torrents had made impassable." After a short while, the road became so rough that the passengers were forced to get out of the carriage and walk.[44] Farther north, where the land was more densely settled, the roads were marginally better, but they were still confusing and often abandoned. William Moraley, for one, got lost just outside Philadelphia, having followed a road straight into a "wood of pines, that grow close together, overshadows the road, and prevents communication with the sky."[45] He traveled down this road for eight miles, and not once did he see a house. He was scared out of his mind.

And yet Aitken's escape was successful. It was an amazing feat, and it marks him as a man of real cunning. His accomplishment becomes all the more remarkable when we consider the distances he was able to cover in a strange and inhospitable land. Assuming that he made it as far north as New York, he would have traveled some 385 miles; if, as is less likely, he proceeded on to Boston, he would have traveled more than 600 miles, a count that does not include his eventual passage by ship back to North Carolina.

Aitken does not tell us how he did all this, but the stories of other successful escapees offer some clues. Most men in his shoes wanted nothing so much as to return to Britain as soon as possible, and it was for this reason that almost all of them gravitated toward ports frequented by ocean-going vessels. The incorrigible James Dalton escaped twice, each time making a beeline for a port where he was unlikely to be recognized. The first time he stole a skiff, sinking it upon reaching the other side of the river. Then he stole a horse, riding it until he reached an unnamed port on the Potomac. There, after skulking about for three weeks, he managed to find employment on a ship headed back to England. The second time he stole a pass from a Scottish servant who was himself plotting to escape; this he used to head north, eventually finding employment on a ship about to depart from New York.[46] When an indentured servant named James Patterson first ran away, he changed his name and, like Dalton, he headed straight for a ship. The plan, however, backfired, and he was returned to his master. When he ran away a second time, his master took the understandable precaution of warning ship captains against hiring him.[47] When William Fogg, another indentured servant, ran away a year later, in 1774, it was simply assumed that he would make for South Carolina, presumably to Charleston and its busy port.[48]

Aitken, however, did not head straight to the nearest port. Instead, he headed north, to Philadelphia. He genuinely wanted to stay in America—and he was curious by nature. We know that in England he once made a special trip to Cambridge, in part because he was fearful of being arrested in London, but in part because he had a "desire to see that university."[49] It was curiosity that later took him to Oxford, where he would overhear the conversation that gave him the idea to burn down the royal dockyards.

Mr. Graham seems to have made little or no effort to pursue Aitken. This is curious, as most masters whose servants ran away thought nothing of offering rewards "from thirty shillings to five pounds," in addition to posting "printed and written advertisements . . . against the trees and public places in the town. . . ."[50] And unlike most other cheated masters, Mr. Graham did not take out an advertisement in *The Virginia Gazette*, even though Aitken's accent—not to mention his stammering—was a dead giveaway. "You are not an American by your dialect, and I presume that you have never been there," Deane would tell Aitken when they first met.[51] This was after Aitken had spent two long years in America. Accents were always a dead giveaway. When a servant named John Driver ran away in 1773, it was noted that he "calls himself an Englishman, but has the Irish accent."[52] When Solomon Burnham ran away in 1775, it was noted that he was "born in *Yorkshire*, and speaks in that dialect."[53] Such accents stood out like sore thumbs, making it all but impossible for their bearers to pass themselves off as native-born. Not only did Americans speak with an accent that was distinct—and surprisingly homogeneous—their usage also tended to be uniform, making it all the harder for British newcomers to blend into the general population. "The propriety of language here surprised me much, the English tongue being spoken by all ranks, in a degree of purity and perfection, surpassing any, but the polite part of London." This from a British officer who visited America in 1764.[54] A "uniformity of language prevails not only on the coast, where Europeans form a considerable mass of the people, but likewise in the interior parts, where population has made but slow advances. . . . " This from William Eddis, who made the trip in 1769.[55]

Based on accent alone, it mattered little where Aitken went after leaving Mr. Graham's. Wherever he went, he would always be regarded as a foreigner—and an unwelcome one at that. To that extent, America was no different than southern England. And if he thought that he might do better as a journeyman painter than he had in England, he was sadly mistaken. In Philadelphia, the largest of the American cities, times were hard, and had been so since the end of the Seven Years' War in 1763. Jobs were scarce, and prices were rising faster than real wages, all of which spelled trouble for men like Aitken.[56] This was true in each of the cities he visited. New York City, for example, was "overstocked" with laborers in the years just before the Revolution, a surplus that one contemporary blamed on "the arrival of so many adventurers from Britain and Ireland."[57] The implications were dire. Unable to find full-time employment, American journeymen, no less than their British counterparts, were increasingly in the habit of wandering from place to place in search of work.[58] Perhaps we now know why Aitken continued to move from town to town even after he had put several hundred miles between himself and Mr. Graham.

He was drawn to Philadelphia. The city, with its crisp, broad streets and obvious wealth, invariably made a good first impression. William Moraley gushed. (It was "one of the most delightful cities upon earth.")[59] Pehr Kalm gushed. (Its "fine appearance, good regulations, agreeable location, natural advantages, trade, riches and power are by no means inferior to those of any, even of the most ancient, towns in Europe.")[60] Colonel Adam Gordon, who visited the city in 1764, gushed. (It was "perhaps one of the wonders of the world," "the first town in America," and a "rival [to] almost any in Europe.")[61] And even Nicholas Cresswell, who was otherwise very bitter about his experiences in America, gushed. ("This is the most regular, neat and convenient city I ever was in and has made the most rapid progress to its present greatness.")[62]

Aitken, too, must have liked what he saw, for he spent more time in Philadelphia than in any other town or city in America. No doubt it helped that the city had a sizeable enclave of Scots-Irish immigrants.[63] Unfortunately, there were perhaps too many reminders of home. Behind the neat and orderly neighborhoods that made such a good impression on visitors were slums every bit as awful as those in Edinburgh and London. To the north, along the Delaware River, there were ramshackle wooden boarding houses where sailors and unmarried laborers rented rooms, and everywhere poorer families doubled up and took in single men as lodgers.[64] And still the immigrants came, building houses closer and closer together, and scrambling for jobs and wages no better than those in the Old World.

Aitken could not have chosen a worse time to come to Philadelphia. War was in the air, businesses were not hiring, and his life was starting to look very much the way it had back in London. In time, he came to realize the hopelessness of his situation, and once again he moved on, more disillusioned than ever.

His next stop was Perth Amboy, or so he would claim in one of his confessions. Perth Amboy was not exactly a household name, and the fact that Aitken was able to name it suggests that he did in fact spend some time there. The surrounding area was extensively cultivated, and according to one pleased visitor, it "very much" resembled England.[65] This, combined with the presence of a Scottish community, probably made Aitken feel vaguely at home. Patrick M'Robert was there just before the war broke out, and being a fond Scot, he was delighted to discover that the area "still retains the name of *Scots Plains*."[66]

The same confession has Aitken next stopping in New York City, which, given its proximity to Perth Amboy, is plausible enough. After Philadelphia, New York invariably disappointed, being, in the words of one visitor, "not so regular... nor so extensive."[67] But it was a very good place to catch a ship back to England, and this, with war now imminent, was something that increasing numbers of Britons were doing. Among them was Nicholas Cresswell, who arrived in New York "determined to get a passage in the first vessel that sails for England if I can."

The same story that places Aitken in New York next places him in Boston, the most radical of all the American cities. The prose is the first thing that rings false. Pompous, stiff, and absurdly formulaic, it betrays the hand of an editor intent on casting Aitken as a picaresque revolutionary:

Upon hearing of the riots at Boston, the restlessness of my disposition would not suffer me to remain any longer at New York; and meeting with a companion whose curiosity was equally excited with my own, we agreed to set out together for that place; and I cannot deny being very active in those riots, particularly in sinking the tea, and insulting the friends of the government, in which I did not escape the notice of many principal persons among the Americans.[68]

The claim is laughable. It places Aitken in Boston in December of 1773, and it assumes, even more improbably, that he found ready acceptance among the city's famously clannish patriots.[69] If Aitken did in fact make it to Boston, he would have discovered that Scots were no more welcome there than they were elsewhere in the colonies, although one Scot, James Swann, is supposed to have participated in the Boston Tea Party, while another, William Hyslop, is supposed to have helped in planning it.[70] Hyslop, however, had been living in Massachusetts since 1746; Aitken, by contrast, would have just arrived. By his own admission, Aitken did not leave for Virginia until 1773, arriving either later in the same year or even in 1774. Assuming that he did in fact arrive in 1773, he would have been operating under a very tight schedule, one that took him from Virginia almost as soon as he landed, and still allowed him enough time to make his way up the eastern seaboard, pausing to work in Philadelphia, Perth Amboy, and New York.

In any event, there is only one source for this claim: the confession dictated to a clerk working for Sir John Fielding. This confession, as we will see, was extracted under duress, from a man who was cornered and afraid. It is possible that he told some lies in an attempt to salvage his pride—and that the editor inserted some lies of his own in an attempt to increase sales of the published confession.

The likelier sequence of events is this: from Perth Amboy, Aitken went to New York, an easy enough trip, and from there he took a ship to North Carolina. But why North Carolina? The answer seems obvious enough: North Carolina was rumored to have a sizeable enclave of loyalists, many of whom were Scots. This made it, in the eyes of many, a safe haven for fleeing loyalists. Even its royal governor thought, erroneously as it turns out, that he could hold the colony, having convinced himself that "loyal subjects yet abound and infinitely outnumber the seditious throughout all the very populous western counties of this Province."[71] In any event, the fact that Aitken chose to flee to North Carolina tells us that he was still very far from committed to the cause of American independence.

Even if his sympathies already lay with the Americans, it would have been almost impossible for him to gain their trust. This was because he was a Scot. The Americans, it seems, blamed the Scots for everything—for the war, for the unreasonableness of George III, and most of all, for the fact that their notoriously spendthrift planters were forever getting into debt, mostly to Scottish merchants. To make matters worse, few Scots stayed in America after amassing fortunes of their own. Instead, they bided their time, waiting for the day when they could return to Scotland.[72] This, too, was a source of resentment and mistrust. The Americans wanted nothing to do with the Scots, and the Scots, it seems, wanted nothing to do with them.

Matters had come to a head in the early 1770s. First, in 1772, came the collapse of the Scottish banking system, which was the reason why Aitken left Scotland in the first place. But its consequences were also felt as far afield as America, where Scottish creditors, their own funds now in jeopardy, started to call in the debts owed by planters. Then, even as the first crisis subsided, another, that of the impending revolution, took its place.[73] Knowing that their days in America were numbered, Scottish creditors continued to call in their debts, and in so doing further antagonized the colonies' influential (albeit insolvent) planters. Nor did it help that most Scots remained loyal to their king, even as the crisis deepened and the position of loyalists in America became increasingly untenable.

The journals of Britons who happened to be in America at the time abound with stories of persecution—if not of themselves, then of their compatriots. Janet Schaw's brother had to flee for his life.[74] Nicholas Cresswell also had to flee for his life when a local committee suspected him of being a spy. And Patrick M'Robert, who found himself stranded in New York City in May of 1775, worried for the many loyalists who lived there. "Many fine industrious families, lately in affluence now do not know where to turn to avoid the dreadful stroke of a desolating war: all is confusion."[75]

Aitken, too, was caught up in the confusion of the time. Once again it was his bad luck to be punished for the sins, some real and some imaginary, of Scots far wealthier and more powerful than himself. It mattered little that he was poor and inconsequential, for he was, simply and inescapably, Scottish. His last several months in America must have been hellish. In December of 1774, in what was to be a harbinger of things to come, a certain Malachi Macalle managed to get three hundred Virginians to sign a petition "for expelling out of the country all *Scotchmen*."[76] In January of 1775, a "Gentleman in Virginia" reported that a "Scotsman is in danger of his life (at least being tarred and feathered) if he says a word that does not please them."[77] "The provincials are said to have taken a dislike to the Scots," *The Scots Magazine* reported in 1776, almost as an afterthought.[78] When Ezra Stiles, future president of Yale University, looked for someone to blame for the war, he knew who was responsible: "Let us boldly say, for history will say it, that the whole of this war is so far chargeable to the Scotch councils, and to the Scotch as a nation (for they have nationally come into it) as that had it not been for them, this quarrel had never happened."[79] And unfortunately for Aitken and every other Scot who happened to be in America at the time, the revolutionaries thought the world of John Wilkes, the man who had inflamed anti-Scots prejudice in England.[80]

The year 1775 witnessed a mass exodus of Scottish loyalists. Their numbers included the insufferable Janet Schaw, who cowered on a royal frigate just outside Wilmington, North Carolina, all the while complaining that it was "crowded beyond any thing that was ever seen with people flying from this land of nominal freedom and real slavery." And their numbers also included young James Aitken. He had wanted to stay in America—he had, after all, chosen to go to North Carolina, a presumed bastion of loyalists, instead of returning directly home. He arrived there in January or February of 1775, by which time the colony's loyalists were already in full flight.

Aitken had no choice but to join them, and no sooner had he arrived than he prevailed on a certain Captain Wright to take him back to England.[81] This time he did not have to pay his way. Ship's captains had a hard enough time finding crews for the voyage back to Britain, and with talk of war in the air, sailors, fearful of being taken up by press gangs, were already making themselves scarce.[82] Aitken, who had no nautical skills whatsoever, was probably taken on as a cook or steward, in which capacity he worked his way back to England. His skills were too few to merit his being paid. William Moraley, for one, worked his way back as a cook. He had to be taught everything, including the proper techniques for splitting wood.[83]

And so James Aitken left America, no richer than when he had arrived just two years earlier. Whatever illusions he might have had about the New World had been dashed, all of which makes it very difficult to account for his subsequent infatuation with the

American Revolution. It was one thing to romanticize America from afar, as so many French aristocrats were wont to do; it was quite another to romanticize it after having spent two years there with nothing to show.[84] Aside from the farcical claim of having participated in the Boston Tea Party, there is nothing to suggest that he developed any partisan sympathies in America. He admitted as much when he later forced himself on Silas Deane. Deane, writing several months after their first meeting, quoted Aitken as saying:

> I foolishly took the part of government. I was very, very harshly used for it by the people, on which I went and joined Lord Dunmore, who made me fair promises, but treated me worse than the Americans had done; this opened my eyes and shewed me that the Americans were right, and that they fought for liberty, but I could not join them in that country after what had passed, so I came to England, where I am resolved to serve them and their cause most effectually....[85]

The Lord Dunmore whom Aitken mentions was John Murray Dunmore, a Scot and the royal governor of Virginia from 1771 until he was driven out in 1775. After that and with the help of loyalists, Dunmore launched guerilla raids in Virginia, and it was in the course of one such raid that the town of Norfolk was burnt to the ground. The irony of this was not wasted on the ever-caustic Horace Walpole. Informed of Aitken's attempt to burn down the royal dockyard at Portsmouth, he quipped, "This comes of teaching the Americans to burn towns!"[86] However, it is unlikely that Dunmore's and Aitken's paths ever crossed. For one thing, the timing is all wrong: Aitken had already left America when Dunmore was attempting to form a militia of his own. (Among others, he enlisted at least three hundred slaves.)[87] It is just possible that

Aitken volunteered for one of Dunmore's earlier adventures, an expedition that took place in 1774; if so, he would have found himself deep in the back country fighting Shawnee warriors. This is very hard to picture.

The story about Dunmore is drivel. But it speaks volumes about Aitken's true ambitions: more than anything, he wanted to be an officer. In Edinburgh, he had dreamt of receiving a commission; in America, he had offered to serve in the British army, but only as an officer; and in due time, despairing of ever receiving a commission in the British army, he would offer his services to the fledgling American army.

CHAPTER FOUR

His Return to England

BY THE middle of 1775, Aitken was once more back in England. One account, his own, has it that he landed in Liverpool in the first week of May; another, that of a man who knew of Aitken only in passing, has it that he landed in Emsworth, Hampshire, in September or October of that year.[1] On this, Aitken is to be trusted, for in both of his confessions he volunteered details about the route that he took and the crimes that he committed along the way. Two things are certain: he returned penniless and had no intention of going back to Scotland.[2] If he was anything like Nicholas Cresswell, who was also reduced to working his way back from America, his mood was low. Depressed and more than a little bitter, Cresswell did as so many others have done, and vented his sorrows in a journal. "The thought of returning to my native country a beggar is more than I can support with becoming fortitude," he wrote. "It casts such an unusual damp upon my spirits that I am more dead than alive."[3] There is a whiff of melodrama in all this, but the feeling, and the disappointed young man behind it, are real nonetheless. Like Aitken, he had returned not in triumph but in failure.

Aitken's first order of business was to get a shave and procure a halfway decent suit of clothes. Without these, he could not possibly hope to find employment, let alone pass through the countryside without arousing suspicion or being picked up by the press gangs that were already forcing men into service. William Moraley, who

The Recruiting Sergeant, *circa 1790, by Thomas Rowlandson (1756–1827). Two potential recruits, both ragged and skinny, are bedazzled by the uniform and considerable girth of the recruiting sergeant.* COURTESY OF THE YALE CENTER FOR BRITISH ART.

worked his way back to England in 1734, remembered looking the very "picture of *Robinson Crusoe*" when he first landed. At the time he was wearing the shirt that he had worn for the past fourteen or fifteen weeks, "a miserable pair of breeches, adorn'd with many living companions, two torn waistcoats, no coat, a coarse, lousy, woolen cap," an old hat given him in Ireland, a pair of torn stockings, and "a bad pair of shoes supported by packthread."[4] His beard, moreover, was shaggy, having gone untrimmed for the fourteen weeks that he was at sea. He was exceedingly grateful when a kind soul gave him a shave, along with some decent, if ill-fitting, used clothes.

Aitken solved his immediate financial and sartorial problems by joining the army, in return for which he received an enlistment bonus of twenty-six shillings, just enough to buy some passable used clothes. In most cases, men joined the army only when they had exhausted all other options, and this was undeniably true of Aitken at this juncture. The typical British recruit was drawn from the same desperate class as indentured servants.[5] He was in his early to mid-twenties and single, came from a town or city, and had been taught a trade but was unable to find steady employment.[6] All of these things were true of Aitken, but he differed from the profile in two important respects: he was literate, something that very few enlisted men were, and he had an extensive criminal past, something that surprisingly few recruits seem to have had.[7]

He first joined the army in Liverpool, almost immediately after landing. The war had now started and recruiting parties were busily scouring the town. Aitken soon fell in with one. Its sergeant was delighted, and he conducted the preliminaries with a practiced bonhomie, plying Aitken with liquor and talking up the nonexistent charms of a soldier's life. For his part, Aitken played along, glad, no doubt, of the free food and drink. When he was asked whether he was "free, able, and willing to serve his majesty, King George the Third," he said that he most certainly was. With that, he received his enlistment bonus and found himself a private in the British army. In principle, he was expected to serve for life—that is, until he was killed, dropped dead from disease, or was simply too old or too crippled to be useful.[8] Two days later, he deserted.

It was a stratagem that he would use on at least two other occasions, each time signing on with a new regiment, pocketing his enlistment bonus, and deserting at the earliest opportunity. In October, when he happened to be back in Gravesend, he enlisted as a private in the Thirty-second Foot Regiment, and was marched off to Chatham before finding the means to escape.[9] Sometime after that, in December of 1775 or early in 1776, he enlisted in the Thirteenth Foot Regiment, and he even remained put "for some time, supposing the change of clothes would prevent my being apprehended for some or other of the innumerable robberies I had committed."[10] On one occasion, he absconded at three in the morning, "leaving my comrades asleep in bed."[11] As luck would have it, at least one of the regiments that Aitken is supposed to have joined—the Thirty-seventh Foot—was sent to America shortly after he had quitted its ranks.[12]

Desertion was a very serious (if understandably common) offense, and those who were caught were almost always brutally flogged. This prospect so unnerved one deserter, a marine private by the name of Isaiah Bayes, that he insisted on being executed, a mercy that was nonetheless denied him. Instead, Bayes was sentenced to a thousand lashes, which the Admiralty, in a rare moment of "lenity," reduced to six hundred.[13] Aitken, however, never got caught. He was stealthier than the unfortunate Bayes— and he was smarter, using a different alias each time he enlisted. As an added precaution, he burned the indenture papers he had received upon completing his apprenticeship.[14] These identified him by name, and by now they had become a liability.

Aliases suited him. They were of obvious use to a man engaged in criminal activities, but they also played to a certain fantastical streak, allowing him to assume identities unburdened by the accident of birth. He was to use aliases for the next two years, and it was under one of them, James Hill, that he was later tried and convicted. As far as we know, he used his real name on only three occasions after returning to England: when he forced himself on Silas Deane in Paris; when he showed up at the London house of Dr. Edward Bancroft (a friend of Deane's); and in the last four days of his life.

Aitken used at least three aliases—James Hill, James Boswell, and James Hinde—all of which were mangled by the press, who added and subtracted letters at will. One, *The London Magazine*, even identified him as James Hell.[15] The most curious alias was that of James Boswell. At first blush, it sounds like a sly tribute to his fellow Scot. This, however, seems unlikely, if only because Boswell was still far from famous in the 1770s. The name probably occurred to Aitken because it combined his Christian name with his mother's maiden name of *Boswell*. There may, however, have been a certain playfulness behind another of his aliases: James Hinde. This happened to be the name of a famous highwayman who was executed for high treason in 1652.[16]

The proletarian sobriquet of John the Painter was a later addition, and it was not of Aitken's devising or choosing. If anything, he resented it keenly, for it identified him as a mere worker, and a lowly one at that. It first surfaces in December of 1776, after Aitken had set fire to the Portsmouth rope house.[17] It is easy to see how it came about. He told various people that his name was John and that he was a painter; if they remembered him at all—and few did—it was as John the Painter. A former employer, for example, remembered only that he "went by the name of John." One is reminded of Jude the Obscure, moving unseen among the scholars at Christminster. "He was a young workman in a white blouse, and with stone-dust in the creases of his clothes; and in passing him they did not even see him, or hear him, rather saw through him as through a pane of glass at their familiars beyond."

In each town and village he was free to make up a new name and a new story to go with it. This, at least, is what William Moraley did as he made his way across the English countryside, changing his name and identity at will to find favor with the people he met. Once Moraley passed himself off as a Mr. Ridley, and once he managed to convince a man that they had a friend in common.[18] Aitken, too, made up stories to gratify his listeners and his own vanity. Hence the story that he had been wounded "in the wars."[19]

On the surface, Aitken's life looked much the way it had back in 1773. As before, he alternated between crime and legitimate employment, sometimes robbing and sometimes working as a journeyman painter. His movements, however, betray a new restlessness. During this time, from 1775 to 1776, he was to crisscross much of the English countryside, allowing him to boast, at the end of his life, that he had committed a crime in almost every county in England. His perambulations took him to Shrewsbury, Birmingham, Coventry, London, Cambridge, and Oxford. He lingered only in London, where, under the proverbial influence of "some women of the town," he committed "a number of street robberies," in addition to breaking into a house in the fashionable neighborhood of Kensington."[30] After Cambridge, he "made a circle round the northern part of England," thieving as he went, and after that, he headed south once more.

The crimes that he committed were opportunistic. Sometimes he broke into houses, and sometimes he held up coaches. He

broke into a house outside Coventry and another outside Warrington, each time stealing money and small objects.[21] Once he broke
into a glazier's, in a small Hampshire town, and stole two dia-
monds used for cutting glass. On another occasion, probably in
August of 1776, he held up a coach just outside Cambridge, having already committed several other highway robberies on the
busy road running from London to Southampton. Each time he
acted alone.

In several towns, including Birmingham, Havant, Exeter,
Titchfield, Warrington, "and many other places," he worked as
journeyman painter. In each place his status was little better than
that of a day laborer. He was "looked on as an itinerant journeyman in search of daily employ," and each time he resumed his
journeys, no one knew "whither he went, or what road he took."[22]

He ran enormous risks in these months. He could be taken up
for desertion; he could be taken up for any of his crimes; and, if he
were especially unlucky, he could be taken up by a press gang.
Press gangs were to be found in all the major maritime towns and
on many of the roads leading away from them, and their constant
presence may be one of the reasons why Aitken seems to have
favored inland towns and villages after returning to England in
1775.[23] Press gangs were very much on his mind when he took
lodgings in Portsmouth in December of 1776. Was there any press-
ing? he asked his roommate. "Yes," he was told, "they press very
hot." Aitken was spooked. "Suppose they were to take up such a
man as me? I can give no account of myself."[24] Was he "not afraid of
the press?" another man once asked him. No, Aitken responded,
just a little too quickly and just a little too emphatically.[25]

It was that way wherever he went. He saw himself as a man of
superior talents—which in many ways he was—but the people
he met on his journeys saw rather less. To some, he was cannon

fodder, to others he was a common thief, and to still others he was a common laborer. Every day, they ran into other young men like him—underemployed, single, and lacking in prospects. Armies and navies wanted young men like James Aitken, but for their ranks and not for their officer corps.

It was the label of common criminal that bothered him the most. He was proud of his two great crimes—the fires in Portsmouth and Bristol—but when it came to his many lesser crimes, he became touchy and defensive. When, for example, he ran into a former employer, he apologized profusely for having robbed him of four guineas, explaining that he "did it more out of revenge . . . than for want."[26] Elsewhere, he insisted that he "never committed or attempted to commit any robberies but when he was like to be drove short of money."[27]

* * *

When Aitken had left England in 1773, the political landscape was flat and distinctly unpromising for anyone who was poor and propertyless. He belonged to the vast majority of Britons who could not vote, and of the various radical factions, none had an agenda that even remotely spoke to his needs and aspirations.[28] Wilkes and his faction were virulently anti-Scots; Wilkes's movement, moreover, appealed to tradesmen and shopkeepers—and not to propertyless journeymen like James Aitken.[29] The self-styled "Real Whigs" were no better. Otherwise known as the "Commonwealthmen," they were men of property.[30] They had no interest in overthrowing the existing system. The king could stay, provided that they got a bigger slice of the political pie. Nor were the scattered radicals among his own class an option. These men would not come into their own until the 1790s, and when they did, they stood for the very things that Aitken despised—the workaday virtues of thrift, sobriety, and self-discipline.[31]

When Aitken returned to England in 1775, the political landscape was unchanged, and the radical factions were much as they had been before. But Aitken himself was changed. In America, where he had spent two wretched years, it was impossible to avoid talk of revolution, and if it did not immediately convert him, it inevitably engaged and excited him in ways that British politics never could. The American Revolution itself provided him with something that he could latch onto. It was dramatic and momentous—exactly the sort of cause that appealed to young men who were bored or dissatisfied with life.[32] The words, for those who lacked them, were to be found in *Common Sense*, Thomas Paine's masterpiece. "The sun never shined on a cause of greater worth." "'Tis not the concern of a day, a year, or an age; posterity are virtually involved in the contest, and will be more or less affected, even to the end of time, by the proceedings now." "We have it in our power to begin the world again. A situation, similar to the present, hath not happened since the days of Noah until now."[33]

Stirring words indeed. But did Aitken read them? The odds are that he did. *Common Sense* was a best-seller in Britain, although its publisher was careful to censor its more inflammatory passages.[34] We know that Aitken read Richard Price's *Observations on the Nature of Civil Liberty, the Principles of Government, and the Justice and Policy of the War with America*. He read it, as did sixty thousand other people, none of whom interpreted it as a call to take up arms against their country.[35] It is not obvious how one gets from the writings of a leftist Unitarian minister to acts that endangered the lives of thousands of innocent people. Everybody agreed that Dr. Price was a good and kindly man, even if his politics were too radical for most. When he walked, children sang. "Make way, make way, make way for the good Dr. Price!"[36] Certainly Price upheld the right of Americans to defend themselves and to have their liberty. "They have risen in their own defence, and repelled force by force. They deny the plenitude of our power over them; and insist upon being treated as free communities."[37] But at no point did Price encourage Britons to take up arms on behalf of America. Still less did he act on his words.[38] That idea would be Aitken's alone. Moreover, Price was something that Aitken was not: a true republican.

Aitken's growing—and not entirely coherent—sympathy for America was not widely shared in Scotland. Even as he was discovering his calling as an American partisan, more than seventy Scottish towns and councils sent petitions to George III, urging him to use force against the rebellious colonies. This was nearly equal to the number sent by their counterparts in England, where the population was five times larger.[39] And unlike their counterparts in England, not a single Scottish town or county sent a petition in favor of a peaceful solution to the conflict. Among Scotland's representatives in Parliament, only one, George Perth, openly opposed the government's policies in America.[40]

This is not to say that all Scots favored the war, or that public opinion was unvarying over time, or even that it was represented in Parliament. For obvious reasons, Glasgow's tobacco merchants had always opposed the war, though the city, like Edinburgh, remained pointedly neutral when war broke out, petitioning neither for war nor peace. And certain intellectuals opposed the war from the beginning, among them David Hume, Adam Smith, and James Boswell. Boswell's sympathies were perhaps the most predictable given his earlier interest in Corsican independence. The most consistent opposition, however, came from the evangelical wing of the Kirk. Chief among them was the Reverend John

Erskine, whose parishoners, it will be recalled, had included Aitken, and whose pro-American pamphlet, *Shall I Go to War with my American Brethren?*, was reissued in 1776. Other evangelical clergymen showed their opposition by refusing to pray for victory, while others ignored official fast days.

Perhaps Erskine and the evangelicals influenced Aitken. The fact is that we do not know why Aitken became passionately pro-American. There was no inkling of this during his days in America. The timing of the revolution was as big a factor as any, with the war becoming news in England just as Aitken's life had hit rock bottom. Even so, he was not an immediate convert. The war had already started by the time he returned in 1775, and for several months, he wandered aimlessly, becoming more reckless with each passing week. This much is clear: before he embraced the American Revolution, his wanderings had no purpose; after he embraced it, they did.

At some point, presumably toward the end of 1775, his thinking progressed from favoring the American Revolution to wanting to play a part in it. This was a step that other British radicals, Price included, were not willing to take. It did not occur to Aitken that he might be able to do something on his side of the Atlantic until he overheard an otherwise innocent conversation. "It is amazing with what force this conversation kept possession of my mind," he was later quoted as saying. "I believe it never left me afterwards."

The circumstances were harmless enough. Several men were gathered in a public house in Oxford, talking about the war. Aitken hung on their every word. The Royal Navy, they all agreed, depended on the royal dockyards; take away these, and the war was as good as lost.[41] The conversation's effect on Aitken was electrifying. It was then and there that he set himself the task of hobbling the Royal Navy by destroying the dockyards that kept it afloat.

It was an ambitious undertaking, especially for just one man. But therein lay its appeal. It gave him a challenge. The destruction of just one dockyard would prove an enormous undertaking, one that would use all his talents. The skills that he would employ were the skills that he already had, starting with the two things he had learned as an apprentice: how to draw and how to grind colors and mix paints. He would use the first in making elaborate sketches of his targets, along with designs for incendiary devices, and he would use the second in manufacturing his own combustibles. He was forever grinding unlikely substances, often prevailing on unsuspecting painters to lend him their stones.[42] His background as a painter probably explains why he favored turpentine over other combustibles. The skills that he had acquired as a burglar would also serve him well, allowing him to move about without drawing attention to himself, slipping in and out of buildings and storehouses. It helped, too, that he was the sort of man whom nobody seemed to notice anyway.

His expectations soon acquired a life of their own, and he started to become slightly unhinged. He relived the same scenario, again and again: with the dockyards destroyed, America would win the war by default, and he would return there an officer and a hero. The indignities, obscurity and crushing commonness of his past life would all be behind him.

There was a caveat. Although he desperately wanted fame, he did not want to work too hard or long to achieve it. In this we can detect the impatience and impulsiveness of a very young man. From this perspective, he had come up with just the right project. It was nothing if not economical of his time, with ten months all told for gathering information, and perhaps two months, if everything fell into place, for burning down each of the major dockyards: Portsmouth in the southwest, Plymouth in the west, and Chatham, Woolwich, and Deptford outside London.

His thinking became increasingly elaborate. At night, his mind raced, "a thousand ideas" playing upon his imagination. He embarked on a tour of the major dockyards, making sketches and taking copious notes as he went. He started with the largest in Portsmouth. This was in January or February of 1776. To support himself and to provide cover for his frequent trips in and out of the dockyard, he found employment as a journeyman painter in Titchfield, a town just outside Portsmouth. There he worked for a painter by the name of Golding, or Goulding, sharing a room with a young carpenter named John Monday.[43]

Strictly speaking, Aitken's destination was not Portsmouth but its sprawling suburb, Portsea. The latter had grown up just outside the town's massive fortifications, and it was home to the famous royal dockyard. By 1775, Portsea was already the larger of the two towns, with a population of perhaps nine thousand. These included most of the men who worked in the dockyard (there were thousands of them, along with their families and apprentices), and at any one time the suburb was also home to hundreds or even thousands of transients, mostly sailors and soldiers who were about to go to sea or who had just returned.

In his spare time, Aitken would wander down to the dockyard, feigning a particular interest in the painters' shop. He made a point of attempting to ingratiate himself with the dockyard workers, including a boyish-looking carpenter by the name of William Weston.[44] Later, at Aitken's trial, Weston was incorrectly identified as an apprentice shipwright.[45] He was in fact a journeyman carpenter, and despite his youth he sensed almost at once that something was not quite right about Aitken. This is our first account of Aitken interacting with someone else. The encounter started innocently enough. Weston was coming out of a repair shop when Aitken approached him, a little too aggressively, explaining that he was a visitor to the dockyard and had never been there before. On the face of it, this was unremarkable. People were always visiting the famous dockyard. But as Weston started to walk away, Aitken followed, all the while plying him with questions about the painters' shop. Weston volunteered to point it out. Aitken next asked whether beer was sold inside the dockyard. Yes it was. Could he buy Weston a beer? The offer, coming as it did from a complete stranger, struck Weston as excessive, and he turned it down. He was relieved when they came within sight of the painters' shop, and pointing to it, he made a hasty exit. The script would be repeated again and again: Aitken would try too hard, presume too much, and the people he importuned extricated themselves as quickly as they could.

In any event, Aitken's attempts to deflect suspicion were needlessly elaborate. Portsmouth saw thousands of transients like him every year, making their way on or off the warships that lay anchored in the harbor. They crowded the town's numerous public houses and generally terrorized its inhabitants. When, for example, the *Blake* set sail in 1808, only 304 of her crew of 585 were English. There were 154 Irish and 45 Scots, followed by men of every possible nationality—one from China, three from Brazil, one from Poland, and so on.[46]

In and out he went, an unremarkable man. He was always headed in the same direction, to the dockyard's largest and most famous building: the great rope house, the largest in Britain and the pride of the Navy Board. It measured 1,094 feet by 54, making it, in the words of one astonished visitor, "near a quarter of a mile long."[47] After the ships themselves, it was the star attraction for the dockyard's many tourists. Defoe was one such tourist, and George III another.[48] The king had last visited the dockyard in 1773, and just afterward he wrote a letter to Lord Sandwich, the

First Lord of the Admiralty, in which he expressed "great curiosity to know the process in making ropes, no one branch in the dock at Portsmouth having seemed more curious to me."[49] What the king and so many other tourists saw were dozens of ropemakers, eighty to a hundred at a time, each performing backbreaking labor, so backbreaking, in fact, that they could only work four hours a day.

Aitken set his sights on the rope house because it was centrally located and housed vast quantities of highly flammable materials—hemp, rope, and the like. It ran nearly the length of the dockyard, and to its south lay another tinderbox: the south hemp house. Together the two buildings contained enough fuel to spark a general conflagration. The dockyard, moreover, did not have its own water supply, and because of this, valuable time was lost each time a fire started.[50] Faced with these obstacles, the Navy Board, which was responsible for the day-to-day management of the dockyards, put its energies into prevention. Workers were not allowed to smoke or even have tobacco in the dockyard; night watchmen were posted to spot fires; and fire engines were held in readiness.[51]

Despite these precautions, there had been a major fire in 1760, followed by an even larger fire in 1770. Both incidents revealed just how vulnerable the dockyard was; at the same time, they also revealed the benefits of redundant dockyards, any of which could supply the fleet in the event of a shutdown at any other. This was more by accident than by design—the Navy Board had inherited half a dozen dockyards and had made no real attempt to consolidate some or close others—but the net effect was to make it impossible to cripple the Royal Navy by destroying just one of its dockyards. Aitken's plan, which aimed at the destruction of the five major dockyards, anticipated as much. What it did not anticipate was that an attack on one dockyard would inevitably put all remaining dockyards on alert, making it all but impossible to attack them in succession. In order to succeed, his plan required a simultaneous attack on all the major dockyards. This, however, required recruiting and working with a group of like-minded partisans, a task for which Aitken was patently unfit.

The fire of 1760 had destroyed the original wooden rope house, along with several nearby buildings. At least two people were killed, and several more were injured.[52] Arson was not suspected, and the Navy Board, anxious to cut costs, rebuilt the rope house with timber.[53] It proved to be a foolish economy when the rope house again went up in flames in 1770. As before, the fire engulfed several nearby buildings.[54] Damage was extensive—one estimate put it at an astronomical £150,000—and this time arson was suspected. Some blamed foreigners; others blamed unemployed workers.[55] Suspicion, however, soon settled on the French, several of whose frigates had been seen lurking outside the harbor just before the fire.[56] One rumor even supplied them with a motive: revenge for a Scot caught spying on the French naval installations at Brest.[57] Shortly after that, a "Romish priest" was arrested in Plymouth.[58] For several weeks, the various royal dockyards were on a heightened state of alert, and in Portsea citizens patrolled the streets at night, convinced that there were "lurking villains or spies still about."[59] The Admiralty was no less alarmed, offering a reward of £1,000 for information leading to the arrest of the perpetrators.[60] This had the desired effect. A man, hoping to claim the reward, came forward and said that the mysterious priest had paid him to set the fire. This revelation was suspiciously faithful to the newspaper accounts, as were his next two revelations: that the priest was a French agent and that a French frigate had lain in wait at the time of the fire.[61] A month passed before the ministry realized that it had been duped and that the man in custody was slightly mad.[62] In the end, arson, while strongly suspected, was never proved, and once again the Navy Board dropped its guard.

The board did, however, learn from one of its mistakes, and this time the rope house and the buildings around it were rebuilt with brick.[63] This precaution could not prevent a fire, but it could, with luck, prevent it from spreading. No serious attempts were made to limit access to the dockyard, however, and it was because of this laxness that Aitken was able to come and go at will.

In many ways, he was merely using the skills that he had perfected as a burglar, which is to say that he was looking for the "neglects" that Sir John Fielding was forever warning homeowners against. When, for example, Aitken was contemplating breaking into a shop in Calne, he passed "backwards and forwards a number of times by the shop door," each time trying to take in as much information as he possibly could.[64] The Portsmouth dockyard was in fact an easier target than the average house, and Aitken immediately found its one point of vulnerability. By land, there was only one entrance into the dockyard, all other landward approaches being sealed off by a high wall, but the gate was loosely guarded, and, as Aitken discovered, almost anyone could pass through it unchallenged.[65] The gate was manned by watchmen selected from among the dockyard's older workers, and they were under orders to challenge anyone they did not recognize.[66] In Aitken's case, the system failed repeatedly. There were two reasons. First, no one, from the Navy Board down, took the possibility of sabotage seriously. This, in the wake of the fire of 1770, was a serious oversight. Such security measures as the Board did take were merely designed to stop workers from pilfering. Workers' bags were examined when they left the dockyard, but not when they entered.[67] Because of this, Aitken was later able to bring large quantities of combustibles into the dockyard without being challenged.

The problem of pilfering—which by all accounts was endemic—brings us to the second point. Morale among the dockyard workers was very low, and with good reason. Shortly before Aitken appeared on the scene, there had been a punishing strike, and while workers were now back on the job, labor relations were still tense.[68] The watchmen who let Aitken come and go at will were not disloyal. Nor was it in their interest to see their livelihoods destroyed along with the dockyard. But in 1776, the year when James Aitken came among them, they were not doing their jobs with an excess of zeal.

In the course of coming and going, Aitken saw something that no one else saw: that the dockyard, for all of its conventional fortifications, was entirely vulnerable to destruction from within. What made this insight brilliant was that it ignored the fortifications altogether. This was something that had never occurred to conventional military planners. Admirals held back from attacking by sea because their ships "must come directly under Southsea Castle, and be afterwards exposed to a long train of cannon from the town and the block-house, which must rake them fore and aft, for a mile together, before they reach the haven's mouth; and when stopped there, liable to their accumulated and constant fire." And generals held back from attacking by land because their forces would encounter "a town [Portsmouth] regularly fortified in the modern style; and the common [Portsea], the dockyard, and the gun-wharf, are likewise so effectually secured, that it would necessarily require a very numerous army to invest and besiege it; nor could it then be taken without affording time sufficient for its relief."[69]

The author of these proud words was Daniel Defoe, who visited Portsmouth and its dockyard in the early 1720s. He is to be forgiven for concluding that an attack, "at least in our days, is not easy to conceive." The best minds in Paris and Madrid had reached exactly the same conclusion. So, too, had the best minds in London. But if Britain's enemies were guilty of showing a lack of imagination, its leaders were guilty of something much worse: complacency. Having spent a great deal of money in modernizing the town's defenses, the Admiralty then placed its entire faith in them. In doing so it overlooked the simplest of military truths: that defenses are only as good as their defenders. The Navy Board in particular deserved blame. It was responsible for administering the dockyards, and it had a bad habit of treating its employees badly, paying them poorly and never on time. In the end, it was the carelessness and indifference of these workers that allowed Aitken to do as much damage as he did.[70]

Aitken left Portsmouth in an exalted mood, confident that its dockyard could be destroyed from within.[71] His next stop was Plymouth, the second largest of the royal dockyards. This, too, he found poorly guarded. It was probably during this time that he worked in nearby Exeter. From Plymouth he headed east toward London and the dockyards at Chatham, Woolwich, and Deptford. In each, through "his own art and through the carelessness of the sentinels," he managed to get "an exact account of the several garrisons in this kingdom, their present state, the number of guns and men at each, and also an account of the shipping in the service of the navy, their tonnage, guns, &c."[72]

For ten months he wandered, planning and taking notes. He was more restless than ever. At one point, in July, he returned to Portsmouth; a day later, he was gone. When he did not think about his plan, he thought about its aftermath: his triumphant return to America and the gratitude and fame that would be his. There he would be awarded the one thing that mattered to him: an officer's commission. This one wish speaks volumes. It is not the wish of a republican; it is the wish of an elitist, of a man who wishes to be at the top of the social hierarchy and not at its bottom. The man in the shabby brown coat does not hate the *ancien régime*; he loves it all too well.[73]

CHAPTER FIVE

His Meeting with the American Envoy to France

A ITKEN'S WANDERINGS next took him to Paris. All told, he spent a month there in 1776, from the middle of October to the middle of November. The trip was not part of his original plan, which had been to return to America and present his proposal to the Continental Congress. [1] The war, however, stood in his way, and he was no more able to pay for his passage now than he had been in 1773. This was something he had not counted on. For a brief time, it looked as if all his hard work had been in vain, and the thought so discouraged him that he succumbed to "a fit of disappointment and despair." But within a short time he came up with a plan every bit as ambitious as the first. He would go to Paris and meet Silas Deane, the new American Congress's representative in France.

Even as he set out, dozens of other foreign adventurers, most of them failed aristocrats, were also wending their way toward the new American mission. Each wanted what Aitken wanted—a commission in the fledgling American army. Very few inspired confidence. They included the Marquis de Lafayette, then just nineteen years old, but for the most part they consisted of unemployed officers. Lafayette, with his "high birth, his alliances," and "his considerable estates" was promising; most of the others were not. [2] Claude Robin, a French army chaplain, despised them. As far as he was concerned, they were charlatans, pure and simple: "By assuming titles and fictitious names, they obtained distinguished ranks in the American army. . . . The simplicity of the Americans, added to their little experience, rendered these villainies less liable to be detected."[3] It helped, perhaps, that so few of these adventurers knew English—and that so few Americans knew any other language. One, an Hungarian by the name of Michaël Kôváts de Fabricÿ, struggled to find a common language, and in the end the only one that he could find was Latin.[4]

Few of them were more qualified than Aitken to lead men, but at least they looked and acted the part. In fairness, Aitken did *act* the part. The part of a junior officer. Prickly, immature, and quick to take offense, junior officers were forever flying off the handle. The people of Portsmouth positively hated them. In 1776 alone there were three separate incidents involving marine lieutenants, and in each instance the assailant had drawn his sword on a civilian.[5] It was bad in Britain, but it was worse in America, where the relative flatness of the social hierarchy made junior officers even more insecure on points of status and rank. The fact that so few of them knew anything about soldiering only added to their insecurities. "We were all young," one of them wrote years later, "and in a manner unacquainted with human nature, quite novices in military matters, had every thing to learn, and no one to instruct us who knew any better than ourselves."[6] In this respect, Aitken was no better and no worse than any other young officer in Washington's army.

But Aitken did not *look* the part, and his appearance continued to mock his ambitions, as, for that matter, did his stammering. By October, he was in Dover, looking for a passage across the Channel. He was fearful of being stopped and questioned, although it is unlikely that anyone paid the slightest attention to him. Polite Britons perhaps clutched their purses more tightly when he came among them, but never would they have taken him for a man bent on doing them a much larger harm. Even so, he took the precaution of secreting his sketches and plans in "a private part" of his clothes.[7] In Dover, he dawdled for two days, in an agony over how to catch a boat to France without drawing attention to himself and his scheme. In the end, he decided that the safest course was to charter a small sailboat to take him to Calais. The boat was so small that it carried just two hands in addition to Aitken, and the voyage, lasting almost nine hours, was harrowing. Benjamin Franklin, who made the passage in 1767, did not succumb to seasickness, but his fellow passengers did. "Take my advice," he wrote Mary Stevenson, "and live sparingly a day or two beforehand."[8]

In France, as in England and America, he showed his customary talent for finding his way in unfamiliar territory. He would later claim that he had "a tolerable knowledge of French."[9] If so, he was an autodidact. In Edinburgh, French was taught only in the colleges that prepared the privileged few for university.[10] It was not taught at Heriot's, and even young James Boswell, who enjoyed every possible advantage over Aitken, started his own grand tour "hardly knowing a word of French."[11]

From Calais, Aitken proceeded straight to Paris, "sometimes taking the advantage of a carriage, and sometimes walking on foot." Franklin, traveling by coach, found the roads "equally good with ours in England, in some places pav'd with smooth stone like our new streets for many miles together, and rows of trees on each side. . . ." Once in Paris, Aitken somehow managed to find Deane's residence at the Hôtel d'Entragues. Inside were two men, a master and his valet. Their roles should have been reversed, for the valet, who was fluent in English and versed in several other languages, was the wiser of the two; he was probably also a spy, but that is incidental. At the time, Deane was just thirty-nine years old, and completely out of his depth. He was originally from Groton,

Connecticut, and his father, like Aitken's, was a blacksmith. Deane was embarrassed by his humble roots, so much so that he changed his name from Dean to Deane. He somehow managed to get into Yale, where he graduated twenty-second in a class of thirty-four. That was in 1758. The brief experience of working for a living convinced him that he had to marry well, and he did so twice. Once married, he started climbing the social ladder, no longer a Dean but a Deane, and to the extent that he supported himself during these years he did so by speculating in real estate, not all of it his own. In 1774 and 1775, he was sent to the Continental Congress as a delegate, a position to which he was not re-elected. In the meantime, however, he was already laying the groundwork for his newest sideline: profiteering. This was a logical extension of his earlier efforts to procure military supplies for the Continental Congress, and it was in this capacity that he was sent to France in March of 1776, ostensibly as a commercial agent. It was a mission that required great delicacy. Deane's first task was to purchase much-needed supplies for the American army. His second was to forge an alliance with France. All of this had to be done without giving the British grounds for declaring war on France. Later, Deane would be joined by Franklin and the Virginia gentleman Arthur Lee, both of whom were far more capable, but for now he was on his own.[12] "I am about to enter on the great stage of Europe," he wrote his second wife, "and the consideration of the importance of quitting myself well weighs me down."[13]

As well it should have. He had no diplomatic experience, no staff to advise him, and he was under orders to win over the Comte de Vergennes, a seasoned diplomat with thirty-seven years' experience in the courts of Europe. For the past two years, Vergennes had been serving as France's minister of foreign affairs, and for the past thirteen years he had been waiting for an opportunity to regain the power and influence that France had lost after the Seven Years' War.[14] To that extent, he wanted to help Deane, even if he did not like or respect him, but he could not yet risk openly siding with America.[15]

There was yet another reason for Vergennes's coolness toward Deane. The British ambassador, Lord Stormont, was watching their every move. His spies were everywhere, as Franklin acknowledged in one of his letters to Juliana Ritchie. He was laughing as he wrote, "If I was sure . . . that my *valet de place* was a spy, as probably he is, I think I should not discharge him for that, if in other respects I lik'd him."[16] Even Deane knew that he was being watched. In his case, what Stormont's spies saw, day after day, was a steady procession of foreign adventurers traipsing in and out of the Hôtel d'Entragues.

James Aitken, however, slipped past them not once but several times, all but invisible in his shabby brown coat. No one, neither Stormont's spies nor Deane's valet, took him for an unemployed officer or an American agent. For a while, it looked like Aitken would not get to see Deane at all, and it was only through sheer persistence that he managed to secure an interview.

The two men met twice, and each has left an account of what transpired. Their stories are remarkably consistent. Deane's account, written two or more years after the fact, is the more detailed. In it, the little things that signify rank and status—speech, clothes, and conversation—take center stage. Twice Aitken showed up at the Hôtel d'Entragues, and twice Deane's valet turned him away, deeming him "a person of an odd and suspicious look and appearance." The third time, Aitken refused to take no for an answer, and pushed his way past. Deane's curiosity was aroused by the scuffle outside his study, and ignoring his valet's advice, he asked that Aitken be shown in. The valet balked.

"You never saw a worse looking fellow in your life," he warned, adding that in his estimation the young man had come either to beg or do some mischief.[17]

Aitken's clothes made a bad impression on the valet; his speech, whether his accent or stammering or both, made an even worse impression. "I can hardly understand him," the valet complained. But Deane was adamant, at which point the valet, still very alarmed, asked to remain "within hearing if anything happens."

For several minutes, Aitken was unable to speak coherently. Deane did not know this, but Aitken was tongue-tied because he believed himself to be in the presence of one of the great men of his day. Deane was a bumpkin, but this is not what Aitken saw. He saw, to use his own words, "a fine and clever fellow," "the honestest man in the world," the one man who could recognize his many talents and give them their proper due. His blind, foolish adulation of Silas Deane began then and there, and not once would his loyalty waiver.

But to return to Deane's story. Even as Aitken stammered and gawked, the object of his admiration was pointedly staring at his watch, and Aitken, taking the hint, started talking with something approaching coherence. As he talked he warmed to his subject and Deane noticed his eyes. They were the eyes of a zealot or a madman—"sparkling and wild," and given to "rolling wildly." Even so, Deane listened patiently enough, making no attempt to call for his valet even as the conversation took an increasingly bizarre turn. Aitken, who was by now in a highly agitated state, alluded to the purpose of his visit. "Pray, sir, if a man is ill used, has he not a right to resent it and to seek revenge or retaliation on those who have injured him?"

Deane took the bait, but his irritation was already starting to show. "This is a droll question for you to trouble me with; go into the fields and tread on the meanest insect and see if it do not at least try to turn upon you, and if it be a serpent he will sting you and effectually revenge himself; this is the voice, the law of nature extending thro' all her animal creation." This answer, for all its banality, merely encouraged Aitken, who responded, "Right! Right!" His next question was the one that Deane had heard and answered so many times before. Would Congress "give rewards and honors to those who serve them voluntarily"? Yes, Deane responded wearily, and growing impatient and perhaps more than a little alarmed, he asked Aitken to get to the point. With that, Aitken told him a story, most of it untrue: that he had lived in America (true); that he had offered his services to the loyalists (probably true); that the governor of Virginia, Lord Dunmore, had made him "fair promises" and broken every one of them (not true); that "this opened my eyes and showed me that the Americans were right" (not true); that he could "not join them in that country after what had passed" (not quite—he had left because Scots, like other Britons, were no longer safe in the colonies).

It was an astonishing story. Even more astonishing was Aitken's next boast. It was right by half. "Though I may appear to your honor a very weak and insignificant creature, yet if you will give me another audience I will show you from the intelligence which I can give you that I can strike a blow, ay, such a blow as will need no repetition." He also let slip that he had recently visited each of "the principal ports" in England, and could give Deane "some intelligence of importance." But he refused to reveal his plan as long as the hovering valet was in earshot, and it was at this point that the conversation started to loop, with "some further incoherent conversation" in which Aitken repeated his wish to be revenged, "and that in no common or ordinary way." He said, again and again, that he was a friend of America.

Perhaps Deane was amused; perhaps he was intrigued; and perhaps he was simply a man with no sense at all. But for whatever reason, he agreed to a second meeting the following morning. He also agreed to Aitken's request that they meet privately.[18] Deane's explanation is plausible enough:

> Struck with the singularity of this *rencontre*, and wishing to know more fully what the man aimed at, for, tho' in his looks he appeared wild, his conversation show'd plainly that his mind laboured with some purpose or project more than common which shook his whole frame, I wished from curiosity, more than from any other motive, to know more of the man and something of his views, of which he had as yet disclosed nothing.

That is where Deane's account ends. A later hand removed his account of their second meeting, in which Deane gave his blessing to the destruction of the dockyards. Here we must rely on Aitken's account, which complements Deane's to a surprising degree. Aitken admitted that he called twice at the Hôtel d'Entragues before actually getting to see Deane. But instead of calling a third time, he waited outside for Deane, following him as far as the Pont Neuf. There he waylaid him and asked for "a private interview, having some information to communicate of great importance to America." Deane, he had to admit, treated him "at first with great caution and indifference."

Aitken continues. For whatever reason, Deane agreed to a second meeting, at which time Aitken, to make himself "of as much consequence as possible, and to appear a little above the common class," told him a lie: that he once had a plantation in America. This fits with Deane's account, which also has Aitken making up a story.[19] It was during this second meeting that Aitken revealed his plan, and when he did, even Deane, foolish man though he was, could not "help looking upon it as an enterprise bordering upon madness." He raised several objections. The plan was impractical. Someone would suspect Aitken. The fires would break out before he could get away. It was this last possibility that concerned Deane the most, and it was at this point that Aitken revealed his blueprint for a pocket-sized incendiary device that could smolder for hours before bursting into flames. This device, he claimed, could be manufactured cheaply and in "a large quantity." Deane was finally convinced.

In Aitken's account, Deane was skeptical at first and gullible in the end. This rings true. In another account, penned by someone who was not there, Deane was considerably more sanguine. Deane, he wrote, "greatly applauded [Aitken's] zeal," and after raising some initial objections, he "was amazed... and... fully convinced of the probability of his scheme."[20] This almost certainly overstates Deane's position. All of the evidence points in the same direction: that Deane took neither Aitken nor his plan seriously. He did, however, appreciate the plan's potential to cripple the Royal Navy, and to that extent he gave it his blessing, never believing that it would actually yield results. Nor could he have anticipated that Aitken would depart from his original plan and attempt to burn down a nonmilitary target.

Later, when he was in trouble for a good many other things, Deane made light of Aitken. But he never apologized for taking the war to the enemy. Aitken, he allowed, might have been subject to the laws of Britain, but he, as an American and a combatant, was not. "I am confident," he wrote, "that every one of common sense and impartiality must acquit me, nay more though they rejoice at the defeat of the enterprize they must approve of the motives, which influenced me to engage in it, motives no less than

John the Painter

John the Painter, 1777. A thoroughly inaccurate likeness, from the hat (Aitken's was fan-tailed) to the spurs (as far as we know, he never rode a horse in his life). In his hand is a promissory note for £300, to be paid by Edward Bancroft. On the crudely drawn table is Silas Deane's calling card. COURTESY OF THE BODLEIAN LIBRARY, UNIVERSITY OF OXFORD, G. PAMPH. 1580(5).

a desire to weaken a declared enemy, and to preserve my country, by every means in my power, from the horrors, and distress of fire and desolation."[21]

Just what did Deane offer Aitken? Not much really: money, but not enough to cover even a fraction of his expenses; a passport that served no real purpose; and most importantly, the name of a man in London whom Aitken might call on for protection and additional funds. That man was Dr. Edward Bancroft, who was not all that he seemed to be.

First for the money that Deane actually placed in Aitken's hands. It amounted to just seventy-two *livres*, or "about three pound."[22] It was a tiny amount, so small as to be insulting, and it meant that Aitken, with no funds of his own, would have to finance his scheme himself. Deane never asked Aitken how he proposed to do this. The smallness of the amount shows that Deane did not take the plan seriously enough to subsidize it. Still, it *was* money, and once it changed hands Aitken was in some loose sense in the employ of the American Congress. If Aitken is to be believed, Deane also gave him a promissary note for £300, to be paid by his contact in London. But we only have Aitken's word for this.

The passport is simply odd. Deane came up with this idea on his own, and the document itself was signed by Vergennes in the king's name and dated 13 November 1776. It was valid for one month, and it was specifically limited to Aitken's "going to England."[23] The document was of little practical use, but it meant a great deal to him nonetheless, so much so that he could not bring himself to destroy it upon returning to England. Instead, he kept the document, only to abandon it later, along with his bundle of treasured books, in a moment of panic. He kept it, we can only assume, because it reassured him that he was engaged in a great undertaking. Certainly he was aware of its incriminating potential, for he worried endlessly after leaving it behind in Portsmouth. When his pursuers discovered the passport two months later, they were flabbergasted, and asked themselves if they had stumbled on a plot that reached all the way back to Versailles.

It was a fair question. How much did Vergennes know when, at Deane's request, he signed the document that authorized Aitken to return to England and set about destroying the royal dockyards? The answer, it seems, is that for once in his long career Vergennes knew nothing. The alternative is too preposterous. Neither he nor Louis XVI had any intention of risking war with Britain at this juncture, and this by itself would have discouraged them from implicating France in an attack on British soil.

At some point, probably just after Aitken was arrested and had become an embarrassment, Deane gave Aitken something else: a code name. It was the number zero.[24] Surely the choice was not random. Was Deane being ironic or merely cruel? Aitken himself knew nothing of this, as the code only appears, almost as a snide joke, in the correspondence between Deane and Bancroft. "I found means last Sunday to see 0," Bancroft mentioned in one of his letters to Deane. In that one line, Bancroft said more about James Aitken and his predicament than he could possibly have known.

In the meantime, Aitken was already on his way back to England. Deane gave the matter no further thought—until he himself was implicated in the plot—and such was his lack of faith in Aitken's plan that he made no attempt to contact Bancroft and tell him what was afoot.

CHAPTER SIX

His Attempt to Burn Down the Town and Dockyard of Portsmouth

U PON LEAVING Paris, Aitken retraced his steps, arriving back in Dover toward the end of November 1776. From there he made his way to Canterbury, where he arranged to have three incendiary devices built from the blueprint he had shown Deane. By all accounts, he was impatient and edgy, and he had great difficulties in communicating his design. First he approached a master brazier, but "finding it impossible to make him understand my directions," he prevailed upon a mere apprentice, a boy by the name of William Teach, to do the work.[1] The boy's inexperience showed. When the device was later found, it failed to impress. The device was examined by several people, and they all agreed that it had been made by "some person not furnished with proper tools for the purpose."[2] Even Teach, when presented with his handiwork, had to admit that it was "very bad soldered."[3]

In fairness to Teach, he was working from a design that was poorly communicated. Obviously, Aitken could not tell him its real purpose. And it had to serve several contradictory functions. It had to be small enough to fit inside his coat, look harmless, and give him enough time to light it and get away. It is clear that Aitken had given each of these functions a great deal of thought. The finished product was a canister that measured just ten inches by three by three-and-three-quarters. Its various tin plates were "put together with very small brads," and the whole looked very much like a lantern or a half-pound tea tin. Despite its homespun appearance,

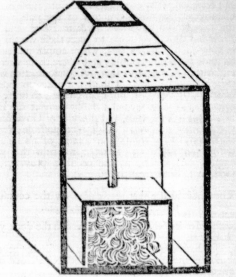

The figure following reprefents the tin cafe, which is made in a long fquare form. A little wooden box is made to fit the cafe, which having a hole through the centre, admits the bottom of a candle into it, which when lighted has vent and air by means of fome fmall holes towards

the top of the tin cafe or cannifter. The box is filled with combuftibles of different kinds, which, when the candle is nearly burnt out, take fire, and by means of the matches placed round, communicate the flames to every thing they touch. Q. Did

A crudely rendered illustration of the incendiary device crafted by William Teach. COURTESY OF THE PORTSMOUTH MUSEUM AND RECORDS SERVICE.

the canister seems to have been designed well enough to function as a slow-fuse device. The top was bored with air holes, and its chamber accommodated a candle. Beneath this, there was a space for matches. The idea was for the candle to burn down until its flame lit the matches. Once lit, the matches were supposed to spark the various combustibles packed into a wooden box at the canister's base.[4]

Only one was ever built. Another apprentice, John Fisher, was given the task of making two more, but he dawdled, and Aitken, nervous and impatient, left before they were completed.[5]

He needlessly drew attention to himself in Canterbury. From an apprentice surgeon and apothecary by the name of John Illenden, he purchased two ounces of turpentine and four ounces of saltpeter (potassium nitrate), and from his landlady, Mary Bishop, he got the name of someone who might fashion wooden inserts for his canisters.[6] The first such insert was subsequently delivered to Aitken at his lodgings, where he was at great pains to conceal it from the prying eyes of Mrs. Bishop. His attempts, of course, merely piqued her interest. In the White Horse, a nearby public house, he got into a fight with two dragoons: Edward Evans and James Wilson.[7] Both men noticed that Aitken had "something bright under his coat that glistened like tin." For whatever reason, Aitken told Mrs. Bishop about the fight; he also told her that he had come "from America on account of the disturbances."

From Canterbury, he made his way to the royal dockyard at Chatham, where he spent two days making further notes. In London, his next stop, he purchased a pair of screw-barrel pistols, "resolving, if any man should detect or molest me, to kill him on the spot."[8] There he also bought tinder, a gallon of turpentine, and an unspecified quantity of saltpeter. Then he headed south to Portsmouth with the two pistols and his canister secreted in his coat. On his back, in his customary bundle, were items more curious still—turpentine, gunpowder, dirty clothes, and, as always, books for a restless mind. In one pocket he carried a watch. It was no doubt stolen.

He reached Portsmouth on 5 December 1776. His plan was to set fires in three separate places: one in the dockyard itself, and two in residential neighborhoods. Three simultaneous fires, he reasoned, would be almost impossible to put out, and with any luck, they would destroy not only the dockyard, but the entire town:

> I concluded, that in so large and populous a place, a number of fire-engines were most probably kept, and that on the first alarm, they would fly to the assistance of the dock, and perhaps extinguish the fire, before any considerable damage could be done. To prevent this, I thought it would be necessary to set the town on fire at the same time in two different parts, imagining that the surprise and consternation which it would naturally occasion, would prevent people from giving assistance to either, 'till the flames had made such progress as not to be got under.[9]

This statement appears in the confession that Aitken later dictated to one of Sir John Fielding's clerks. The exact words are not Aitken's, but this was his plan.

That night, instead of finding lodgings, he prowled the streets of Portsea. He was looking for places to set diversionary fires, and it was for this reason that he paid particular attention to houses built mostly of timber. In the morning, when the gates to Portsmouth were opened, he entered the town and continued his search. There he found what he was looking for: a somewhat dilapidated lodging house at 10 Barracks Street. He knocked on the door.

It was opened by Mrs. Elizabeth Boxell. She was still young enough to bear children—one, described as "a young child," was "at her breast" when she was later called on to testify against Aitken—and both she and her husband were known to have "extreme good characters."[10] She agreed to rent Aitken a room, and he left his bundle with her, saying that he would return that evening. Exhausted from his nocturnal peregrinations, he headed for a public house, had a drink, and fell fast asleep. It was when

Mrs. Boxell opened his bundle, ostensibly to send his clothes out to be washed, that she began to suspect that something was amiss. In it she found an old shirt, a pair of leather breeches, and the mysterious canister. It was the canister that caught her eye. By her own admission, she spent a quarter of an hour examining it, unable to determine what it might be.[11]

Aitken was none the wiser when he returned to pick up his canister. He had already made one trip to the dockyard, and as before no one had challenged him at the gate. At two that afternoon, he returned to the dockyard, his canister and combustibles in tow. Again no one challenged him. His first stop was the south hemp house. It was here that raw hemp, arriving from Scandinavia in the late summer, was aged before being processed and then spun into rope.[12] There were several workers in the building at the time, but no one saw him hide Teach's canister in a pile of loose hemp.[13] He had packed the device's wooden base with tar, oil, and matches, and just outside it he left paper and, for good measure, an uncorked bottle of turpentine.[14] The latter, with its telltale smell, was perhaps not the wisest choice, but most fortunately for Aitken, it went completely unnoticed. Nor did anyone notice him when he emerged from the hemp house, his brown coat fairly bristling with bits of hemp.

He crossed the laneway and entered the rope house. The ropemakers were gone for the day, and he had the building to himself. Having already left his one canister in the hemp house, he was forced to improvise. He decided to start fires in three separate locations. This time he used vials filled with turpentine, laying each on its side and replacing the cork with hemp. Just outside each bottle he left a piece of paper with gunpowder and hemp strewn on top. For added effect, he saturated the surrounding area with turpentine.[15]

All that remained was for him to light the three vials of turpentine and get out as quickly as possible. After that, he would return to the hemp house and light Teach's canister. If all went according to plan, he would return to his lodgings on Barracks Street and start a diversionary fire there. Had any of his matches worked, he might even have succeeded. He struck one after another, and it was only when he had exhausted his supply that he realized that night had fallen and he was locked in the rope house. He was frantic. "I went," he later recalled, "from one end of the building to the other, which was of a prodigious length, and tried every door I could find; but all was fast. I went upstairs very gently for fear of being heard, intending to make my escape from one of the windows; but this I also found impossible."[16]

Finally, in desperation he started banging on a door. The first person to respond was Edward Carey. He refused to let Aitken out, telling him that he must instead "abide there all night."[17] The second person was a boy. Who was there? he wanted to know. "A friend," replied Aitken, adding that curiosity had brought him (as it had so many others) to the dockyard. The boy accepted this explanation and went to find someone with keys to the rope house. He returned with two men: Richard Voke and Richard Faithful. It was Voke's job to fix the ropemakers' tools, and it was Faithful's to make sure that the rope house was locked and properly secured at the end of the workday. Faithful was the older of the two caretakers, being in his late thirties or early forties, and he was sufficiently established to have his own house, at 46 King's Street in Portsea.[18] It was Faithful who let Aitken out, a mistake for which both he and Voke would later lose their jobs. At the time, they suspected nothing, quite possibly because Aitken, convinced that he was about to be apprehended, went out of his way to appear "very ignorant in every respect," asking "a number of simple questions."[19]

He walked out of the dockyard and into the night. His nerves were frayed, and to steady them he stopped for a drink before returning to his lodgings. By the time he returned to Mrs. Boxell's, his roommate, a blacksmith by the name of William Abram, was already preparing for bed. Abram was probably just a little younger than Aitken. A document from the Navy Board implies as much, calling him a "lad." He must have looked young for his age, because the Board only later discovered that he was too old to be an apprentice.[20]

The following morning, Abram rose before dawn and left for work. Aitken had the room to himself, and he used the time to start a diversionary fire before returning to the rope house. He succeeded in setting fire to some rags, and then prepared to leave the room and lock the door behind him.[21]

He had not counted on Mrs. Boxell. No sooner did she detect smoke than she charged up the stairs, barging into the room in what Aitken later described as "a violent passion." She could scarcely believe her eyes. Smoke had already filled the room, and Aitken, far from apologizing or offering an excuse, did as he had done with Faithful and Voke. He pretended to be simple. What was he doing? she wanted to know. Was he trying to set her house on fire? Oh, and what was she afraid of? Aitken asked. The sheer lunacy of his answer took her aback. She stated the obvious: that she was afraid of fire. She opened a window and left the room in a huff. She returned a few moments later, only to discover that Aitken had shut it. This time she told him off: "I said I would not have my window shut by him or any other man, that if I chose to have it open it should be open." She told him to get out, and following him out into the middle of the street, she kept her eye on him as he walked away. That was between six and seven in the morning.

He headed in the direction of Portsea and the dockyard. Toward seven he stopped at the White Hart on Queen Street, just outside the dockyard. It was run by John Courtney and his wife, Anne. John Courtney surfaces twice in the town's court papers, once to post a recognizance for a friend charged with wife-beating, and once to answer a charge for kicking a servant and turning her out without paying her back wages.[22] When asked to recall that morning, the first thing that he remembered was Aitken's bundle. Aitken was carrying it at the time, and he asked Courtney to look after it for him. He then called for a glass of gin and a half-pint of beer. He mixed the two (a common enough cocktail), and warming it over the fire, he called for a teaspoon of sugar, which he added to the drink.[23] He was cold, and hovered around the fireplace. His actions attracted the attention of two ropemakers who had stopped for a drink. Their names were William Baldy and John Mortimer, and both lived nearby.[24] It was Mortimer who struck up a conversation. "What," he asked, "are you come from a journey?" Aitken answered the question literally. He had just come from Portsmouth, but before that he had indeed "come from a journey."[25]

Around ten in the morning, he stopped at a lodging house at 5 North Street, just a few blocks away from the dockyard. He settled on this house because it was near the dockyard and built mostly of timber, making it a good spot to set a diversionary fire. Its owner, a widow by the name of Anne Cole, agreed to rent him a room, and after that he left, explaining that he was "going a little way out of town."[26] He asked her to look after his bundle until he returned. "Did you open that bundle?" the crown prosecutor wanted to know. "It was not tied close, and I saw it a little way open," she had to admit. "What did you see in the bundle?" "I saw some books and other things," she answered, adding that she did not untie it.[27] Aitken never returned for his bundle. Days became weeks, and

Anne Cole kept the mysterious bundle "unopened, expecting him to call every day for it." For his part, Aitken could barely remember her—he had, after all, talked with her for only a few minutes—and at one point during his trial he confused her with Mrs. Boxell.

From North Street, he set out to replenish his supply of matches, and this brought him to a chandler's shop on Havant Street. It was run by an old woman by the name of Elizabeth Gentell.[28] "He came to my house," she later testified, "and asked for a half-pennyworth of matches; I took down two bunches and put them upon the counter; he asked me if they would take fire quick; and he desired me to change one of the bunches, which I did." Even during his trial, when he was loaded down with chains and had ceased to look threatening, Aitken made her nervous. Throughout, she avoided making eye contact with him, prompting Aitken to taunt her for taking "so small a time . . . to look at me."[29]

From Havant Street, it was a short walk to the dockyard itself. He stopped for a pint of beer toward 11:15 in the morning, after which he once again entered the dockyard.[30] His coat now bulged with cheap matches and a potpourri of combustibles, but still nobody challenged him. Everything was going according to plan until he had the bad luck to be spotted by William Baldy, one of the ropemakers who had seen him earlier that morning at the White Hart. By now it was 11:30, and Baldy, seated on a barrel, was already eating his lunch. Making the best of a bad situation, Aitken once again tried to pass himself off as a fool. He picked up a small stone, and showing it to Baldy, he asked, "Pray, sir, do you make use of these things in making cables?"

Baldy had never heard anything so ignorant in his life, and looking Aitken "very full in the face," he answered the question with more tact than it deserved. "I suppose, sir, that some must have come from the clay which these barrels are filled with."

"Oh," Aitken answered, "I thought that you did not make use of such things," and with that he walked away.[31]

As luck would have it, the next person he ran into was none other than William Weston, the man he had met back in January or February. It was now noon, and Weston was talking to Baldy. As before, Aitken's manner was fulsome. He was clearly agitated, and Baldy, misreading the situation, assumed that Aitken and Weston were long lost friends. Aitken put out both his hands, and shaking Weston's, exclaimed not once, but repeatedly, "How d'ye do? How d'ye do?" This was altogether too effusive, as was Aitken's insistence that they go for a drink. Once again, Weston declined.

The day, it seemed, was full of encounters. No sooner had Weston extricated himself from Aitken than two other men, John Norris and John Furmidge, ran into him. Both were tar-heaters, and they spotted Aitken skulking around the entrance to the tar cellar sometime between noon and one in the afternoon. Furmidge came from a family that had been established in Portsmouth since at least 1703, at which time an ancestor, Francis Furmidge, was charged with assault.[32] The Furmidges, it seems, had a positive talent for getting into fights, with Furmidge after Furmidge, male as well as female, appearing before the town's magistrates in the years that followed. But it was Norris who challenged Aitken. Again Aitken played the fool. "Is that pitch?" he wanted to know, pointing to a vat of tar. Norris was prepared to humor Aitken; Furmidge was not. He must lock up, he said. In hurrying along his workmate, Furmidge unwittingly helped avert a major catastrophe, for it is clear that Aitken was even then planning to set fire to the dockyard's stores of tar. They walked with him for a short distance, and Aitken invited them to have a drink. Like Weston, they declined.

The fact that Aitken drank throughout the day was not unusual—people drank whenever they could—but his sad and always desperate invitations were. They served no practical purpose, not for a man intent on committing a spectacular crime and getting away with it. He asked complete strangers to drink with him because he was lonely, and loneliness overrode his reason. His invitations always came too quickly, and his conversation and his manner were always just a little off.

From the tar cellar he proceeded to the south hemp house. His canister was exactly where he had left it, but his cheap matches failed one after another. After several tries, he gave up, and decided to try his luck in the rope house.[33] He was down to his last matches. The ropemakers were gone for the day, and the house boys had already finished sweeping up after them.[24] For an hour or more, Aitken did nothing at all, and as he waited, the tide started to come in. This was a detail that he had overlooked. Had he waited until the next low tide, he would almost certainly have caused a great deal more damage, if only because nearby ships, each loaded with gunpowder, would have been unmovable; but had he waited until evening, he would have found himself locked inside the dockyard again. At about 3:30 that afternoon, he used his remaining matches to set three separate fires in the rope house. Controlling his fear and agitation, he left the rope house and walked into the waning afternoon. No one challenged him as he headed toward the Hard, the thoroughfare just outside the dockyard.

He had not been alone in the rope house. Richard Voke and Richard Faithful, the two men whom he had met the previous night, were still there, Voke working in the little garret that passed for his shop, and Faithful making his usual rounds. It was customary for the ropemakers to leave every fourth or fifth window open before leaving, and as Faithful went about shutting these, he noticed a light, but made nothing of it. That was at 3:55. Just a few minutes before 4:30, he went upstairs to chat with Voke; Faithful remembered the time because Voke, eager to quit for the day, had pulled out his watch to check the time. It was as his companion was putting on his coat that Faithful smelled smoke. Then Voke, too, smelled it. Voke was able to walk only a few steps before the smoke overwhelmed him. "Christ God!" he cried out. "The toppings are on fire!"[35]

CHAPTER SEVEN

His Meeting with a British Spy

As AITKEN was leaving the dockyard, he ran into a man he had known in Titchfield.[1] He was sure that this man was watching him "very steadfastly." The chance encounter completely unnerved him, even though there were no signs of fire yet. Aitken was spooked nonetheless, and in his fright he abandoned his original plan, which had been to rush back to Anne Cole's house, pick up his bundle, and start a diversionary fire before leaving Portsmouth to its fate.

Landladies were very much on his mind, Mrs. Boxell most of all. By now she would have told her neighbors about his attempt to burn down her house, and it was only a matter of time before she linked him to the destruction of the rope house. He needed somewhere to hide, and set his sights on London. Edward Bancroft, Silas Deane's friend, lived there, and surely he would welcome Aitken with open arms.

He headed out of town, running most of the way, and reached a public house in Buckland, just outside Portsmouth, at about four in the afternoon. Aitken was, in the words of one witness, "very much out of breath" when he got there. When he saw a woman driving a tilted cart, he accosted her and somehow prevailed upon her to give him a ride. Her name was Anne Hopkins, and she was on her way home from the market. "Do, ma'am, drive as fast as you can," he begged her, jumping up into the cart and seating himself beside her.[2] He told her that he would "make her any satisfaction" if only she would take him to Petersfield.[3] There, with any luck, he could spend the night and catch the coach to London the following morning.[4]

Anne Hopkins, however, had other plans. She would take him only as far as her home and not one step farther. Dusk was already falling, she was alone with a strange young man, and she had no intention of driving in the dark any longer than necessary. The first inkling of trouble came at the village of Cosham, where much against Aitken's wishes, she stopped to buy a new pair of pattens. Aitken went into the shop with her, and, anxious to expedite the transaction, he fished sixpence out of his pocket and slammed the money down on the counter. They continued their journey. Just before Hopkins reached her house, she stopped again, this time to water her horse at a pond. Aitken took advantage of the moment to look back in the direction of Portsmouth. There, on the far horizon, he could discern a fire. He bolted without a word, running, he later claimed, "for near four miles on the road to Petersfield, being still under great apprehension of Mrs. Boxell's giving intelligence of me, and of being pursued."[5] Anne Hopkins was oblivious to the day's events. She gave the matter no further thought, and probably would have forgotten it altogether had she not been tracked down and called upon to testify against Aitken three months later.

She last saw Aitken running down the main road to London. He continued, on foot, for the rest of the night, arriving in Kingston upon Thames between ten and eleven the following morning. He had covered forty-four miles in seventeen hours, excluding the four or more miles between Anne Hopkins's house and Petersfield. He was exhausted and hungry, and his nerves were on edge. When two dogs started barking at him, somewhere outside Kingston, he snapped. He shot at them, wounding or killing one. He stayed in Kingston until late in the afternoon, too exhausted to continue. By the end of the afternoon, he was sufficiently recovered to continue his trip to London, now just eleven miles away. He had walked for two miles when a post chaise passed him. He called on its driver, a boy, to stop, only to be "disregarded and laughed at," whether because of his clothes, his speech, or both. Aitken flew into a rage and shot into a side window of the coach at close range. Inside were two gentlemen "who appeared very much frightened" but were otherwise unhurt.[6]

Shortly after this outburst, Aitken managed to catch a ride with a hackney stage, arriving in London just after dark. All told, he had covered seventy-two miles in just over twenty-four hours, mostly on foot, and mostly in the dark. It was a testimony to his sheer determination—and to his exuberant good health. His mind, too, proved resilient, for he quickly recovered his composure upon reaching the capital. Here he could be quite sure that there was nobody who could link him to the fire, and with any luck he could pass unnoticed among the thousands of other impoverished Scots who lived and worked in the capital.

Had he done nothing more, or simply bided his time, it is almost certain that his spectacular crime would have gone unsolved. But he had no intention of returning to a life of workaday obscurity. Flushed with success and desperate to get word to Deane, he sought out Bancroft almost immediately, pausing only to have a drink and clean himself at a public house in Westminster. Even so, he cut a very sorry figure when he showed up at Bancroft's house at number 4 Downing Street.

Bancroft was thirty-one years old. He had grown up in Westfield, Massachusetts, and as a teenager he had been tutored by Silas Deane. He was much brighter than his tutor, restless, and utterly unscrupulous. From 1760 to 1763, he had been apprenticed to a physician, but at the age of eighteen he ran away, first to Barbados, and then to Suriname. There he found employment with a surgeon from Edinburgh, devoting his spare time to studying tropical flora and fauna. He began to make a study of the various colors and poisons that could be extracted from local plants. In 1767, when he was just twenty-two, he published his results in *An Essay on the Natural History of Guiana*. People, Benjamin Franklin included, started to take notice, and in 1773, with Franklin's help and that of the Astronomer Royal and the king's physician, he became a founding member of the Royal Medical Society of London (he had begun a formal study of medicine in 1767, and in 1774 he was awarded a degree in medicine from the University of Aberdeen). There was no doubt that he was a brilliant young man.

Among Americans, at least, he was widely admired.[7] With the notable exception of Arthur Lee, who later joined him in Paris, none suspected that he might have been less than sympathetic to the country he had left so many years ago. Franklin held him in high regard and trusted him implicitly, as did Jefferson, John Adams, and his old tutor Silas Deane. Had his compatriots taken the time to read the more obscure passages of his famous *Essay*, they might have caught hints of a darker side to his personality. One passage in particular stands out. In it, Bancroft describes how the natives of Suriname used to bide their time before poisoning their enemies:

They always feign an insensibility of the injury which they intend to revenge, and even repay it with services and acts of friendship, until they have destroyed all distrust and apprehension of danger in the destined victim of their vengeance. When this is effected, they meet him at some festival, and engage him to drink with them, drinking first themselves to obviate suspicion, and afterwards secretly dropping the poison, ready concealed under their nails, which are usually long, into the drink.[8]

Edward Bancroft was not a poisoner, even if he did bring back alarming quantities of curare and other poisons from his expeditions into the Surinamese jungle. But he was something just as sinister: a double agent. He had been recruited by Paul Wentworth, a close relation of John Wentworth, the governor of New Hampshire and a distant relation of Charles Watson Wentworth, the Marquess of Rockingham. Bancroft and Paul Wentworth first met in Suriname, where the Wentworths owned property. Both were American expatriates, and both preferred England to New England. In 1769, the same year that Bancroft published his *Essay*, they collaborated to produce a rambling treatise on the worsening crisis between Britain and her colonies.[9] It steered what was then a middle course, opposing the Stamp Act, along with Parliament's right to tax the colonies, but upholding Parliament's right to control their external commerce, and placed ultimate authority over the colonies in the king's hands.[10]

Whether by coincidence or not, the name *Wentworth* was to make an appearance in yet another of Bancroft's endeavors: an epistolary novel called *The History of Charles Wentworth*. It is, as its subtitle promises, "interspersed with a variety of important reflections calculated to improve morality, and promote the economy of human life." This, surely, was an area where Edward Bancroft had no standing. And alas, fiction was the one thing for which he had no talent. He admitted as much in the preface, albeit unwittingly: "The letters themselves are generally written in a style, not confined by stiffness or formality, nor yet relaxed into that affected ease and carelessness, and that ridiculous familiarity of expression, which has lately been introduced, from an abuse of a rule which enjoined us 'to write as we would speak.'"[11]

Bancroft's career as a double agent began when the Continental Congress dispatched Deane to Paris in early 1776. Deane was under orders to write to Bancroft upon arriving, ostensibly "on the score of old acquaintance." Bancroft, it was hoped, would supply "a good deal of information of what is now going forward in England," toward which end the two men were to settle on a discreet "mode of continuing a correspondence." Deane did as he was told—he genuinely liked and trusted his old pupil—and in July of 1776 Bancroft paid him a visit in Paris. There they renewed their friendship, and Deane, suspecting nothing, revealed everything. Upon returning to London Bancroft went straight to Paul Wentworth, and offered to share the correspondence to which he would now be privy. This included, most notably, Deane's correspondence with the Continental Congress, the progress of their negotiations with the French, and the movements of American ships and privateers. The only real issue was how much Wentworth would pay Bancroft, and after some haggling they settled on £500 up front and an annual stipend of £400. In the meantime, Bancroft continued to receive a much smaller salary from Deane.[12]

It was a cozy arrangement. And it might have continued indefinitely had James Aitken not shown up at Edward Bancroft's doorstep one evening, demanding to speak with him in private. Despite his shabby appearance, Aitken was led into the parlor and joined by Bancroft a few minutes later. Aitken was feeling very pleased with himself, and he wasted no time in telling Bancroft exactly what he had done. He told him everything: that his name was James Aitken and that he had been "sent by Mr. Deane from Paris, to burn and destroy the dockyards and shipping belonging to the government." He had already accomplished part of his mission—did Mr. Bancroft know that the Portsmouth dockyard was even then on fire?—and it was Mr. Deane's express wish that Mr. Bancroft supply him with as much money as he needed to complete his good work. There was more. He needed a place to hide. Could he stay at 4 Downing Street?[13]

Bancroft could scarcely believe his ears. As he listened, he weighed his options. If he helped Aitken, he risked being exposed as an American spy, and if he refused to help, he risked being exposed as a British spy. Wentworth paid him more than Deane; he liked life in London; and Deane had been duped once and could be duped again. And so he made the most logical choice. He would find some way to explain his actions to Deane, but in the meantime, the troublesome young man would have to go. This, of course, is not what he told Aitken. He said only that he would not help him and would not be a party to his plot. Bancroft became increasingly curt. Saying that he had company, he told Aitken to leave.

He did, however, agree to a second meeting. And he chose a most unlikely spot: the Salopian Coffeehouse on Charing Cross Road. It was just yards away from the Admiralty's offices, making it a favorite haunt of "military heroes" who were down on their luck.[14] His reasons for selecting this particular location are not clear. Nor are his reasons for agreeing to a second meeting. Perhaps he hoped that he could dissuade Aitken from completing his mission, or perhaps he was simply looking for information that he might pass on to Wentworth. In any event, his second meeting with Aitken, either later that evening or the following morning, went no better than the first. Bancroft was still leery, or, in Aitken's words, "shy."

Later, when Bancroft was under suspicion in England for his part in the plot, he would claim that in both of their meetings

Aitken had merely "dropped several vague and obscure insinuations of having mischievous purposes, but said nothing which could discover either their nature, or whether they were already effected or not."[15] Bancroft, however, had ample motive to lie; Aitken did not, and in this particular instance his version of their second and more extended meeting is the more trustworthy. His account, albeit in a highly edited form, appears in the confession that he later dictated to one of Sir John Fielding's clerks:

> I related to him my whole conversation with Mr. Deane, my success at Portsmouth, which he would see confirmed in the papers of tomorrow, and my reliance on him for money, and such other assistance as I should want in the continuance of this scheme. After a short conversation, Dr. Bancroft told me, that though he wished Mr. Deane very well, and entertained a great friendship for him, yet he would not have to do with any of his schemes. That he lived and got his bread under this government, and must therefore be excused from meddling in this affair; nor would he encourage me in my proceedings, and desired me not to call at his house, or trouble him any more. I answered, that I would not; but was sorry to find Mr. Deane was so much deceived in him; and that though he was such a friend to Great Britain, I declared myself an utter enemy to it, and told him he would soon hear more of my works at Plymouth to convince him of it, and wished him a good night.[16]

This much is certain: the two men parted knowing that the other had the power to destroy him. Of the two, only Bancroft promised that he would not report their conversations. And for once in his life, he kept his word.

* * *

In Portsmouth, meanwhile, Richard Faithful and Richard Voke found themselves trapped inside a burning building. Voke's first instinct was to run back upstairs to rescue his tools, which he succeeded in doing, but the smoke was by now so thick that he was blocked from bringing them downstairs. This sent him scurrying to the nearest window, which he straddled while onlookers gathered below and "pulled off their clothes for the man to fall upon." A ladder, however, was soon found, and Voke scrambled down to safety.[17] Faithful, in the meantime, had cut and run, and, battling the smoke, he made it the ground floor, where he pushed open a door and emerged, coughing violently.

At the same time, workers in nearby buildings were also becoming aware of the fire. James Russell, a sub-clerk in the rope house, was working in his office, just ten yards away from the rope house itself, when he heard the dockyard bell ring at 4:35. He thought this odd, but he did not go out to investigate. Seven or eight minutes later, the dockyard was in an uproar. People were running past his office, and when he heard "a sound (though an indistinct one) of fire, he went to the office door, and looking at the middle story, opposite the door, [he] saw plainly the rigging loft in flames through the bottom and sides of the window shutters.... "

These same events were also witnessed by John Eddowes, the clerk of the rope house and James Russell's supervisor. Of the 1,707 men listed among Portsea's ratepayers in 1775, only ten were of sufficiently exalted social status to merit the title of mister. *Mr.* John Eddowes was one. He was paid a hundred pounds a year, hardly a princely sum, but he was also provided with a house, free of charge, inside the dockyard.[18] It was located just eight or ten

James Gambier, 1773, by John Singleton Copley (1738–1815). The portrait dates from Gambier's second sojourn in America. It shows him in happier days, before his nervous breakdown, and before he had been taken to task "for not in the least appearing to have taken any steps of inquiry into the cause of the [Portsmouth] fire." COURTESY OF THE MUSEUM OF FINE ARTS, BOSTON, GIFT OF MISS AMELIA PEABODY.

yards away from the rope house. Mr. Eddowes was feeling poorly that day, and it was from his parlor window that he saw smoke billowing out of a shutter in the rope house. Rushing outside, he was greeted by the sight of Richard Voke, clinging to a window and screaming for dear life. Eddowes knew a thing or two about fires. Six years ago, following the great fire of 1770, his housekeeper had "died of fright."[19]

The next person to become aware of the fire was the commissioner of the dockyard. Each dockyard was supervised by a commissioner who reported directly to the Navy Board, and at this time the Portsmouth post was held by James Gambier, a career naval officer. He received his first command in 1746, during the War of Austrian Succession, and was twice posted to North America, first during the Seven Years' War and then from 1766 to 1773. In 1773, after a brief stint as comptroller of victualling, he was appointed resident commissioner of the royal dockyard at Portsmouth. He was lucky to have the job—it was peacetime and he could have been put out to pasture on half pay—but that is not how he saw it. His was fifty-three years old; his career was stalled; and he did not get along with his superiors at the Navy Board. Time and time again he went over their heads and dealt directly with their superiors in the Admiralty. There was a certain logic in this—Gambier was a career navy man, and the commands and promotions that he sought were to be gotten from the Admiralty and not from the Navy Board—but these priorities came at the expense of doing his current job with anything approaching professionalism.

His house was directly across from the rope house, and he was at home when the fire broke out. He remembered running to the spot "on the almost instant of the fires being discovered."[20] It was probably Gambier who ordered the *Albion*, which was then at dock, to put out to sea at once.[21] It was a wise move. The brig was carrying

The Arrival of the Fire Engine *by Thomas Rowlandson (1756–1827). These simple pumps proved surprisingly effective in putting out the Portsmouth and Bristol fires.* COURTESY OF THE YALE CENTER FOR BRITISH ART.

two thousand barrels of gunpowder, enough to level the dockyard and much of Portsea; unfortunately for Aitken, it was high tide when the fire broke out, and the *Albion* was able to clear the dock in a few minutes.

The hard work of fighting the fire fell to the thousands of workers, sailors, and marines who happened to be in the vicinity at the time. Of these, the dockyard workers were the most numerous. They were also the first on the scene.[22] When the fire broke out, the ropemakers were already gone for the day, but thousands of other workers were still on hand. (It was a Saturday, and work did not stop until five.)[23] They were joined, about an hour later, by sailors who were rowed in from ships anchored at Spithead.[24] In the meantime, marines and veterans, the latter being assigned to garrison duty in Portsmouth, came streaming in. It was a large and disparate group of men, and they worked with admirable efficiency, some clearing away fire hazards, others pumping water through the dockyard's primitive fire engines. Thanks to their efforts, the fire was quickly contained, and a few hours later it began to subside.

It could have been much worse. The rope house was gutted, and the rigging for the *Princess Amelia* and the *Deal Castle* were lost, but the dockyard was saved. The initial estimate put the total damage at just over £14,200, not including such incidental outlays as £275 for clearing away the debris.[25] The estimate proved low, and was later revised upward to just under £20,000. This included a niggardly £134 in payments to the men who had put out the fire.[26]

Aitken's failure to do more serious damage can in large part be attributed to lessons learned from the disastrous fire of 1770. In its wake, the rope house had been rebuilt in brick, and thanks to this precaution much of the structure remained standing after Aitken's fire. George III noted as much in a memo the day after the fire, and Gambier went so far as to say that only the roof needed replacing.[27] This was too optimistic. The walls were later found to be unstable and had to be demolished. But they did help contain the fire, as did the policy, implemented after 1770, of storing more of each ship's excess cordage on board instead of in the dockyard.[28]

In the end, though, luck was as important a factor as any in averting what could have been a major catastrophe. There was no wind that night, and most of Aitken's matches had failed.[29] If only he had waited. The workers would have been gone for the day, and the receding tide would have left the *Albion* stranded and vulnerable.

* * *

The day after the fire, the rope house, now in ruins, continued to smolder. Fearing that the fire might yet spread to adjacent buildings, Gambier ordered his shipwrights "and other necessary people" to spend the night in the dockyard, with fire engines at the ready. As an additional precaution, fifty marines from the Portsmouth Division were deployed to keep order.[30] After that, things very quickly started to get back to normal. By the ninth of December, just two days after the fire, nearby ships were already being used as temporary shops.[31] By the twelfth, arrangements had been made to reassign surplus ropemakers to the dockyards at Woolwich, Chatham, and, most importantly, Plymouth.[32] (Among those later reassigned to Chatham were the ill-fated Richard Voke and Richard Faithful.)[33] Those who were not reassigned had their hours cut, and with them, their wages. Despite this, several workers, whether "through infirmities or choice... prefer'd biding at home" until the rope house was rebuilt.[34] They had good reason to be optimistic. By 20 December, less than two weeks after the rope house had burnt down, materials were already being purchased for its reconstruction. These included 300,000 bricks, 300 loads of lime, and 407 lintels.

Men returned to work, carts of bricks arrived in endless succession, and Gambier and the commissioners of the Navy Board resumed their feud. It was the commissioners who fired the first salvo in this newest round. A few days after the cleanup had begun, they decided that the sailors who were helping out were being paid too much. The sailors were incidental to their decision. The commissioners were merely trying to get back at Gambier, who had taken it upon himself to pay them each sixpence a day. In an attempt to bring him to heel, he was ordered not to "suffer them to be employed longer than is absolutely necessary."[35]

For his part, Gambier wanted nothing so much as to put the whole incident behind him. The facts, however, stood in his way. Several witnesses had come forward with the same story: that the fire had actually started as three separate fires, each becoming visible at more or less the same time, and only later converging. There was only one possible explanation: arson. Moreover, the fact that three separate fires had been set in such rapid succession suggested that the destruction of the rope house was the work of not one arsonist but several.

The skeptics, Gambier included, were soon overruled. When news of the fire reached Whitehall, Lord Weymouth, mindful, perhaps, of the hysteria that had surrounded the fire of 1770, pooh-poohed the loss of the rope house as an unfortunate accident. He was about to say more when he was cut off in mid-sentence by the king, who said that as far as he was concerned the fire was the work of arsonists.[36] Lord Sandwich, the first Lord of the Admiralty, took the hint, and on 9 December, just two days after the fire, he opened an investigation.[37] At the same time, several Bow Street Runners were dispatched to Portsmouth. Their task was to find and arrest "several suspicious persons that are imagined to have had some hand in setting fire to the dockyard."[38] The first to be arrested was the hapless Richard Voke. His presence in the rope house at the time of the fire made him an obvious suspect, as did the fact that for several days after his harrowing escape he was in a state of shock—"speechless and insensible"—and thus unable to account for his actions.[39] Gambier's guess was that Voke had meant to pilfer from the rope house and that his lantern "by accident occasioned this conflagration."[40] The other two suspects were not named, but they must have included Richard Faithful, whose actions just before the fire were as suspicious as Voke's.

On the eleventh of December, the three suspects, along with ten other men and four boys (the youngest was just seven), were questioned by Gambier and two commissioners whom the Navy Board had sent down to assist in the investigation. For whatever reason, Faithful and Voke neglected to mention their encounter with Aitken on the sixth of December. All three suspects were cleared and released.

The investigation almost stopped there. Perhaps the fire was an accident after all. On the twelfth of December, Gambier, along with two commissioners from the Navy Board, filed a preliminary report. All three declared that they were unable to "ascertain whether the misfortune arose from accident or design." "We are," they added, "at a loss to form an opinion upon the matter," this despite "the most strict interrogation."[41] Gambier, of course, was hoping that the fire had been accidental, as any other cause would reflect poorly on his administration of the dockyard. In the meantime, nothing was left to chance, and the other dockyards were instructed not to admit strangers.[42] This precaution was to prove fortuitous, for even then Aitken was on his way to Plymouth, the second of his five targets.

CHAPTER EIGHT

His Many Attempts to Burn Down the City of Bristol

THE MATTER might have rested there had William Weston not got to thinking. Weston was the carpenter Aitken had button-holed on two separate occasions, first in January or February of 1776, and, more recently, just hours before the Portsmouth fire. Weston remembered that everything about the man was just a little off—his unctuous manners, his excessive interest in the dockyard, and now his sudden reappearance just before the rope house went up in flames. He could not remember the painter's surname— probably none had been given—but he did remember that he went by the name of John, and that he had worked for a while in Titch-field. There was something about Aitken's fulsome manner that made Weston stop and think. He decided to tell his story to Gambier.

To be safe, Gambier dispatched his deputy purveyor to Titch-field. His name was Thomas Nichols, and he hardly knew where to begin. He was looking for someone known only as John, who was either "a gardener or a painter."[1] These scant details were over-heard by a certain Reverend Croker, who was enjoying a drink when Nichols showed up at a local public house and started asking questions. A terrible thought occurred to Croker. Perhaps the sus-pect was "an enthusiast," devoting "himself, like a French *elire au martyre,* for this particular business."[2] Perhaps, too, he would "make similar attempts at every dockyard in the kingdom." Filled with alarm, Croker dashed off a letter to Gambier, urging him to send "an exact description" of the suspect to the other dockyards.[3] On Christmas day, Gambier did just that, dispatching a memorandum to his fellow commissioners at Deptford, Woolwich, and Plymouth.[4]

In the meantime, Gambier's investigation was proceeding at a snail's pace. In fairness, he had bigger things to worry about, starting with his ongoing feud with the Navy Board. Very quickly, the issue became not the investigation but his conduct of it. It was bad enough that the fire had occurred on his watch. But Gambier made matters worse when he sent copies of witnesses' statements straight to the Lords of the Admiralty, again bypassing his superiors on the Navy Board. His motives are obvious—he was trying to salvage his reputation with the men who really mattered—but this time he went too far. The Navy Board commissioners sent him a stiffly worded rebuke: "It has been the constant practice for all correspondence relating to the business of the yard to be carried through the channel of this board, and unless this is clearly observed, it cannot be conducted with regularity and propriety."

The rebuke sent Gambier to the dockyard's archives. There he spent the next few days combing through the correspondence of his predecessors, looking for proof that they had been as highhanded in their dealings with the Navy Board. His work suffered, and Aitken's trail grew cold, but after an exhaustive search Gambier found what he wanted. This time he was prompt to report his findings to the commissioners in London:

I take leave . . . to assure you, gentlemen, that I have most attentively studied the duty and office of his Majesty's Commissioner by his patent for the affairs of this dockyard, from every tract and vestige in the official records ever since the Duke of York's time to the present, and after having most minutely and duly digested and considered every part, as well as my own separate particulars, as that of every individual member of the Navy Board, and that also, of the whole body as a Board; I hold it most religiously my duty, strictly to obey the orders of the Admiralty Board, under whom I act, and to whom I am amenable and responsible, by communicating to them every transaction of consequence in the said department, under my care and superintendence.... [5]

But it was not this claim, outrageous though it was, that ultimately got him into trouble. It was the claim that there was no point in pursuing the investigation any further. Referring to Aitken, Gambier wrote, "I do not see what further enquiry can possibly be made after the man before mentioned or further endeavoured to trace him, or ascertain if he is the person seen in the rope house on the day of the fire." The remark would come back to haunt him, and he had no one else to blame when he was later accused of being less than diligent in pursuing Aitken.

Shortly after posting this letter, Gambier, "unable to suffer [his] conduct in any shape whatever to be arraigned," suffered a nervous breakdown. [6] He took to his bed, complaining of gout. One morning he woke up and found that he could not write. That task now fell to his wife, to whom he dictated letters from his sickbed. [7] Later, when he was somewhat recovered but just as intent on garnering sympathy, he told Sandwich that he was well enough to write but that he did so with a shaking hand. [8] James Gambier's ordeal had only begun.

The commissioners took over the investigation. The first thing they did was to send Gambier's deputy-purveyor, Thomas Nichols, back to Titchfield. [9] This time Nichols exerted himself, stopping at each of the town's public houses and calling on its two master painters, Messrs. Golding and Baker. [10] He found two people who had known Aitken: a Captain King, whose house Aitken had painted back in January or February, and John Monday, Aitken's former roommate. King remembered "a macaroni painter," one who appeared, "for his occupation, above the common degree." Other than that, "he was a thin man, with light hair, about twenty-five or twenty-six years of age." Monday's description was the more useful of the two, and it was to appear in the ads later run by the Navy Board. Quite by accident, Monday had run into Aitken again six or seven weeks before the fire, and from that encounter he remembered a man "about five feet seven inches high," wearing "his own hair, sandy and loose." Several other features stood out: the man was "about twenty-six years of age," had on "a fantail hat and a brown coat" and a "long watch chain," and was carrying "a bundle at his back."[11] Someone, probably Monday, volunteered another distinguishing feature: the man in question had "whitish" eyelids.[12] One other distinguishing feature was deliberately omitted: Aitken's telltale Scottish accent.

*   *   *

James Gambier was not the only man feeling slighted. Bancroft's refusal to help Aitken in any way had left him "highly disconcerted ... and vexed at the disappointment of receiving a sum of money." That night, he could not sleep, and the following morning he got up early and started walking in a westerly direction. He stopped briefly at an alehouse in Hammersmith, where he wrote Bancroft an angry letter. "You will soon hear more of my handiwork," he boasted.[13]

He traveled sometimes by foot and sometimes by coach, and when he went by coach he would only travel short distances for fear of being noticed by his fellow passengers. Aside from worrying that he might be arrested, his biggest concern was feeding himself. Bancroft's refusal to give him money meant that he was again penniless, and as before, he supported himself by thieving. In High Wycombe, he broke into a house and took "a few linens, consisting of caps, handkerchiefs, but nothing of value." In Avington, he tried but failed to break into two houses. In Hungerford, he worked for a Mr. Smith for ten days, only to break into his house and rob him of four guineas. In Fairford, he committed a burglary.

A few days before Christmas, he arrived in Bristol. As luck would have it, he arrived just as its citizens were debating whether they should sign a petition supporting the war and the king's handling of it.[14] Local Tories were trying to ram the petition through the city's Common Council, and local Whigs were trying to block it. Ironically, Aitken's attempt to burn down the city would tip the balance in favor of the pro-war faction. He could not have chosen a worse place to advance the cause of American independence.

But that had not been part of his original plan. He had merely wanted to find a place to hide for a few days before proceeding to Plymouth, and Bristol, with a population roughly the size of Edinburgh's, was as good a spot as any. Like London and Portsmouth, the city had a sizable enclave of transients and poor laborers, and it was among them that Aitken hid. He headed straight to the old town, and there, in its dense maze of poorly built houses and dark alleys, he was as good as invisible.[15] Even so, he was convinced that someone might recognize him. He made a point of never lodging "in one house two nights together, unless he was certain that he was not suspected."[16]

It had not occurred to him that he might want to burn down Bristol. A few days in the old town convinced him otherwise. The area was poorly lit, many of its buildings were built of wood, and all were closely jumbled together.[17] It was the perfect target. But it was only one of many. Beyond the old town lay the city's quay. The quay was about a mile long, and it was ringed by warehouses, merchants' counting houses, sugar refineries, taverns, and coffee-houses. Each was a firetrap. So, too, were the hundreds of wooden ships that lined the quay.[18]

Aitken lingered for about a week in Bristol, looking for places where he could "do the most mischief."[19] He started to pay particular attention to merchant ships, and to two in particular: the *Savanna la Mar* and the *Active*. Each, he noticed, carried a dozen canons and eight swivel-guns.[20] Where there were guns there was gunpowder—enough, he hoped, to spark a succession of deadly explosions up and down the quay.

Aitken's grand plan, no less than his mental state, was starting to come unraveled. He thought about setting fire to the ships that crowded Bristol's quay; he thought about sticking to his original plan of burning down the dockyard at Plymouth; and he thought about trying his luck at the dockyard at Woolwich, on the other side of England. In the end, he decided to stick to his original plan, and shortly after Christmas he set off for Plymouth. Bristol was spared—for now. On his way to Plymouth he stopped briefly in Exeter, arriving there on 28 December and leaving on New Year's Eve. He knew some people in the town, having worked there for four months in 1776, and he could not resist showing off. He announced that he was "going to Plymouth dock."[21]

He was becoming increasingly reckless. His meeting with Bancroft had spooked him, and he was convinced that he would soon be caught and hanged for his crimes. Reverend Croker had been more prescient than anyone could have realized: Aitken *was* starting to play the part of the martyr.

Further disappointments awaited him in Plymouth. Because as many as ninety ropemakers from Portsmouth had been temporarily reassigned there, he worried that someone might recognize him.[22] The dockyard, moreover, was on high alert. Aitken was not recognized when he showed up at the gate, but he was turned away, and unable to enter the dockyard by any other means, he started making a ladder out of rope. He had been surrounded by rope ladders at sea, and it occurred to him that one might be used to scale the wall surrounding the dockyard.[23] The task of making the ladder took him all of a day, and no questions were asked when he paid a smith to fashion two scaling hooks. He waited until dark to put his ladder to use.

His versions of what happened next differ. He told one man that everything went wrong, and that after one attempt he gave up. He was unable to latch his ladder to the wall; sentinels were nearby; the moon was bright; and because there was snow, he was in mortal terror of leaving tracks.[24] But he told another man that he had no difficulties fastening his ladder to the wall, and that he did so in several places. Each time, however, he was rattled by sentinels, and when he dislodged some bricks, he finally gave up for the night and ran away. The same version has him spending the remainder of the night walking the streets of Plymouth, cursing both the cold and his bad luck. In the morning, he went to an alehouse. Exhausted, he slept there until evening, and as night fell he once again set out with his rope ladder, determined to get inside the dockyard and set fire to its stores of pitch and tar. He very nearly succeeded, or so he claimed. Managing to get "down into the yard, without any noise or difficulty," he "proceeded very gently towards the magazine of pitch and tar," only to be deterred by two soldiers marching back and forth. He next made his way to the hemp house, but was again frightened off by a guard. When he heard "several voices in earnest conversation," he was convinced that he had been spotted, and coming out into the open, he ran in the direction of his ladder, scrambling over the wall and then running until he was well out of town.

Both versions have Aitken returning to Exeter, running much of the way. There he asked a master painter, a certain James Mason, if he could use one of his stones to grind charcoal. Perhaps Aitken looked desperate, for Mason took pity on him, offering him food and drink. Aitken eagerly accepted. After eating, Aitken lingered for some time at Mason's shop.[25] The two men spoke as Aitken worked away at Mason's stone, grinding not charcoal but a new mix of combustibles. Was he part of a press gang? Mason wanted to know. "No, sir, I be not," Aitken replied. What did Aitken "think of the American affairs"? Something in Mason's question piqued Aitken's vanity, because he told him the same lie that he had told Deane. "I have lost a plantation there," he said.[26] This, coming from an impoverished journeyman painter, seemed highly implausible, but Mason was a kind man and he had the tact to let the matter drop.

That night, Aitken took lodgings on the outskirts of town. Again his vanity got the better of him. Alluding to some future great deed, he told several people that he was about to "set off for London, from which place they should soon hear from him, if he was not dead or in prison, and that they might expect to see his name made public in a remarkable manner."[27]

But he did not set off for London. Instead, he returned to Bristol, arriving on the thirteenth of January and spending the next two days paying particular attention to the merchantmen that lay at anchor. At night, he continued his walks, familiarizing himself with the city's streets and lanes, and looking for additional targets.[28] In the old town, where the lighting was bad, he passed unnoticed. He might have passed completely unnoticed had he not repeated the same mistake that he had made in Portsmouth: setting fires in his room. It was while he was burning one of his shirts that he attracted a man's attention. The two men recognized each other at once—they had met in Portsmouth—and Aitken bolted, leaving behind a bundle that aroused even more suspicion. In it were his singed shirt, a quantity of combustibles, assorted tin cases, and, most damning of all, his newest "little library," consisting of Voltaire's *Henriade* and two pamphlets, both pro-American, by Richard Price.[29]

Still no one pursued him, and in a short time he recovered his nerve. He struck on the night of the fifteenth, toward midnight. Moving freely through the deserted city, he placed homemade incendiary devices on three separate merchantmen: the *Savanna la Mar*, the *Fame*, and the *Hibernia*. Still undetected, he broke into a warehouse belonging to a druggist, hoping to use its stores of oils and spirits as fuel. There he deposited yet another homemade incendiary device, and having lit it, he returned to the three ships, setting fire to each in rapid succession.

Confident that he had set in motion "the destruction of the whole town, or at least that part of it which was of most consequence," he left Bristol just before dawn.[30] No sooner had he departed than its citizens woke to the news that fires had been set in several locations, and that combustibles had been left behind at each. They were found because each of his fires had failed to catch. A major catastrophe had been averted, but the city was nonetheless on edge. Andrew Pope, the Tory mayor, cited "attempts . . . made in several places at the same time" as proof of a "design to destroy the whole city."[31] Another citizen shuddered to think of what might have been—"the general conflagration of this city, the loss of many lives, and the total ruin of thousands."[32]

The response of the injured parties was immediate. Each offered a reward for the arrest and conviction of the perpetrators (the fact that fires had broken out in several places at more or less the same time fooled everyone into believing that they were the work of several men). The mayor and aldermen offered a hundred guineas, as did the Merchant Venturers and each of the men whose property had been targeted. Embarrassed at having been caught napping, the city's fire wardens offered an even larger reward: 150 guineas.[33] A few days later, after Aitken had set still more fires in Bristol, the king himself stepped in, offering the princely sum of £1,000 for information leading to the arrest and conviction of the perpetrators. Whitehall had not been unduly alarmed by the Portsmouth fire. But the Bristol fires put the latter in a new light. People began to suspect that they were in some way linked. The targets, moreover, had a common denominator. One was a naval port, the other a commercial port, and together they suggested that the nation's shipping was being targeted. Bristol was also England's second largest city, and the prospect that it might be so easily destroyed had everyone rattled.

*   *   *

The first night had not been a success. When he had recovered his composure, three or four miles outside Bristol, Aitken looked back, expecting to see a mighty blaze. The accounts of what he saw differ. One has it that he saw nothing at all, and spent the rest of the day walking aimlessly back and forth and cursing his bad luck.[34] Another has it that he saw just the opposite, a dreadful fire, and that he was unable to resist the temptation to return and admire his handiwork.[35] This much is certain: he returned, and came face to face with the people whose lives and livelihoods he had endangered. He found "the whole city in consternation, and terror." Unmoved, he redoubled his efforts, and over the next three days he made several more attempts to burn down Bristol, always striking at night.

But it was not as easy as it had been on the first night. He was now thwarted at almost every turn by the city's watchmen. Once they almost caught him. "Observing two of them coming towards" him, he darted into "a passage about two yards wide," and flattened himself against the wall. One of the men followed him into the passage, and passed by him twice without touching or noticing him.[36] The incident so unnerved Aitken that he left Bristol the following morning, only to return later in the day.

In his idle moments he built increasingly fantastical incendiary devices. He made them himself, relying on his wits and whatever materials were at hand. The crude boxes he had left behind on the three merchantmen had been failures, but within a few days' time he managed to construct a far more sophisticated—and far more effective—device. It was, in the words of a man who saw it, "a globular machine, about the size of a six-pound ball, form'd of wire, cover'd with brown paper, pitch and rosin." It had "been fill'd with combustibles," and these, once ignited, caused it to explode.[37] Edmund Burke, who represented Bristol in Parliament at the time, described it as a firework, an "engine of mischief," and suggested that it be sent to the Ordnance Office for further analysis.[38]

It was with this new device, on 19 January 1777, that Aitken finally succeeded in causing real damage in Bristol. That morning, Bristol woke up to yet another fire. It broke out in the vicinity of Quay Lane, and before it was extinguished, several warehouses and residences in the immediate area were in ruins. Watchmen had passed the area at six in the morning and had noticed nothing unusual; thirty minutes later, the fire was burning out of control, and at one point it threatened to spread to two nearby streets.[39]

The actual damage was minor. Fire engines were quickly brought to bear on the fire, and as in Portsmouth, they worked surprisingly well.[40] Help also came from the various recruiting parties in the city at the time. There was a certain irony in this, as the parties, representing seven different regiments, were looking for men to send over to fight in America.[41] All told, 112 soldiers and marines were on hand, including thirteen sergeants. Matthew Purnell, a private, lost his musket and bayonet in the course of fighting the fire; his socks, too, were destroyed, suggesting that he had come very close to being burned himself. The town council proved considerably more generous than the Navy Board, authorizing payments of five shillings to each sergeant, three shillings sixpence to each corporal, and two shillings sixpence to each private. A local merchant, grateful that at least some of his wares had been rescued, took it upon himself to give an additional sixpence to each soldier who had lent a hand.

It was the last fire that Aitken ever set. The newly energized watchmen were taking a toll on his nerves, and he left Bristol that day, the nineteenth of January, never to return. That same day the mayor took the extraordinary step of asking that "a troop or two of dragoons" be dispatched to the city.[42] Whitehall was only too glad to comply, sending not two companies of troops but three, to be placed under the mayor's direction.[43]

The actual losses were not that great. And they were not nearly as extensive as they might have been. As in Portsmouth, ordinary people pitched in to put out the fires, and calm weather favored their efforts.[44] No lives were lost, and none of the ships that had been targeted was seriously damaged. The greatest damage occurred to the *Savanna la Mar*, which lost its mizzenmast and sustained other losses, all of them minor.[45] When Aitken saw this for himself, he was bitterly disappointed. The fires set on the morning of the nineteenth were the most costly, causing, by one estimate, damages in the range of £15,000.[46] Another put the damages at just £5,000.[47]

The real damage was psychological. Long after Aitken had left for good, the citizens of Bristol continued to believe that neither they nor their belongings were safe. "We are all in confusion," one correspondent wrote on the morning of the nineteenth. The same correspondent reported that owners of shops and warehouses were removing their merchandise from the city's core.[48] That morning, too, the city's "most respectable" citizens formed patrols, going out at night and challenging anyone who looked even remotely suspicious.[49] They made several arrests. One suspect, who seems to have been every bit as unstable as Aitken, told the constables arresting him that "he would discover something of moment," and true to his word, "he took out of his pocket a tinderbox and some gunpowder, and said that it was intended to set fire to an alderman's house."[50] All but two of the suspects were released after being questioned.[51] Two more suspects, one of them an American sailor, were produced by a man identified only as Perry, but they, too, were released. Only then did the local authorities settle on Aitken himself. They knew next to nothing about him, only that he was "a stranger who had lodgings in the Pithay for a night or two, but who cannot now be found."[52] Even then, they continued to pursue other suspects. No one man, they reasoned, could have set so many fires in so many different places. And as in Portsmouth, the Bow Street Runners were dispatched to the scene. This time they were sent on a wild goose chase after three more suspects, one of whom was "supposed to be concealed in the environs of London."[53] They may have been acting on Aitken's boast that he was about to "set off for London."

It was only with the last and most spectacular of the Bristol fires that the city's famous representative, Edmund Burke, was roused to take an interest in the affairs of his constituents. Burke was one of two members of parliament representing the city, and things had started badly when, just after being elected in 1774, he declared that legislators should follow the dictates of their own consciences—and not those of their constituents.[54] This did not sit well with the citizens of Bristol, and from that time forward he kept them at arm's length, visiting the city as little as possible. When news of the fires reached him at his home in London, his initial reaction was one of concern. But he downplayed the possibility of arson, possibly because he already foresaw the ways in which such charges could be exploited by his enemies among the city's Tories.[55] Such fires, he observed, "are very common, and that this providentially has not been very considerable."

At some point, however, Burke felt the need to make a concession to his constituents, for on the first of February, he belatedly took out an ad in *Felix Farley's Bristol Journal*, offering a reward of fifty guineas for information leading to the arrest and conviction of the "atrocious offender" responsible for the fires.[56] The ad had the additional advantage of getting back at Pope, the mayor, who had conveniently ignored Burke's earlier offer of the same reward.[57]

Aitken was long gone and still the city continued to be plagued by strange events. Soon there were copycats, who could only have been Tory pranksters. In any event, this was the one group that stood to gain from fostering the impression that arsonists, all of them working on behalf of America, were still at large and just as dangerous as ever. The first week in February, bundles of paper, candles, and tow were found in several different places in Bristol; it was unclear whether this had been done "with design of mischief, or only to terrify the neighbours."[58] Their appearance coincided with that of several anonymous letters. These, predictably enough, linked local Whigs, many of whom were known to favor American independence, with Aitken's fires. The letters, with their transparent political references and studied lapses in grammar and spelling, were clearly a hoax, and an inflammatory one at that. Burke saw this at once, and cried foul when they were published.[59] Others, including the city's Tory mayor, took the letters seriously, and at his initiative a copy of the most threatening letter was forwarded to Whitehall for further examination. It alluded to a much larger conspiracy, and for a while it had a good many people in London fooled:

> I dare say you are as sorry as myselfe on account of our il sucess, but I trust Fortune will be more favorable in time to come & ourselvs more wise and successful Wee need not fear...we shall be much better paid if we doe wel be of good Courag & fear not wee must all stand or fal together Wee must all stand or fal together You rember what our good Chief sayd when we saw him last that heel go to helgate but heel turn the Constitutione & rase the Wegs up again Pray god the day may come for tho we don't prosper to our wishes in America, I beleev our scemes here there's a general plot laid & we nid not fear less Goverment forces....[60]

The letters, much as their author or authors had intended, helped prolong the crisis by several weeks. When, for example, a fire was discovered and quickly extinguished in a cooperage near the famous church of Saint Mary Redcliffe, Felix Farley took the occasion to warn his readers that "this city is not in such perfect security, as to justify the least abatement of that vigilance which the inhabitants have every night observed, since the late dreadful alarm."[61] "The incendiaries," it was reported elsewhere, "did their business with skill and industry."[62] There was another fire in Well's Sugar House, and yet another in a hay loft, and in both places investigators reportedly found a candle, lit at both ends and nestled among highly flammable shavings.[63]

Soon another and even more sinister rumor gained credence. According to a letter posted on 19 February, someone had attempted to poison the city's water supply, and had very nearly succeeded. The culprit was a "stranger" who had reportedly broken into a shop and stolen a vial of arsenic; this he then gave to a boy, telling him to empty it into a reservoir or conduit. The plot (if that is what it was) fell apart when the boy began to suspect that something was amiss.[64]

For the city's Tories, the fires were a godsend. Seizing the moment, the mayor and his allies let it be known that the fires were the work of "persons deputed by the Congress in America to distress England"; by implication, anyone who sympathized with America was complicit in the fires that had terrorized the city's inhabitants.[65] This applied equally to those who had opposed signing the petition urging the king to stand firm. Hence the sly disclaimer, published while the city was still in an uproar: "It was an ill-judged thing to present an address to his Majesty on the success of his arms at this critical time, for we have a number of Americans amongst us, men of capital fortunes, who strongly opposed the address; it has bred more mischief amongst us, than ever Wilkes did in the City of London, and of much more fatal consequence.... "[66] The contentious petition was approved. When one man dared to oppose it, "he was turned out by some near him, and it was then unanimously agreed to and signed."[67]

*　*　*

The same day that Aitken first struck in Bristol, another of his incendiary devices was discovered by accident in Portsmouth. It was the canister made by William Teach. Its discovery came about when workers were removing defective hemp from the south hemp house. James Russell was present, as were John Major, a master ropemaker, and John Thomas, a representative of the company that had sold the hemp.[68] It was Russell who first spotted the object. At first they thought that it was a canister of tea, but all three quickly realized that it was in fact an incendiary device. This sent them digging among the surrounding hemp, where they quickly unearthed the canister's wooden insert, along with an ominous array of matches and combustible materials—tar, oil, brimstone, and a bottle of turpentine.[69] With the discovery of Teach's canister, the possibility that the fire had been accidental was ruled out. It *had been* arson and the intention had been to burn down the entire dockyard—and not just the rope house.

Gambier was still confined to bed. For obvious reasons, he had hoped that the fire was accidental. He had, moreover, been less than alacritous in investigating its causes. With the discovery of the canister, he realized at once that both his management of the dockyard and his conduct of the investigation would inevitably come under scrutiny. Making the best of a bad situation, he dispatched Russell, the canister, and a self-serving letter to Sandwich, once again bypassing the Navy Board in an attempt to curry favor with the Admiralty.[70]

With the discovery of incendiary devices in both Portsmouth and Bristol, the two cases became linked. And with this, a general panic set in, starting in Whitehall. "Administration are exceedingly alarmed at the accounts of the late premeditated villainous conflagrations at Bristol," *The General Evening Post* reported. "Several councils have been held at Buckingham House . . . and his Majesty has expressed the utmost anxiety for the safety of that city, and the loyal part of the inhabitants thereof, who seem to be the innocent objects of this deliberate villainy."[71] The prime minister, Lord North, was shocked to receive an anonymous letter. Its sender, identifying himself only by the initials "G.W.H.," claimed to be a friend, but what he had to say was distinctly unfriendly. "I am," he wrote, "well assured there is a design to destroy his Majesty's dock-yards and store houses. My Lord, take care of them. The schemes are deeply and most secretly carried on and are as artful from giving suspicion, as the devil himself."[72]

The linkage of the two cases had another consequence: it confirmed in many people's minds that the fires were the work of an organized and dangerous group. Suspicion naturally fell on Americans and their sympathizers. The fires were the work of "our enemies," one newspaper insisted. "Nothing," it added, "is more certain than their diabolical intentions."[73] Another newspaper supplied them with a motive. Knowing that Britain was "likely to gain a decisive victory in the field," they were "endeavouring, by the most hellish plots, to undermine her glory, and prevent her success."[74] Inevitably, the fires had a chilling effect on the many Britons who were sympathetic to American independence, as was gleefully noted by *The General Evening Post*. "These fires," it observed, "have served to *cool* those mistaken zealots, who had espoused the unnatural cause of ungrateful children, against a too indulgent parent."[75]

The Americans were the prime suspects, but some people believed that French or Spanish agents had set the fires. They were the usual suspects, having been blamed for the fire that destroyed the Portsmouth rope house in 1770. This theory was put forth in a letter published in *The St. James's Chronicle*. Its author, writing under the coy pseudonym of "Matter of Fact," observed that "whenever a war with France and Spain was about to commence, the destruction of the dockyards of England was always attempted by fire."[76] For the briefest of moments, there was talk of a certain "Mr. Jacques," a shadowy Frenchman who made a sudden appearance in Portsmouth toward the end of January, demanding to see the dockyard.[77]

The sighting of a Frenchman was just one of many troubling events in Portsmouth. When "some persons" asked too many questions about a magazine then under construction, they immediately "excited some suspicion of villainy." When a fire broke out in a shed behind an inn, it was immediately "supposed to have been maliciously set on fire."[78] When a man wearing a mask showed up one night he was immediately taken into custody. He aroused still further suspicion when he "refused to unmask, or give any answer, but to the commissioner himself." Gambier agreed to speak to him, and they were reportedly "closeted together some time."[79]

Soon other towns in England were wracked with fear and plagued by strange events. One newspaper story reported an attempt on Salisbury's water supply, although in this case the editors seem to have confused Salisbury with Bristol.[80] A correspondent from Exeter, jealous, perhaps, of the attention being lavished on Bristol, reported that "Bristol is not the only place in the west of England which has been the object of the dire incendiaries." "Exeter, the ancient loyal city of Exeter," now shared in that unhappy distinction, having "more than once been attempted by them, though happily with little damage."[81] The authorities in Liverpool were taking no chances. As soon as they heard about the fires in Bristol, "it was unanimously ordered and resolved that a strong and sufficient watch be set every night from five o'clock in the evening, till seven o'clock in the morning, to patrol through the docks, and round the town, for the safety thereof." At the same meeting, "a great number of the gentlemen present voluntarily offered themselves to be upon the guard, by rotation each night," and everyone agreed that it was a good idea "to keep a strict look out on all loitering persons being in or coming to the town." Landlords in particular were advised to report "any lodgers or inmates in their houses, whom they have just cause to suspect...."[82]

Next came more copycats, some real and some imaginary. An attempt was made on the royal dockyard at Harwich, but was "happily prevented."[83] That same week, a "very wicked design" was uncovered in Gravesend. There a tiny garrison stood guard over much of the gunpowder used by the Royal Navy. As in Portsmouth, the garrison, such as it was, consisted of veterans in varying states of decay, making the site vulnerable to sabotage. A man reportedly paid a second man fifty guineas to sprinkle gunpowder around the magazine and start a fire. The first man got away, but the second did not, and when he was arrested, he had the "impudence to declare . . . that if it had not been discovered, he should have made us all sleep very soundly."[84] The threat so unnerved local authorities that they asked Whitehall to send them more troops. And in Portsmouth a sailor went mad. He had planted an incendiary device much like Aitken's on the *Terrible*, and in a moment of regret or despondency, he unburdened himself to an officer. After that, yet more men were dispatched to guard Portsmouth's own magazine.[85] As an additional precaution, the garrisons at each of the royal dockyards were also reinforced.[86]

As the panic spread, so did outrage over the heinousness of the fires. Surely these were crimes of such extraordinary evil that they fell outside the existing criminal code. "Of all bad characters, an incendiary is the foulest," wrote one correspondent. "He acts as an assassin armed with the most dreadful of mischiefs, and in executing his diabolical purposes, involves the innocent and the guilty in the same ruin."[87] It followed that existing punishments were inadequate. It is hard to imagine how else Aitken might have been punished, as just about every crime he committed was a hanging offense, but one concerned citizen had a novel suggestion: find the perpetrators and burn them alive:

The crime of an incendiary, does so far exceed every other species of villainy in the aggregate sum, that one might, without appearing an advocate for cruelty, wish to see the righteous law of Moses of "*an eye for an eye*," &c. adopted with respect to it, by procuring a law to be enacted for the punishment of such professed agents of the devil, and enemies of God and man, by the same raging element wherewith they dare attempt to perpetrate so horrid a crime. A penalty so terrible, wou'd certainly operate more strongly on such abandoned, diabolical minds, than that of the gallows only; a punishment becomes regarded, from the frequency of examples, rather with contempt than dread![88]

The real beneficiary of these events was Lord Germain, the colonial secretary and a staunch foe of American independence. He had been looking for the right time to introduce legislation allowing the ministry to detain American combatants without charging them. Aitken provided him with the perfect opportunity. (There had been an earlier attempt to suspend habeas corpus in Bristol, but the measure was blocked by the city's more moderate councilmen.)[89] The primary targets of the "American High Treason Bill" were American privateers, but the bill was also a source of great anxiety among Americans living in Britain. They feared, and not without reason, that the law might be used against them as well.[90] Their position was rendered all the more tenuous by talk of American incendiaries, and on 7 February, Germain, confident that he had the nation behind him, introduced his bill. Among the reasons given for suspending habeas corpus was the need to deal with persons who "have been or may be brought into this kingdom, and into other parts of his Majesty's dominions." In the ominous words of the bill itself, "it may be inconvenient in many such cases to proceed forthwith to the trial of such criminals, and at the same time of evil example to suffer them to go at large...."[91]

In the heated debates that followed, Aitken (then known only as John the Painter) was mentioned, albeit only in passing. Charles Fox, who was pro-American, mentioned him, as did North, each to prove a point against the other. Fox objected in vain. The bill enjoyed the full support of the ministry and a jittery public, and on 24 February it passed by an overwhelming majority. In Aitken's case, it proved unnecessary. When he was later arrested, there was more than enough evidence to charge him with burglary, and it was on this charge that he was held while his more serious crimes were investigated.

In the meantime, more resources were thrown into the investigation. The Navy Board dispatched a commissioner to Portsmouth to examine the mysterious canister and find out everything that he could.[92] Not counting the commissioner's own inquiry, there were now four separate investigations going on, with almost no coordination between them. The king's deputy solicitor was back in Portsmouth, pursuing leads of his own; the Bow Street Runners had been dispatched; Andrew Pope, the mayor of Bristol, was heading up a third investigation; and Gambier, anxious not to be shown up, had reopened his own inquiry. He did so with conspicuous enthusiasm, letting it be known that he had posted "emissaries in every quarter in the neighbourhood to gather all possible intelligence."[93] He may have been stirred into action, but this did not mean he had any intention of cooperating with the Navy Board.

It was not until the third week in January that the Navy Board posted a description of the man who was still only known as John the Painter. At the same time, it offered a reward of fifty pounds for his capture.[94] The amount was paltry, too little to yield results, but it was an important first step. At the same time, the Navy Board offered another reward, totaling twenty guineas, to anyone who could find the maker of the canister left behind in the hemp house. It was assumed that this person lived in or around Portsmouth, and the notices were posted there. In the meantime, the famous canister, having made the rounds in London, was sent back to Gambier, who was instructed to show it only to people who might know something about it.[95]

* * *

By the end of January, the nation was in a state of panic. The arsonists —for everyone assumed there was more than one—were still on the loose and able to strike anywhere at anytime; everybody's nerves, from the king's down, were on edge; and the various men pursuing Aitken, their careers and reputations on the line, had nothing to show for their efforts. Under the circumstances, it was only a matter of time before someone would be arrested. That unhappy distinction fell to a certain Francis Hobbs. It was his bad luck to fit Aitken's profile. He was young, although at twenty he was four years younger than Aitken; he was by trade a painter; and now that people thought about it, they were sure that they had seen him in Portsmouth at about the time of the fire. His employer, a master painter by the name of Wiss or Wise, had sent him to Southampton to purchase silverleaf. On the way, Hobbs had passed through Portsmouth, only to return to Newport, on the Isle of Wight, the day before the rope house went up in flames.[96] This is exactly what Hobbs told Gambier, who then sent for Weston. Did Weston recognize the man? He did not. Gambier was satisfied and let Hobbs go. Someone, however, overruled Gambier, and two days later Hobbs was taken under heavy guard to London.[97] There he doubtless spent several miserable days before he was released.

The investigation was foundering, and professional jealousies were starting to become a real and increasing problem. It was at this point that the Admiralty intervened, taking over from the Navy Board. Less than a week after the Bristol fires, the Lords of the Admiralty summoned before them the one man in England who knew something about how to conduct a proper criminal investigation: Sir John Fielding.[98] He told them exactly what they needed to do.

CHAPTER NINE

His Capture and Subsequent Imprisonment

S IR JOHN'S advice was simplicity itself. The best way to solve a crime was to offer a "proper reward"—and not the paltry fifty pounds offered by the Navy Board.[1] The Lords did as they were told and offered £1,000 for information leading to the arrest and conviction of the persons responsible for burning down the Portsmouth rope house. Any accomplices would be pardoned, but only if they gave up their confederates and the actual arsonist. The Admiralty's reward, when added to the other rewards already on offer, brought the total price on Aitken's head to £2,735. It was a small fortune. James Russell, a sub-clerk, could have worked for the next thirty years and still made less, and Thomas Nichols, the deputy purveyor Gambier had sent to Titchfield, could have worked until he dropped dead and never earned as much.[2]

In addition to putting up £1,000 in reward money, the Admiralty placed ads in ten consecutive issues of *The London Gazette* and twelve consecutive issues of *The Morning Chronicle, The Gazetteer, The Daily Advertiser, The Public Advertiser, The St. James's Chronicle,* and *The London Evening-Post.*[3] Sir John did his bit by running the advertisement in *The Hue and Cry,* and this, combined with the wide reach of London's newspapers, guaranteed that the reward would be seen—and coveted—by law-enforcement officials and newspaper readers across England.[4] Less than one week after the reward was first posted, Aitken was in custody.

* * *

On 19 January, Aitken left Bristol and headed east. His plan, to the extent that he still had one, was to report back to Deane in Paris before attacking the navy's other dockyards.[5] He had little to show for his efforts. The Portsmouth dockyard was still operational, the Plymouth dockyard was untouched, and Bristol had survived his repeated attempts to burn the town down. He brooded over his failures and continued to be angry with Bancroft.

He stopped in Sodbury, and after that, in Marshfield and Chippenham. At some point he passed through Andover. There he was spotted by John Dalby, the keeper of the local bridewell (house of correction). His next stop was the market town of Calne. There he noticed a haberdasher's shop that "might be easily broke open." He walked "backwards and forwards a number of times," looking inside the shop but not entering.[6] That night, while its owner slept, he pried open a shutter, and holding on to a window sash, he let himself in and proceeded to take whatever he could carry. Something, however, must have frightened him, for upon fleeing Calne he left behind a pistol, one of a pair purchased in Bristol.[7]

He had chosen the wrong shop to rob. It belonged to a man named James Lowe, and when Lowe woke up the following morning and found that his shop had been broken into, he was livid. He talked to his wife. Now that she thought about it, she had seen a young man pacing back and forth outside the shop just yesterday. Wasting no time, Lowe saddled his horse and set out in pursuit.

He was not alone. John Dalby, the keeper of the Andover bridewell, was already on Aitken's trail.[8] Dalby set off with high hopes. He had seen Aitken and he had seen the description of John the Painter in *The Hue and Cry*. There was no doubt in his mind: the man he had seen was John the Painter.

Aitken's gimlet, powder flask, and bottle of turpentine. These, along with a pistol, two bundles of matches, and a pair of scissors, were found on his person when he was arrested by John Dalby, the keeper of the Andover bridewell. Later, when questioned by Sir John Fielding, Aitken acknowledged that the items were his, but refused to elaborate.

COURTESY OF THE PORTSMOUTH MUSEUM AND RECORDS SERVICE.

He pursued him to the Hampshire village of Odiham. There, on 27 January 1777, Aitken surrendered without a struggle. He was armed—he still had one of the pistols he had purchased in Bristol—but he was too exhausted to resist. Perhaps, too, he was already reconciled to his fate. Lowe showed up a few minutes later and identified Aitken as the man seen lurking outside his shop. When Dalby opened Aitken's bundle, he could barely contain his excitement. In it he found an arsonist's medley: a powder horn, two boxes of tinder, two bundles of matches, a half-empty bottle of turpentine, a pair of scissors, and a large gimlet.[9]

The bundle also contained several items stolen from Lowe, and it was on the basis of these that Aitken was charged with burglary and held in the village bridewell. It was probably here that he was relieved of the money he was carrying—just over eight pounds. At some point, either in Odiham or London, he was put

One of the two pistols Aitken purchased in Bristol. The hammer was lost when the children of its next owner used it as a toy. COURTESY OF THE PORTSMOUTH MUSEUM AND RECORDS SERVICE.

in shackles, and these remained on him until just before he was hanged. The shackles were loathsome. They ruined clothes and cut into the flesh. But most of all, they were heavy. John Motherhill, who was charged with rape in 1786, said that his weighed seventeen pounds.[10] The practice appalled at least one contemporary, the reformer and philanthropist John Howard. "Loading prisoners with HEAVY IRONS," he wrote, "which [makes] their walking, and even lying down to sleep, difficult and painful, is another custom which I cannot but condemn."[11] Howard had just completed an inspection of virtually every prison and lockup in England and Wales. He was especially horrified by what he saw in the nation's bridewells—"prisoners, covered (hardly covered) with rags; almost famished; and sick of diseases," "many criminals...half starved... scarce able to move, and for weeks incapable of any labour," "emaciated dejected objects," and so on.[12]

The Odiham bridewell was one of the worst that Howard visited. It had just three rooms, the largest of which was occupied by the keeper. The two other rooms were each twelve feet by eleven, housing, between them, eight prisoners in February of 1776.

Prisoners with no funds of their own slept on the floor, with neither bedding nor straw. The food was equally Spartan: one pound
of bread a day for each prisoner.

*   *   *

News of Aitken's arrest spread quickly, and within days the
Odiham bridewell was besieged with visitors from Bristol, London,
and Portsmouth.[13] Among them were William Weston and William
Abram, who the Navy Board had sent to make a positive identifica-
tion. They immediately recognized Aitken.[14]

He told his visitors nothing, not even his real name. Everyone
thought his name was James Hill—his last known alias—and it was
under this name that he was questioned and later tried. He had,
however, already made two slips at the time of his arrest. Forgetting
himself, he had asked Dalby whether he was a king's messenger. As
Bancroft pointed out in a letter to Deane, this amounted to "a tacit
acknowledgment of some state crime."[15] Aitken made his second
slip with Lowe, telling him that he had once worked in Titchfield.

His luck had run out. The same week that he was apprehended,
two crucial witnesses came forward. The first was the man who had
seen Aitken first in Portsmouth and later in Bristol, and the second
was Elizabeth Boxell, Aitken's first landlady in Portsmouth.[16] Aitken
had guessed right: no sooner had he vanished from her sight than
she told her neighbors about his attempt to burn down her house.
At their urging she had gone to see the famous canister when it was
later found in the south hemp house. She recognized it at once.[17]

By the end of the month, it was clear that the prisoner in the
Odiham bridewell was in fact John the Painter. There was great
excitement in Whitehall. On or about the first of February, a man
named Thomas Randall was sent down from London to escort

Aitken back to the capital.[18] Unlike Dalby, Randall really was a king's messenger, and his presence was an indication of just how seriously Whitehall took the case. As an added precaution, Randall brought with him two Bow Street Runners.[19] The forty-mile trip took perhaps eight hours—coaches traveled at about five miles an hour—and it was late when the party reached its destination: the New Prison at Clerkenwell.[20] Aitken was probably confined in one of the "night charges." (These cells, just above the gateway to the prison, were reserved for prisoners who arrived too late to be examined by a magistrate.)

John Howard visited the New Prison just after it had been rebuilt and expanded in 1775. For once, he was impressed. The new facility featured separate wards for men and women, with a paved courtyard and an open shed for the men's use during the day. In the men's courtyard, as in the women's, there was a pump for washing and cleaning. At night, the prisoners were housed in barracks, with two windows in each room "and backwards three, with iron bars, and shutters; but, very properly, no glass." Aitken was free to mingle with his fellow prisoners, but he chose to keep to himself. He "is a very sober man," one newspaper reported, "[who] does not mix with the prisoners, and confines himself to his own apartment."[21]

Prisoners able to pay three shillings sixpence a week got beds of their own. Aitken was not one of them. When Thomas Lawrence, a prospective publisher, visited him four weeks later, Aitken "appeared much to be in want." Lawrence, eager to gain his trust, slipped him two half-crowns, which he declined at first, explaining that the money taken from him upon entering the prison had been "lately restored to him."[22] In the end, he took the money.

He needed it. Like every other prisoner, he was expected to pay his way. He paid to get in—a garnish up front of one shilling and fourpence plus the usual six shillings "for keeping and discharging every person committed by warrant of commitment"—and he paid, or was supposed to pay, a shilling every time he was questioned by a magistrate.

He spent just under a month in the New Prison, growing thinner and weaker by the day. By way of food he received a penny loaf of bread a day; these, John Howard tells us, could weigh as little as seven ounces. This meager ration was supplemented by gifts of beef and bread from a "salesman" in Smithfield; if the location is any clue, this "generous benefactor" was probably a butcher, and the beef was probably leftover offal.

* * *

For nearly a month he was shuffled back and forth between the New Prison and Sir John's offices on Bow Street, always in shackles and always under heavy guard. In each of Aitken's public appearances before Sir John, the chamber was packed—with newspaper correspondents, curiosity-seekers, and often enough with high-ranking officials from the ministry. When these officials were not present in person, they were watching closely from the sidelines, working hand in hand with Sir John every step of the way. Even before Aitken was hauled before him for the first time, Sir John met with Lord Suffolk, the secretary for northern affairs and a staunch foe of American independence. The two men had "a long conference...relative to the person who was taken up on suspicion of setting fire to the rope-yard at Portsmouth."[23] Later that same day, Sir John met with the Lords of the Admiralty for "near two hours, on the same business." In the weeks that followed, Sir John was in constant communication with them. On 3 February, for example, he wrote to Suffolk, informing him that he had already "examined James Hill several times." He promised to "give every assistance in [his] power to further any enquiry into a business so essential to the public safety...."[24]

* * *

The two men came face to face for the first time on 2 February 1777. Several Lords of the Admiralty were present, and Sir John showed off for their benefit. His opening gambit was dramatic. He confronted Aitken with the pistol and combustibles that Dalby had seized in Odiham. Aitken did not take the bait. He merely acknowledged that the items were his, and let it go at that. Nor did he incriminate himself when three witnesses—William Weston, Richard Faithful, and Richard Voke—said that they remembered him from Portsmouth. His answers to Sir John's other questions were equally exasperating. He denied ever being in Portsmouth, the three eyewitnesses' claims notwithstanding, and he denied ever being in Bristol. When asked whether he had ever been to America, he simply refused to answer. In the words of one witness to the proceedings, he "behaved in a most daring manner during the whole time."[25] The session lasted just under three hours, and Sir John had made no headway at all.

It was that way each time. Sometimes Aitken lied, sometimes he refused to answer questions, and sometimes he told the truth, but only when it could do him no possible harm. There is a partial transcript of one of the later sessions, which shows Aitken getting the better of Sir John:

SIR JOHN: Was you ever at Southampton?
AITKEN: I don't choose to make any answer to that question.
SIR JOHN: Was you ever at Titchfield?

AITKEN: No.

SIR JOHN: Did you paint a Captain King's house there?

AITKEN: I know nothing of the gentleman.

SIR JOHN: Did you never hold a conversation or correspondence with an aide-de-camp to Mr. Washington?

AITKEN: I don't know Mr. Washington.

SIR JOHN: Do you know a man called *General* Washington?

AITKEN: I have *heard* of General Washington.

SIR JOHN: Then you know *General* Washington, but you don't know *Mr.* Washington?

AITKEN: I don't choose to answer the question.[26]

Aitken's obstinacy was much remarked on. "Notwithstanding every means...made use of, he would not give the public the least *sketch of his design*," it was reported in *The Public Advertiser*.[27] At the end of a particularly grueling examination, one person wrote that Aitken had behaved "with his unusual sullenness, and refused answering interrogatories," but another person, witnessing the same proceedings, put a more positive spin on Aitken's caginess: he had "artfully refused to answer any question that was put to him by the bench."[28] Sir John was growing more exasperated with each passing day.

In his next appearance Aitken was confronted with two witnesses from Bristol, each of whom could place him in the city just before his attempts to burn it down. One was a former landlady (landladies were his particular bane), and the other was the gunsmith from whom he had purchased his most recent brace of pistols.[29] In response, Aitken again denied ever having been in Bristol.

Almost a week had passed, and Sir John was getting nowhere. A different tack was called for. Perhaps Aitken might unburden himself to a friend—if only he had one. It was Lord Temple, friend and brother-in-law to the great Pitt, who supplied the perfect candidate:

a Welshman by the name of John Baldwin. Not only had Baldwin spent several years in America—in Philadelphia, Perth Amboy, and New York City—he was also a house painter by trade. Temple arranged for Baldwin to show up at Sir John's offices on 7 February. Aitken was once again being questioned. Did Baldwin know the prisoner? Sir John wanted to know. No, he did not.[30] Baldwin's seeming candor made an immediate impression on Aitken, who bowed to him from the bar. As Aitken was led out of the room, Baldwin made a point of following him.[31] Aitken fell into the trap at once. The two men chatted briefly about mutual acquaintances in Philadelphia, Baldwin told a sad story (that he had a wife who was "very much indisposed"), and Aitken, convinced that he had made a friend, asked Baldwin to visit him in prison.[32] Baldwin paid his first visit that same afternoon.

He was to prove a most assiduous visitor. For the next two weeks, he visited Aitken once and sometimes twice a day, each time relaying the details of their conversations to Temple and Lord Germain. (Germain was the sponsor of the so-called American High Treason Bill, which was then being debated in the House of Commons.) For obvious reasons, he was especially anxious to secure "some confession which might contribute to render the Americans and their friends more odious in England."[33]

Aitken genuinely liked Baldwin, and in an attempt to impress him, he told many lies, most little and some fatuous. Did Baldwin know Silas Deane? No, he answered. "Not know Deane! Silas Deane! Oh, he's a fine fellow, he's employed by the Congress at Paris," Aitken exclaimed. He dropped more names, Franklin's and then Washington's. At one point he told Baldwin that he personally knew Washington, and at another he pontificated about military strategy. It was his opinion that General Washington "was much abler than General Howe; that the former would perplex and harass the latter during the winter, but that the grand campaign was to be in the summer; that America would certainly be victorious; that she had plenty of pitch, tar, and turpentine, and that the back country would furnish stores; that all her army wanted was a few officers, and that France would supply them."[34] Gradually, as Aitken started to let down his guard, he told Baldwin something approaching the truth. But as much as he liked Baldwin, he never fully trusted him. At no point did he tell him his real name; nor did he tell him anything about his family or childhood.

Later, when he learned that he had been betrayed, Aitken claimed that he had been using Baldwin all along—and not vice versa. He had lied, he said, when he told Baldwin that Deane had given him a letter of exchange for £300. He did this "to give himself the greater consequence with Baldwin, and secure his assistance in breaking gaol."[35] There may be some truth to this. If Edward Bancroft is to be believed—always a big if—Baldwin made a show of bringing various "instruments" into the New Prison and parading them before Aitken.[36]

With each passing day, Baldwin managed to draw Aitken out a little more. Glad of a listener and needful of a friend, Aitken talked and talked, giving Baldwin the names of the people he had met over the course of his journeys. No sooner did he do so than the Bow Street Runners were sent out after them. Once these witnesses were found, they were brought back to Bow Street. There they were put face to face with Aitken, always in the hope that he would confess or slip. The sequence in which they appeared was utterly transparent, and yet Aitken suspected nothing.

His sessions before Sir John continued without respite. On 10 February, Aitken "underwent a private examination before Sir John Fielding, in Bow Street, and some gentlemen from the Admiralty." As a special concession, "he was allowed to sit on a stool." Several of Sir John's questions were based on information that could only have come from Baldwin, including several pointed questions about George Washington. It is sad and astonishing that Aitken completely failed to put two and two together.

The next time that he was hauled before Sir John he was brought face to face with Mrs. Boxell, his landlady in Portsmouth, and Mr. Golding, his employer in Titchfield. Mrs. Boxell made a sterling witness. Everybody agreed: "Her evidence was very clear, and seemed to be delivered with great candour and honesty." Throughout, Aitken "appeared very sullen, and refused giving any satisfactory answers."[37] When asked to respond, he flatly denied knowing either witness.[38] He was just as recalcitrant when new witnesses from Bristol identified him.

On the twelfth, Aitken found himself in the company of the more usual sorts of people who appeared before Sir John: James Rogers, who was charged with defrauding Henry Morris of three cheeses; the driver of a hackney coach, who was fined ten shillings "for using indecent language to Mr. Ayton, the banker"; and John Ling, who was accused of escaping from a prison hulk, only to have the charge dropped for lack of evidence. It was Aitken, however, who once again took up most of Sir John's time. This time he was confronted with evidence of his misdeeds in Devonshire and Gloucestershire. He was read a letter from James Carrington, a magistrate in Exeter, who quoted him as boasting: "You shall hear from me in a month, if I am not dead, or in prison. My name will by that time be very remarkable." He was read another from a Mr. Brothers of Fairford, who claimed that goods stolen from his house were subsequently sold in Tetbury by a man "who called himself Hind." Brothers had not seen the suspect, but the others in Tetbury had. They had, in fact, seen too much. In a moment of bravado, Aitken had taken off his shirt and shown them a "scar near his shoulder, which he said was caused by a gunshot." And "he precisely answered the description given of John the Painter in *The Gazette*." Aitken was forced to bare his chest. Just below his right shoulder was a scar that gave every appearance of having been caused by a musket ball. Angry and humiliated, he refused to answer any more questions. Had he ever been in America? No answer. Where was he from? Again no answer.[39]

The ministry was now starting to focus on the most interesting and least understood piece of the puzzle: the American connection. On 13 or 14 February, there was a break in the case: Sandwich received a letter from someone who could actually place Aitken in America. Its sender, Edward Ives, remembered that a man named John had arrived on a ship returning from America in 1775. This John was a painter by trade, and he matched the description then circulating in the newspapers.[40] The revelation was a source of great excitement. There *was* an American connection, and everybody now asked the same tantalizing question: who in America had authorized Aitken to attack Portsmouth and Bristol?

Sandwich himself was present at Aitken's next interrogation, as were "several other noblemen and persons of distinction," including Lord North's son. Again Aitken disappointed his audience. A parade of eyewitnesses from Exeter, Portsmouth, and the smaller towns through which he had passed appeared in rapid succession, each reporting an encounter with the arsonist. And still he "refused giving any satisfactory answer."[41]

Baldwin played his part during his visits to the prison by asking Aitken increasingly pointed questions about his sojourn in America. In one of their very first meetings, Aitken had mentioned the names of prominent Americans—Franklin, Washington, and Deane—but there was nothing to suggest that he actually *knew* any of these men. Baldwin started probing. He was looking for proof, and on or about 19 February he finally got it. Aitken was in a talkative mood, and he told Baldwin about the bundle he had left behind in Portsea. Bragging, he told him of the passport that Vergennes had signed at Deane's request. Baldwin drew him out some more, and Aitken told him of the other things that he had stashed in the bundle: three books (which he named for Baldwin's benefit), a pair of breeches, and a pair of buckles.

The revelation triggered a search back in Portsea. James Jeffreys, Gambier's chief clerk, sent out two subordinates to search all houses in and around North Street. An hour later, they were back, with nothing to show for their efforts. They had knocked on Anne Cole's door at 5 North Street, but gave up when no one answered. The following morning, Jeffreys himself knocked on her door. The bundle was just as Aitken had left it. Anne Cole had peeked inside but taken nothing. The ministry finally had what it wanted: proof that Aitken had been in Portsmouth the first week in December and that he had visited Deane in France shortly before that. One crucial detail, however, was overlooked: the name on the passport. It was not James Hill: it was James Actzen (another version has it as "Iatkins"), misspellings, to be sure, but ones that were nonetheless faithful to Aitken's true surname.[42]

A day or two after the bundle was found, Aitken was once again dragged before Sir John. The bundle was waiting for him, along with its damning contents. Once again he stood his ground. But he was not prepared for Sir John's next question: Did he know Silas Deane? The question flattered him, and he made his first admission. Yes, perhaps Mr. Deane had given him some money.[43]

But it is not what Aitken told Sir John that mattered. It was what he had already told Baldwin. Baldwin's work was done. He stopped calling at the New Prison and spent the next two weeks briefing the team that would prosecute Aitken for burning down the Portsmouth rope house. Thanks to Baldwin, they had more than enough evidence to secure a conviction. Even so, they were leaving nothing to chance. If they failed to convict him for arson, they were prepared to charge him for his various burglaries, any one of which was a hanging offense.[44]

One charge was off the table: treason. Its omission is curious. The punishment would have been the same—hanging—but afterwards the crowds watching the execution would have been treated to an additional spectacle: the drawing and quartering of the corpse.[45] The likeliest explanation is that Whitehall was anxious to avoid executing a Scot for treason, if only because the always dangerous John Wilkes was still capable of causing mischief and would do so by playing on the anti-Scots prejudices of the London mob. National unity, moreover, was very much on people's minds. The nation was at war, and the army was heavily dependent on Scottish recruits. (In 1778, two-thirds of the men who enlisted were of Scottish origin.)[46] It was the worst possible time to make an example of an errant Scot. The government's sensitivity on this point fits with another curious omission. The advertisements offering a reward for Aitken's capture mentioned every possible detail about him save one: his telltale Scottish accent.

* * *

Representatives from the ministry were not the only ones following Aitken's every word. Edward Bancroft was trying to find out as much as he could, convinced that his days were numbered. He had kept his word to Aitken, and had not betrayed him. Now it was Bancroft's turn to worry: would Aitken betray him? Bancroft was a wreck. He wrote to Deane on 7 February, informing him that "a

Thomas Lawrence, Sr., by Thomas Lawrence, Jr. (1769–1830). Lawrence was first in line to get Aitken's dying confession. Sir John Fielding's clerk beat him to it, but it is thanks to Lawrence that we know a great deal about Aitken's final days. COURTESY OF THE NATIONAL PORTRAIT GALLERY, LONDON.

person...described under the name of John the painter" had been arrested and had already been questioned twice. On both occasions the prisoner had "eluded all important questions," but since then a third interrogation had taken place. Bancroft was anxiously awaiting the results.[47] By the thirteenth, his nerves got the better of him, and he went to the New Prison, hoping to meet privately with Aitken. It was a Sunday and he was able to slip in without drawing attention to himself. Bancroft mentions their third and final meeting only in passing, and he does not tell us what they discussed—nor how Aitken reacted. But it is not hard to fill in the blanks. Bancroft pleaded with Aitken to keep silent, citing the damage that any revelations might do to Deane. It was the only card that Bancroft had left to play, and it presented Aitken with a dilemma: how to ruin Bancroft without also ruining Deane.

On his last night in the New Prison, Aitken received another unexpected visitor. His name was Thomas Lawrence and he was hoping to get rich by publishing Aitken's dying confession. There was an enormous market for these so-called confessions, and Aitken's promised to be a best-seller.[48] But Lawrence had to act quickly. There were no appeals from a death sentence, and while most condemned felons were either pardoned or given reduced sentences, those who were not invariably hanged within a week of sentencing.[49] Thanks to a tip from a Bow Street Runner, Lawrence had gotten a jumpstart on the competition.[50] Everyone else was waiting until after the trial, but not Lawrence. He was not only assuming that Aitken would soon be dead; he was banking on it.

He needed the money. He had been trained as a solicitor, but had given up the law to write poetry. When he failed, he set up shop as the landlord of a public house in Bristol, and in 1772, after running this enterprise into the ground, he set up shop in the Black Bear Inn in Devizes, a popular stopover for people en route to Bath.

It was just after seven in the evening when he arrived at the New Prison. He slipped the keeper a bribe and was taken to see Aitken. According to Lawrence, Aitken received him "at first with a reserved civility, but in a very short space of time became more open." Lawrence made no attempt to conceal the reason for his visit. He explained how he had handled the confession of a man who had been hanged a few years ago. Not only had he administered to the man's "wants during the short time he had then to live," he had also promised to attend his burial. Whether he kept his promise he did not say. No matter. Aitken, who "believed he had not long to live," heard what he wanted to hear. Lawrence, to underscore that he was in earnest, slipped him two crowns. The keeper, greased, no doubt, with yet another bribe, then took them upstairs to a room where they might be more comfortable and talk freely. Lawrence called for a bottle of wine. Aitken was curious about the man whose confession Lawrence had taken. How had he died? And "in what manner was he buried"? After a few glasses of wine, he agreed: Lawrence should be the one to have his confession. Their conversation was cut short by the appearance of a Bow Street Runner. It was late, he explained, and he had to be up at five to escort the prisoner to Winchester to stand trial. As they walked downstairs together, Lawrence reminded Aitken of his promise, "whispering him in the ear, and willing him to continue in the same state of mind, respecting his confession and repentance." Just before he left, Lawrence called for another bottle of wine, which Aitken eagerly accepted. He got as drunk as he possibly could and tried to get some sleep.

CHAPTER TEN

His Trial in Winchester

THE MORNING after Thomas Lawrence's ghoulish visit, Aitken was woken before sunrise and placed in the custody of four Bow Street Runners. They were there to escort him to stand trial in Winchester. He evinced "the greatest cheerfulness and alacrity in making the necessary preparations for his journey, and expressed his fullest confidence of an honourable acquittal."[1] It was an impressive display of bravado. We know from Lawrence that Aitken already believed he would hang, although he had no way of knowing for which offense.[2] He would not hear the indictment against him until the start of the assizes; nor, until the day of his trial, would he know the names of the people testifying against him. When he did, he was mortified to find John Baldwin among them.

This was the way it had always been at the assizes. The Crown enjoyed every possible advantage, ambushing prisoners, many of them ill and half-starved, and giving them neither the time nor the resources to mount an adequate defense. Few even bothered.[3]

He traveled by coach, "strongly guarded, and loaded with heavy irons."[4] The ministry spared no expense. The trip alone cost just under thirty-four pounds, easily exceeding the cost of his passage to America.[5] One account, published in several newspapers, reported that he broke down and lost his nerve just outside Winchester, recovering his customary sangfroid a few minutes later. The story could only have come from one of the Bow Street

Runners accompanying him, who no doubt received a handsome payment for it:

> When...he had arrived within six miles of the place where his judges were to be assembled, the apprehension of his deplorable fate seemed to strike him with peculiar force; he trembled exceedingly, and for some time appeared to be in a state of perfect stupefaction. When he reached the gaol, he had recovered his intrepidity, which he maintained till the awful sentence had been pronounced upon him; and so circumspect was he in all his actions, that an inflexible obstinacy was, by many, considered as a proof of conscious innocence.[6]

The story is plausible, but not for the reasons given. If Aitken did in fact collapse just outside Winchester, it was almost certainly more from exhaustion than fear. He had traveled sixty-five miles in just one day, and by the time he reached his destination he was hungry, thirsty, and probably close to fainting.

* * *

As Aitken was being whisked through the Hampshire countryside, hundreds of curiosity-seekers, dignitaries, and newspaper correspondents were also wending their way to Winchester to catch a glimpse of the famous prisoner and the famous dignitaries who would be attending his trial. Sir John Fielding would be there, as would Lord Sandwich and the other Lords of the Admiralty. The assizes were always a big event, attracting both the cream and scum of local society, but on this occasion the "concourse of people... was greater than ever was known."[7]

A new wave of gawkers appeared the Sunday before the trial. They had come from the surrounding countryside, "Sunday being a kind of holiday to the country people." Chief among them were the wives and daughters of local farmers. Aitken refused to leave his cell, and instead sent word that "John the Painter did not see company that day." His refusal and the way in which it was phrased did not sit well with the crowds who were turned away. They all agreed: "he deserved to be hanged, or he would never have behaved so rudely to folk who came so far on purpose to pay him a visit."[8]

The most important dignitaries to attend the trial—Sandwich, the other Lords of the Admiralty, and Sir John himself—had all booked lodgings in advance.[9] So had Thomas Lawrence.[10] Sir John arrived several days before the trial, while the Lords of the Admiralty waited until the last moment, making their appearance on its eve.[11] The two judges, Sir Beaumont Hotham and Sir William Henry Ashurst, arrived on or about 3 March. Both had come from London and knew what the ministry expected. And finally, there were the witnesses the Crown intended to present.[12] One, a woman who lived in Whaddon, a village just outside Salisbury, never made it to Winchester—or so it was reported. So frightening was the prospect of traveling in a coach to Winchester that she "fainted away and died in a few minutes."[13] This is the first and only mention of Whaddon, and the story is almost certainly apocryphal.

Aitken was one of twenty-five prisoners on the docket. As luck would have it, one, Richard Carter, also happened to be charged with arson. His targets—a barn and outhouse, plus two haystacks valued at twelve pounds—were rather more prosaic than Aitken's. Two prisoners, one male and one female, were charged with murder, and another, Henry Cawdrey, was charged with "feloniously... killing and destroying one gelding" belonging to Allen Mason. The

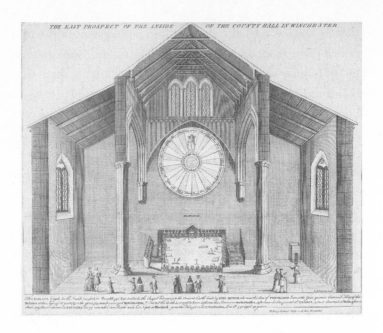

The Interior of the Great Hall at Winchester *by R. Berning, eighteenth century. Pride of place is given to a fourteenth-century forgery of King Arthur's round table.* COURTESY OF THE HAMPSHIRE RECORD OFFICE.

Exterior of the Great Hall at Winchester, *1838.* COURTESY OF THE HAMPSHIRE RECORD OFFICE.

remaining twenty prisoners were variously charged with felonies that Aitken himself had committed on numerous occasions—simple theft, breaking and entering, and highway robbery.[14]

Aitken's, however, was a special case, and because so many important people had come to watch, he went first. He was guilty of dozens of crimes, all of them capital, but in the end he was indicted for only three. These were the destruction of the rope house, the attempted destruction of the south hemp house, and the incidental destruction of naval stores. He was not indicted for his other fires. The omission was probably deliberate, because it saved everyone who had offered rewards after the Bristol fires. The king benefited most of all. He had offered £1,000 of his own money, and everyone who had volunteered information in hopes of collecting it went home empty-handed.

*　*　*

The trial took place on 6 March in Winchester's Great Hall, a magnificent building dating from the early thirteenth century. The hall had originally been part of the Winchester Castle, and it alone was left standing when Cromwell's troops demolished the city's fortifications in 1651. Over the centuries, countless individuals had been tried and condemned there, the most famous being Sir Walter Raleigh, who was found guilty of treason in 1603. (He was later pardoned.) The building was much as it had been in Raleigh's day, and its principal attraction was a large wooden tabletop that hung from one of the walls. It was believed to be King Arthur's round table but it actually dated from the fourteenth century.

The table was a sham, and in its own way it set the stage for the day's events. The trial was a contest between unequals with a foregone conclusion. On one side sat two judges, twelve jurors, and no fewer than five prosecutors, three of whom were seasoned litigators. On the other side and alone stood a dazed, ragged, and not entirely coherent man. After more than a month behind bars, he was dirty, disoriented, probably malnourished, and weighed down with chains, which both slowed and announced his movements.[15] To the well-fed jurors who sat across from him, he *looked* guilty, an impression that was reinforced by the practice of referring to him not by name but simply as "the prisoner." Had Anne Cole kept the bundle that *the prisoner* left behind? a prosecutor wanted to know. And how long did *the prisoner* stay in her house?[16]

Nor did it help that he was identified as a mere *laborer*. This was common practice, but in Aitken's case it was a deliberate insult, especially since everyone knew he was a painter by trade. The prosecution was imprecise on one other point: Aitken's real name. So far, Aitken had revealed it to no one, not even to Baldwin, leaving the prosecution with no other choice than to indict him under all of his known names—"James Hill, otherwise James Hind, otherwise John Hind, otherwise James Acksan."[17] *Acksan*, a crude phonetic approximation of *Aitken*, could only have come from the passport left behind in Anne Cole's house.

He held up better than most defendants. The publisher of *The Hampshire Chronicle* wrote that Aitken "put himself on his trial with great judgment and caution."[18] At one point he even attempted to rattle William Davy, the lead prosecutor, by asking him whether he was "his majesty's counsel." The question caught Davy off guard. "I am. What then?" Aitken continued to mock him: "I only wanted to know if you were his Britannic majesty's counsel, and if you had done with the examination."

Aitken was without counsel. This was standard practice at the assizes, and to this extent Aitken was treated no differently than any other felon on trial for his or her life. Lawrence put it out that "two very respectable council" had volunteered to represent Aitken, but that he had turned them down, explaining that "their service would not avail him."[19] In the absence of counsel, Aitken made several procedural errors, and each time he was rebuked, damning him still further in the eyes of the jurors. Halfway through the trial, one of the judges ran out of patience and stopped to give him a lecture. "Prisoner, I would once for all, without repeating it to you after every witness is called, inform you, that you are at liberty to ask any witness what questions you think fit, after the examination is gone through by the Crown. You know best your own defence."[20]

The advice was less than helpful. Not only had the witnesses been sprung on him, he could not possibly hope to match wits with the seasoned litigators the Crown had hired to prosecute him. He admitted as much when he attempted to mount his own feeble cross-examination of Baldwin. "I am not endowed with oratory," he explained in his frustration.[21]

The other players in court had every possible advantage over Aitken. They were better fed and better dressed. They were also cleaner, and this made them appear more respectable. The jurors were all richer than he (each owned property valued at ten pounds or more) and none was a journeyman or a laborer.[22]

The judges each wore a scarlet robe lined with ermine and a full-bottomed wig.[23] William Ashurst was fifty-two years old, and had been a judge on the Court of King's Bench for only a few years. His rise was less than meteoric. He spoke little during the trial, which was perhaps just as well, as he was not known for his eloquence. Edward Wynne, writing in 1790, observed that Ashurst's "language has no peculiar neatness or brilliancy, but it is perspicuous, pointed, and clear." Wynne continues: Ashurst's oratory "will ever have more weight and influence in a court of English judicature,

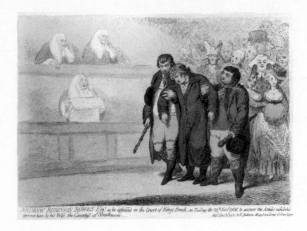

ANDREW ROBINSON BOWES Esqr. as he appeared in the Court of Kings Bench, on Tuesday the 26th Nov 1786, to answer the Articles exhibited against him by his Wife the Countess of Strathmore.

Andrew Robinson Bowes Esqr. as he Appeared in the Court of Kings Bench, *1786, by James Gillray (1756-1815). The prisoner, after just a few weeks in prison, is too weak to stand, let alone defend himself against the charges that are being read to him. The judge in the upper left-hand corner is Sir William Henry Ashurst, one of the judges who presided over Aitken's trial; to his side is his pupil and protégé, Sir Francis Buller, already elevated to the bench. Buller was a prosecutor at Aitken's trial.* COURTESY OF THE NATIONAL PORTRAIT GALLERY, LONDON.

JUDGE THUMB

Judge Thumb, 1782, by James Gillray. Sir Francis Buller, one of the five prosecutors assigned to Aitken's case, acquired the unfortunate sobriquet of "Judge Thumb" after ruling that a husband could beat his wife with a stick provided that it did not exceed the width of his thumb.
COURTESY OF THE NATIONAL PORTRAIT GALLERY, LONDON.

than any one can hope to arrive at, by the mere pomp and splendour of Grecian or of Roman eloquence."[24] This is faint praise, and it is hard to escape the impression that Sir William Henry Ashurst was an uncommonly dull man.

Beaumont Hotham had risen much faster than Ashurst. He was only forty, but he was otherwise a nonentity. He was a *baron* only by virtue of being a Baron of the Exchequer. Wynne tells us that Hotham was utterly lacking in "that fire and brilliancy of genius which irresistibly attracts the notice of mankind," so much so that his "elevation to the Bench not unfrequently produced the mortifying enquiry, 'Who is he? What's his name?'"[25]

Such questions continued to dog Hotham until 1800, when he came to the public's attention by sentencing a boy of ten to hang. The boy had been caught stealing notes from a post office, and Hotham was determined to make an example of him, citing "the infinite danger of its going abroad into the world that a child might commit such a crime with impunity, when it was clear that he knew what he was doing." The crowd in the courtroom listened to this pronouncement in stunned silence, and the defendant, who was dressed for the occasion in an especially childish pinafore, started to wail. (The Home Office was aghast, and the boy's sentence was later commuted.)[26]

There were five prosecutors. Their numbers and credentials speak to the importance that Whitehall attached to the case. Their leader was William Davy, an experienced prosecutor with a reputation for being caustic. Two years earlier, in 1775, he had prosecuted the notorious Mrs. Rudd, who was almost certainly the mastermind behind the most sensational forgery of the century. Davy, it was reported, was "so extremely abrupt, that she burst into tears and was near fainting."[27]

There were three other barristers: Francis Buller, John Fielding (son of the famous author and nephew of Sir John), and the venerable Lord Mansfield. Buller was only eight years older than Aitken and already marked for success. In 1763, at the age of seventeen, he had married an heiress. That same year he began his legal studies in London, where his mentor was Ashurst. A year after prosecuting Aitken, Buller himself became a judge. He was thirty-two.

The oldest and most distinguished member of the team was William Murray, better known as Lord Mansfield. Mansfield was widely regarded as the most brilliant jurist of his day, and he was on hand to make sure that nothing went wrong. The old man (he was already seventy-three) was one of the king's most trusted advisors, and for the past two decades he had served as Lord Chief Justice.

He had been given every advantage in life. He had once observed: "My success in life is not very remarkable; my father was a man of rank and fashion; early in life I was introduced into the best company, and my circumstances enabled me to support the character of a man of fortune." He had only one thing in common with Aitken: he was Scottish.

He frightened people. The spikes atop King's Bench Prison were known as "Lord Mansfield's Teeth."[28] Boswell wanted to like him, but could not:

> His cold reserve and sharpness, too, were still too much for me. It was like being cut with a very, very cold instrument. I have not for a long time experienced that weakness of mind which I had formerly in a woeful degree in the company of the great or the clever. But Lord Mansfield has uncommon power. He chills the most generous blood.[29]

Many people hated him: John Wilkes, the London mob, and almost everyone in America. His opinions were unpopular. He

The able Doctor, or America Swallowing the Bitter Draught.

ABOVE: The able Doctor, or America Swallowing the Bitter Draught, *1774 or 1775. The print first appeared in England, and was later copied by Paul Revere. Lord Mansfield, never a friend to America, holds her down while Lord North forces tea down her throat. The print also lampoons Lord Sandwich, who is shown lifting America's skirt, and the Scottish Lord Bute, who stands at the far right, sword at the ready. The fact that Bute had long since been hounded from office is conveniently overlooked.*
COURTESY OF THE BRITISH MUSEUM.

LEFT: *William Murray, First Earl of Mansfield, 1783, by John Singleton Copley (1737–1815). Mansfield was present at Aitken's trial to make sure that nothing went wrong. "It is," Boswell confided in his journal, "unpleasant to see so high an administrator of justice such a man."*
COURTESY OF THE NATIONAL PORTRAIT
GALLERY, LONDON.

upheld the state's right to press sailors into service, and he had urged George III, as if urging were needed, to make no concessions to his American subjects. In 1775, Mansfield had infuriated everyone in America by arguing that the colonies were in a state of rebellion, and in 1778, even as the war was starting to stall, he continued to press for a military solution to the conflict:

> What a Swedish general said to his men, in the reign of Gustavus Adolphus, is extremely applicable to us at present. Pointing to the enemy, who were marching down to engage them, said he, "My lads, you see those men yonder: if you do not kill them, they will kill you." If we do not...get the better of America, America will get the better of us.[30]

Lastly, there was a Titchfield solicitor on the team by the name of Thomas Missing. He was a former member of Parliament and the son of a wealthy local merchant.[31] He had helped in the initial investigation, back in December, and his command of the facts made the prosecution's task all the easier, as did the copious documentation provided by Sir John.[32] But the prosecution owed even more to Baldwin—far more than any of its members were prepared to admit.

* * *

It was still dark when people started to gather outside the Great Hall. By six, the streets "were as full of people as if it had been noonday."[33] At seven, the doors to the Great Hall were opened, and curiosity-seekers barged and jostled their way in. By 7:15, the hall was completely full, and at eight sharp, Hotham and Ashurst made their entrance. Aitken was brought to the bar and arraigned. He pleaded not guilty.

We have a pretty good idea of what was said that day. This is because at least two people in the audience, Joseph Gurney and William Blanchard, took notes in shorthand. Of the two, Gurney's version is more complete; Blanchard's, while maddeningly elliptic, comes closer to the way people actually spoke.[34] There is another reason for favoring Gurney's version: he was a seasoned and respected court reporter, having transcribed, among others, the trial of the duchess of Kingston in 1776.

The task of reading the indictment fell to Fielding in his capacity as junior counsel. Davy then walked the jurors through the facts. His most difficult task was explaining why the prosecution's case was based almost entirely on the testimony of an informer. (Aitken, who had to this moment suspected nothing, was stunned.) Davy's remarks on this uncomfortable subject were not especially convincing, but if no one was fooled, still less did anyone care. He next recounted nearly everything that Aitken had told Baldwin over the course of their sham friendship. He did so in damning detail. On and on he went:

> The tenth part of these circumstances, which I have opened, would serve, I should think, to decide the fate of any man standing in the prisoner's situation; but it is the wish of the public, it is the wish of government, that all the world should know the infamy of this transaction, and that they should know to whom they are indebted for the sorrows they have felt, and how much they owe to the providence of God, that America has not been able totally to destroy this country, and to make it bow its neck, not only to the yoke of America, but to the most petty sovereign in Europe . . . let

but the English navy be destroyed, and there is an end of all we hold dear and valuable; the importance of the subject, the magnitude, the extraordinary nature of the thing calls for a more particular investigation, than any other subject of what kind soever could demand....[35]

The prosecution called nineteen witnesses, far more than it really needed. All but two—the clerks James Jeffreys and James Russell—could tell of an encounter with Aitken. Six were from Canterbury: Mary Bishop, his landlady; John Illenden, the apothecary who had sold him turpentine and saltpeter; Edward Evans and James Wilson, the two dragoons with whom he had gotten into a fight; and the apprentices William Teach and John Fisher. (A third apprentice, the boy who made the wooden box to fit inside Teach's canister, had since died.)

Ten of the witnesses were from Portsmouth, including four men who could place him in or around the dockyard just before the fire: William Abram, William Baldy, William Weston, and Edward Carey. James Gambier was also on hand, but only as a reluctant observer. At one point he was asked to identify the bundle left behind at Anne Cole's, and at another he was called on to translate the famous French passport, presumably because he grew up in a French-speaking household. Such was his chagrin that he had made no attempt to see or question Aitken after his arrest, and it was not until 6 March, the day of the trial, that he first set eyes on his nemesis. In reality, both men were on trial that day, the one for his crimes, the other for his mismanagement of the dockyard. Davy was relentless. He told the jurors of a botched and indifferent investigation, and while he did not name specific individuals, everyone, Gambier most of all, could fill in the blanks.

There were only three witnesses who were not from Canterbury or Portsmouth. They were James Mason, the painter from Exeter who had lent Aitken his mixing stone; John Dalby, the jailer who had arrested him; and John Baldwin.

Baldwin was the prosecution's star witness, testifying for two hours, or what one weary correspondent described as an "extremely long" time.[36] Aitken lashed out at him repeatedly, much to the delight of onlookers. "He seemed particularly angry with Baldwin," the newspapers gleefully reported.[37] Their exchanges, such as they were, were lopsided. The one would taunt and inveigh; the other would continue as if nothing had been said. "I can't embrace you now, Mr. Baldwin, as I did last Monday sennight."[38] No response. "I remark to the witness that there is a righteous Judge, who also giveth righteous judgement; beware of what you say concerning that Mr. Deane, perjure not yourself, you are in the sight of God, and all this company is." Again no response. Aitken might as well have been talking to a wall.

Baldwin was the cause of several outbursts; so were mentions, most of them disparaging, of Silas Deane. Each time Deane was mocked, Aitken rose to his defense; indeed, he defended Deane with far more passion than he defended himself. The first such outburst occurred early in the trial. Davy was being sarcastic and Aitken took the bait:

DAVY: I wish Mr. Silas Deane were here; a time may come, perhaps, when he and Dr. Franklin may be here.
AITKEN: He is the honestest man in the world.

Later, when Baldwin mentioned Deane, Aitken again interrupted:

AITKEN: Consider in the sight of God what you say concerning Silas Deane.

DAVY: You need not be afraid, Silas Deane is not here, he will be hanged in due time.

AITKEN: I hope not. He is a very honest man.[39]

These outbursts have the advantage of coherence; others do not. They tell us little about Aitken, other than that he was outwitted, outmatched, and exhausted both physically and emotionally. But interspersed among the outbursts and rambling asides are observations and comments that betray a keen native intelligence. Aitken objected, for example, when Gambier was called upon to read the French passport into the record. "State your objection," Hotham demanded. "That they who shall be called to witness for or against me, may not hear the contents of it," Aitken replied and he was right, as Davy acknowledged by agreeing to call no more witnesses.

Aitken tried to cross-examine Baldwin, but his questions fell wide of the mark. Hotham went through the motions of asking Aitken whether he wanted to call any witnesses of his own. This was disingenuous. Aitken had no way of hunting down witnesses or guaranteeing their appearance at his trial. For a man with no friends, no counsel, and no money, it was impossible.

Hotham summed up the evidence for the jurors' benefit. He spent the better part of an hour tying together loose ends in the prosecution's case. Why, he wondered aloud, would any *innocent* man carry a tinderbox full of tinder and a powder horn full of gunpowder? Perhaps the witnesses from Canterbury were a bit fuzzy about dates, but their testimony should be credited nonetheless. And the jurors could take it on his authority that Baldwin's testimony was admissible—anything that Aitken told him was done voluntarily, "without any solicitation whatsoever, and without any promise or engagement of secrecy."

Hotham plodded on in this fashion, hoping all the while to make a good impression on Mansfield. The newspapers, at least, were impressed. *The Public Advertiser,* for one, claimed that he made his summation "with great precision, and made his observations as they occurred, both for and against the prisoner."[40] Hotham admitted that he could find almost nothing to say in Aitken's favor, not that this bothered him: "If I had found myself enabled in my conscience to have stated anything more favourably for him, I would have been the first to have done it."[41]

When the jurors' turn came, they spoke among themselves for about "a second," and to no one's surprise pronounced Aitken guilty.[42] This was abrupt even by the summary standards of eighteenth-century justice, and the newspapers took it as yet further proof of Aitken's absolute guilt.[43]

Aitken's response commands our respect. Everybody was hoping that he would break down. Most defendants did. Aitken did not. Upon hearing the verdict, he merely smiled. One wonders about that smile. Was it the smile, beatific and superior, of a martyr? We do not know. All we know is that his manner became increasingly exalted as the trial came to an end. Even as he was about to be sentenced to death, he refused to kneel, and when asked why sentence of death should not be passed upon him, he made no attempt to plead for his life.[44]

Hotham donned his black sentencing hat, and silence descended on the hall. Rising from his seat, he explained why Aitken must hang. Such speeches were measured by their outcome. If the prisoner started to weep or tremble, the speech was a success. Martin Madan, writing in 1785, used words such as *tears, terror,* and *fainting* to describe the desired effect. If Edward Wynne is to be believed, these macabre speeches were Hotham's one forte. "Baron Hotham is nevertheless respectable upon the Bench; and it has been observed, that whenever called to the administration of *criminal* justice, the humanity, the solemnity, and impressive pathos of his address to prisoners, has melted the most obdurate to contrition and repentance."

Beaumont Hotham gave the speech of his life that day. One account has it that he spoke "in the most solemn manner," "in a strain equally humane and awful," and always with "great feelings of humanity."[45] Thomas Lawrence wrote that he delivered "a most humane, and most affecting exhortation to repentance, and solemn preparation for an awful sudden change."[46]

Hotham professed himself to be at a loss for words to describe Aitken's crimes. They could only have "proceeded from a general malignity of mind, which has broke out in a desire and a design, not only to ruin one devoted individual, but to involve every one of this audience, nay the whole English nation, perhaps, in immediate ruin." He could offer the prisoner no hope of pardon. Of course, he said all this "not to taunt or distress" him, "but merely from motives of humanity and religion." In the same lofty spirit he told Aitken he must die: "For you cannot be suffered to live in this world; you must die, and that within a very few days. And therefore, before you go into eternity, for your soul's sake, do what you can, that that eternity may be an eternity of bliss instead of misery."

His words did not have the desired effect. If anything, they merely emboldened Aitken. Perhaps they flattered him, in the same way that death flatters a martyr. He did not want a pardon, he said. One account has it that he pronounced himself "exceedingly well satisfied" when Hotham concluded his peroration, another that he blurted out the word *joyful*.[47]

His behavior baffled and impressed the people who witnessed it. "The prisoner," it was observed, "seemed little, if at all, affected with his situation."[48] It occurred to no one that this might have been because he was half-starved. Instead, observers attributed his aplomb to a martyr's fanaticism, to an unreasonable "enthusiasm." "Upon the whole," wrote *The General Evening Post*, "his behaviour was not insolent, tho' confident, and apparently careless of danger; he showed some signs of a clear head, but more of a fixed enthusiasm, begot by ignorance and false zeal."[49]

* * *

It had been an unusually long trial, "near seven hours" from start to finish.[50] Hotham was positively fidgety by two that afternoon. "Gentlemen," he remarked with some acerbity, "the trial has lasted already very long; the summing up has also been long...."[51] It was a reasonable complaint, even though he had been the one to sum up the evidence, dawdling at this for more than an hour. The typical eighteenth-century trial was over in minutes. A capital case, such as Aitken's, might take a little longer, but by the end of the day, fifteen to twenty defendants, all or most of them on trial for their lives, would have been tried, one after the other.[52] Thirteen cases, such as Ashurst and Hotham heard on their last day at Winchester, constituted a light workload.[53]

Hotham and Ashurst sentenced three other men to death that week, including the small-time arsonist Richard Carter.[54] None of those condemned had committed murder, and the one convicted murderer, Richard Weeks, got off lightly. For the crime of murdering his wife he was branded on the hand and sentenced to one year's imprisonment in the county jail. Of the four men condemned to die, only two, James Aitken and Richard Carter, did not have their sentences commuted. The judges, it seems, were determined to make an example of arsonists big and small.

John the Painter, from The Life of James Aitken, *1777. The print shows Aitken in his final days, in the Winchester County Jail. The clothes are too natty, and the face too regular, but the heavy chains are true to life, as is the fan-tailed hat.* COURTESY OF THE HAMPSHIRE RECORD OFFICE.

CHAPTER ELEVEN

His Last Day

As soon as the trial ended Aitken was led away, still loaded down with chains.[1] These, along with the crowd that had gathered to see justice done, impeded his progress, reducing his exit to a slow and undignified shuffle. It was at this juncture that a man stepped forward from the crowd, "and touching the prisoner on the shoulder, asked him if he knew him."[2] Aitken did. He was Mr. Smith, a former employer from Hungerford, and Aitken, surrounded by unsympathetic strangers, "seemed exceedingly happy" to see a familiar face. He asked Smith to accompany him, and upon reaching his cell, Aitken asked his old master's forgiveness for stealing four guineas. He also asked Smith to repay a trifling debt, sixpence in total, to a "young man" in Hungerford. Smith acceded to both requests. He might have sought out and paid the young man in question, but this much we know for certain: he sold his story to the publisher of *The Hampshire Chronicle*.

The vultures were descending. For five days, from the conclusion of his trial on the sixth of March to his death by hanging on the tenth, Aitken was besieged by visitors and curiosity-seekers. Some came in hopes of publishing his story; others came out of a morbid curiosity; others, like Mr. Smith, combined business with the guilty pleasure of touching and talking to a man condemned to die. This was the way it had always been. People bribed jailers, and jailers took them to see prisoners who were awaiting execution.[3] The practice was not without its critics. Defoe, writing in 1728, had proposed limiting visitors to "but those that had immediate business, and those not to stay."[4] The proposal fell on deaf ears.

*   *   *

Aitken's last days were dominated by four men. Each took shameless advantage of him. Two were familiar—Thomas Lawrence and Sir John Fielding—and two were new to him: John White, the keeper of the Winchester county jail, and Reverend Westcomb, its chaplain. All four men were after the same thing: Aitken's confession. Only Sir John was not motivated by greed. He was motivated by something far worse: pique.

Thomas Lawrence had left the New Prison in Clerkenwell, London, confident that Aitken's story was his. Aitken was true to his word, and on 28 February, after being transferred to the Winchester county jail, he sent Lawrence a note, asking him to "Come and see me."[5] The note arrived while Lawrence was away on business, and he did not set out for Winchester until the day of the trial. By the time he arrived, it was noon and the trial was entering its fourth hour. Breathless and frantic, he scribbled a note, which a clerk handed to Aitken. Upon reading it, Aitken greeted Lawrence like a long-lost friend. How long had he been in town? And would he visit him after the trial?

Lawrence did, but not before buttonholing someone far more important than Aitken. As the crowd straggled out of the Great Hall, he made a beeline to Sandwich. He introduced himself and offered him an advance copy of the confession that Aitken was about to make. Sandwich was happy to accept. Neither he nor anyone else in the ministry was satisfied that Deane was Aitken's only backer. If Lawrence could gain Aitken's trust and get him to name other Americans in high places, he had Sandwich's blessing.

The other man who stayed behind in Winchester was Sir John Fielding. Aitken had made the tiniest of admissions to him—that he knew Silas Deane—but other than that he had answered almost none of his questions. Sir John was determined to get a full confession before he left Winchester. It was jailkeeper John White's job to keep Aitken from talking to anyone except Sir John's clerk. We do not know the clerk's name, only that he worked for Sir John and that he paid several visits to Aitken. In return, Sir John let White publish Aitken's confession. It was a handsome inducement, and John White proved a most faithful watchdog.

Thomas Lawrence knew nothing of this when he showed up at the county jail that evening, pen and paper in hand. He was let in, but when Aitken started to tell his story, the visit was, in Lawrence's words, "cruelly interrupted, without the least ceremony." Lawrence protested, to no avail, and was told that Sir John wanted to speak to him. When he arrived at Sir John's lodgings, he was kept waiting, and it was only much later in the evening that the two men met. There was only one thing that Sir John wanted to know: had Aitken "confessed anything, and what"?[6] Lawrence read him his notes, and let slip that he would be returning to the county jail the following morning between nine and ten.

Forewarned, Sir John's clerk showed up at the jail just before dawn. This time he gave Aitken a reason to talk: if he made a full confession, Sir John would personally intervene on his behalf, not to spare his life, but to spare his corpse the indignity of being gibbeted. Aitken started talking at once, finishing only minutes before Lawrence arrived to conduct his own interview. As luck would have it, Lawrence and Sir John's clerk passed each other just outside the jail, the one coming with blank sheets of paper, the other leaving with a signed transcript. This was turned over first to Sir John and then to an editor. The edited confession, along with an eyewitness account of Aitken's last words and actions, was subsequently published under the title *The Life of James Aitken.*

It was in White's interest to make sure that this confession was the only one. Lawrence was the competition, and when he showed up for his appointment with Aitken, White turned him away rudely. Lawrence left in a huff, but he did not give up. He told his story to anyone who would listen, and a few hours later he was back at the county jail, two justices of the peace by his side. This time he was allowed in. Aitken told his story all over again, albeit in abbreviated form (by now he was exhausted and quite possibly hoarse), and Lawrence had him sign the completed transcription. And with that, Lawrence was gone.

He had what he wanted, and contrary to his earlier promises, he did nothing whatsoever to help Aitken in his few remaining days. But he did keep his promise to Sandwich. Sandwich got a copy of Aitken's second confession, and it was this version—and not Sir John's—that was forwarded to the king.[7] Lawrence was not able to publish his version in pamphlet form (probably because it was too short), but he did sell it to various newspapers, including *The Hampshire Chronicle* and *Felix Farley's Bristol Journal.*[8]

Sir John behaved no more honorably. If Aitken was under any illusions about the disposition of his body, they were dashed by the appearance of a most unwelcome visitor: a blacksmith who had come to take Aitken's measurements for the iron cage that would hold his body.

The two confessions, White's and Lawrence's, must be read with considerable caution, and always with the knowledge that Aitken was not their author. Lawrence, who was at great pains to establish the authenticity of his version, swore that he had merely transcribed Aitken's confession word for word, but this beggars belief. Aitken could read and write, but in both confessions there is a narrative coherence that rings false. Other publishers freely admitted to improving on the confessions of famous criminals, editing them, in the words of one such ghostwriter, not "to give any undue colouring to facts, but simply to supply the deficiencies of the writer, whose laborious situation in life has denied him those literary advantages indispensable to the writing [of] his story with tolerable propriety."[9] The same publisher, perhaps feeling more than a little defensive, insisted that he had limited his changes to "spelling, style, and disposition," all with an eye toward making the account "clear and fit for perusal."

The most important thing that Aitken revealed was his real name. He was James Aitken once more—not James Hill, James Hinde, James Boswell, or even John the Painter. Along with his old name, he assumed his old identity from Edinburgh. His morality lost its revolutionary edge and became conventional once more. He rediscovered religion. And his defiance gave way to a certain mawkishness. His thoughts turned to his mother, whom he had not seen since leaving Edinburgh in 1772. He told Lawrence that he thought she was still alive, and on the day before his execution, he sent Lawrence one last letter, begging "for the compassion you have for me as a dying man, that you will write to my sorrowful mother concerning my unhappy fate; but in the softest terms possible, as her grief I know will be very great on hearing of it."[10] By now Aitken was under no illusions about Lawrence, and by way of inducement he enclosed "a further confession of some particulars, which with the other I humbly desire you will regulate into a proper style and publish them, for the satisfaction of the world and the clearing of the innocent." Lawrence did as he was asked, or so he claimed, "writing to his supposed surviving afflicted parent in the most comfortable and best manner I was capable."[11]

Aitken fully expected to die. There is no evidence that he shared the common—and not unfounded—hope that he might yet cheat the hangman, whether by receiving a pardon at the last minute or by being sent to a prison hulk. As Baron Hotham had warned, this was out of the question for a man as wicked as Aitken.

The newspapers painted a rather different picture. According to them, Aitken remained hopeful of receiving a pardon in exchange for naming his presumed accomplices. There were, of course, no accomplices, and no one had any intention of offering a pardon, but it made a good story. *The General Evening Post* reported that the execution, scheduled for Monday the tenth, had been postponed.[12] At the same time, *The St. James's Chronicle* reported that Aitken had "some important discoveries to make on a promise of pardon."[13] And *The Public Advertiser* went one step further, informing its readers that Aitken had "accepted the offer of being admitted an evidence on promise of pardon, upon which he had made a genuine discovery of the persons who set him to set fire to Portsmouth Dock, etc. and that the parties are some of them of eminence, and are in France."[14] None of it was true.

* * *

He spent the last two weeks of his life in the Winchester county jail, under the watchful eye of John White. According to John Howard, the jail had been "kept very clean" since two dozen prisoners had died of typhus in a single year. After their deaths, the prison had been modernized, and steps were taken to keep the inmates alive. Under the new regime, they were provided with towels, straw beds, and coverlets, in addition to a threepenny loaf, weighing just under two pounds, every other day.[15] Once a week, thanks to a charitable bequest, they were treated to "an ox's head, four sheep's heads ... about seventeen pints of oatmeal, three pints of salt, twelve loaves the size of twopenny ones, [and] about twenty gallons of table beer." The same charity sent them their left-overs three times a week.

The jail housed both felons and debtors. As in every lockup, everyone was expected to pay his or her own way. A sign, posted at the entrance, spelled out the various fees, with one schedule for debtors and another for felons. The latter had to pay two shillings upon being committed, ostensibly "for cleaning the gaol and find-ing candles and all other common necessaries," plus three shillings a week for bedding, or two "if two lie in the same bed." If they had any money left over, they could, with a payment to Mr. White, "send for any beer, ale and victuals or other necessary food from what place they please and also to have such bedding, linen etc. as ... they shall think fit." In their two meetings in Winchester, Lawrence provided Aitken with small sums for this purpose, and others may also have contributed to his upkeep in hopes of getting him to talk. Lawrence described Aitken's cell as "gloomy," although he never actually set foot in it. Both of their meetings in the Winchester county jail took place in tolerably furnished rooms, the comparative comforts of which doubtless encouraged Aitken to linger and expand upon his tale. It was with this in mind that Lawrence arranged for an even better room the second time around, with "a cheerful fire lighted up, a glass of wine ... and everything comfortably provided before Mr. Aitken was brought in...."[16]

He spent the last days of his life in a drunken haze. It was a com-mon practice, and it continued no matter how many times it was criticized. Defoe complained in vain: "I have known poor wretches that have not seen a sober moment from the time of their sentence to the day of their execution."[17] Bernard Mandeville complained in vain: "They eat and drink what they can purchase."[18] Such drinking was permitted and even encouraged because it lined the pockets of men like John White. Wardens commonly kept a tap room, charging inmates exorbitant prices for beer and wine. There was one such room in London's New Prison, and inmates in the Winchester county jail were free to buy beer and wine from the enterprising Mr. White. Conditions at the Odiham bridewell were laxer still. By law, the keeper was supposed to post a sign forbidding sales of spirituous liquors; when Howard visited, the sign was nowhere to be seen. The largest room, moreover, had been converted into a brewery.[19] It took years to control sales of liquor to inmates, and many more to eliminate them altogether. The Gin Act of 1736 had abolished— but by no means eliminated—sales of gin and other spirits in prisons, and when the so-called "Tap Act" finally did away with prison tap rooms in 1784, wardens cried foul and demanded compensation.[20] One, Richard Akerman, demanded several hundred pounds, citing, as justification, comparable amounts already paid to jailers elsewhere in England.[21]

Before his trial, Aitken was allowed out of his cell for two hours a day, "during which time he was generally visited by great numbers of people, some on motives of friendship, many (of the same principles as himself), with a view to assist him with money, &c. and more merely out of curiosity."[22] His exercise, such as it was, took place in a courtyard, which at the time of Howard's visit in 1776 was "shut up from the jail," rendering it less than conducive to "health and convenience." Even so, White managed to pack in paying visitors. One newspaper, *The Public Advertiser*, reported that Aitken was "surrounded with spectators, to whom he appears very cheerful and facetious, but will give no direct answers to any questions asked."[23] That, however, was before the trial—and before his courage started to flag.

Howard says very little about the "dungeon" in which Aitken spent most of his time, only that it was "down but five steps; it is boarded and has large windows." This was in fact an improvement on "the former destructive dungeon," which was "darker, and down eleven steps." The few comforts available to Aitken were entirely at White's discretion, and cannot have done much to alleviate the horrors of being confined to a small and dark space for hours on end.

He spent much of the time thinking about heaven and hell. We know from Lawrence that Aitken was in mortal terror of being gibbeted, and that the thought of it obsessed him in his final days. He could not bear the thought of being denied a proper burial. Richard Shepherd, who was hanged in 1720, was "solicitous for nothing so much as about his corpse after death, as fearing he should be anatomiz'd; wherefore, in hopes of preventing his carcass from falling into the surgeon's hands, who would have no more mercy on it than the hangman had, he sent his wife the morning he was to die to sell the clothes she had upon her to buy him a coffin."[24] Richard Tobin, who was hanged in 1739, wrote to his former master, begging him to "take some pity on me . . . for my friends is very poor, and my mother is very sick, and I am to die next Wednesday morning, so I hope you be so good as to give my friends a small trifle of money to pay for a coffin and a shroud, for to take my body away from the tree in that I am to die on. . . ."[25]

The prison chaplain, a man named Westcomb, added to his miseries by refusing Aitken communion until he made yet another confession, which could be published on its own or sold to the newspapers. It was a common ruse, and its abuse over the years helps explain why prison chaplains were held in such low esteem.[26] Charles Speckman, who was hanged in 1763, suffered at the hands of one such chaplain, in this case the ordinary of London's

The Idle 'Prentice Executed at Tyburn, *1747, by William Hogarth. The condemned man rides backwards in a tumbrel while a minister, in this case the Ordinary of Newgate, exhorts him to repent. James Aitken was spared this latter indignity, having refused to allow the odious Reverend Westcomb to accompany him to the gallows.*

Newgate Prison: "The Ordinary has...refused me the sacrament, under pretence of not being prepared, but in reality, to get from me an account of my life and transactions, for which he would not give me one farthing, or his charity extended so far towards me, as to furnish me with a little food to keep soul and body together till the time of my death."[27]

For three days, Aitken and Westcomb battled, the one refusing to make yet another confession, the other withholding communion. In the end, Westcomb blinked. On the night before his execution, Aitken narrated a "continuation" of his confession for Westcomb's benefit, but only after he had received communion. We do not know what he told Westcomb, but it was too slight to be published on its own and instead had to be incorporated into the account dictated to Sir John's clerk.[28]

*   *   *

His last day began, appropriately enough, with a final journey back to Portsmouth. Notorious felons were often executed near the scenes of their crimes, to heighten the exemplary value of their deaths. Aitken paid particular attention to his appearance that morning. Tradition demanded no less. The celebrated highwayman Dick Turpin bought a new coat and shoes so that he might look his best on the day he was hanged.[29] Others went to their deaths dressed as bridegrooms. Criminals, Defoe grumbled, "go to execution as neat and trim, as if they were going to a wedding."[30] A foreign visitor was astonished: "He that is to be hang'd or otherwise executed first takes care to get himself shav'd, and handsomely dressed either in mourning or in the dress of a bridegroom."[31] And Swift made fun of the practice in "Clever Tom Clinch, Going to Be Hanged":

His waistcoat, and stockings, and breeches, were white;
His cap had a new cherry ribbon to tie't.
The maids to the doors and the balconies ran,
And said, "Lack-a-day, he's a proper young man!"
But, as from the windows the ladies he spied,
Like a beau in the box, he bow'd low on each side![32]

Aitken was poor and friendless, and he probably went to his death in the clothes he had been wearing for the last six weeks. But he would have done his best to look as clean and presentable as possible, and like Richard Broughton and James Hayes, two Irishmen who were hanged in 1753, he would have refused to take his final journey "without a clean shirt and stockings to be hanged in."[33]

The entourage set out before dawn. A "strong guard" kept watch over Aitken the entire time, and much to his horror, White and Westcomb rode with him in the coach.[34] Anyone with any dignity—Sandwich, the Lords of the Admiralty, and even Sir John—was long since gone, and no one from the ministry attended the execution.

Between eleven and twelve, the coach came to a stop outside the Portsmouth town jail. Here Aitken was finally relieved of the manacles he had been wearing for more than a month. In Newgate, the striking off of shackles was another occasion for a crowd to gather, and it is easy to imagine much the same scene in Portsmouth.[35]

Once his manacles had been struck off, he was hustled into a tumbrel, where he was tied to a chair. Gambier says that Aitken tried at least once to rise from it.[36] In Scotland, condemned felons were spared this final indignity and were allowed to walk, as best they could, to the gallows. Aitken had seen them when he was growing up, shuffling off to the gallows in the Grassmarket. Edward Topham was right: the practice was "more decent... than being thrown into a cart, as in England, and carried, like a beast, to slaughter."[37]

Had Aitken been an ordinary felon, he would have been forced to sit on or beside his own coffin. He was denied this dubious consolation, and with it, the promise of a Christian burial. Even so, he would not let Westcomb join him in the tumbrel or on the scaffold.[38] His adamance on this point was remarked on among those who knew nothing of the history between the two men. Some, including the publisher of *The Hampshire Chronicle*, leapt to the erroneous conclusion that Aitken was a Roman Catholic.[39]

He was done with Westcomb, but he was not yet done with John White. White clambered into the tumbrel, which wended its way toward the dockyard. Once inside the dockyard Aitken was taken straight to the ruins of the rope house. There he could see with his own eyes "the destruction his mischievous hands had wrought." One account quotes him as saying that "he remembered the place perfectly well, and that he was the person who set it on fire; but could now make no reparation, but with his life."[40] Gambier's account quotes him as saying, "I acknowledge the crime and I am sorry for it."[41] Either way, these are the first hints that Aitken had reconciled himself to playing the part expected of him: that of the repentant criminal.

Just after being led around the remains of the rope house, he surprised everyone by asking to speak with Gambier. Gambier came out of his house, rattled and uncertain of what to expect. At first Aitken spoke in platitudes. He started by acknowledging his guilt and expressing the hope that he might yet receive "forgiveness from God almighty through the mercies of Jesus Christ my saviour." Next he asked for Gambier's forgiveness. Gambier is silent on this point, suggesting that he could not bring himself to forgive the man who had caused him so much trouble. So far, Aitken had said nothing untoward. But then, just as the cart was pulling away, he started to speak once more. The cart stopped, and Gambier, to his infinite chagrin, was treated to a lecture on how to do his job: "I have one thing more to observe as a caution to all the commissioners of the dockyards throughout England to be more strict, careful and vigilant for the future because it is in the power of any active and resolute man to do great mischief." Another version quoted Aitken as adding that he had "intended to have given a stab in the side, but it has only been a slight scratch in the hand." Did he have any further advice to give? a weary Gambier wanted to know. He did. "Tell the Lords of the Admiralty to keep a particular eye on the rope house at Plymouth."

It was probably at Gambier's insistence that Aitken was not hanged inside the dockyard, but just outside its walls, on the thoroughfare known as the Hard.[42] Aitken knew that he would hang, but he had no way of knowing that a mizzenmast would be used for this purpose. It was a vindictive gesture, dreamt up by someone in the Navy Board or Admiralty. Its symbolism was wasted on no one, Aitken least of all.

The mast came from the *Arethusa*, a small frigate that was in the dockyard for repairs. The ship was French—it had been built in Le Havre and launched in 1757, only to be captured two years later, in 1759, when her name was changed from *L'Aréthuse* to the *Arethusa*.[43] She had been sent out after American privateers in October and again in December of 1776.[44] The mast was either sixty or sixty-four feet high (accounts differ), and it had the dubious distinction of being "the highest [gallows] ever erected in England."[45] The dockyard probably provided the men to raise it on the Hard. Local ropemakers were probably called on to make rope for the occasion, not only for the noose, but also for the pulleys that would be used to raise Aitken's body nearly sixty feet in the air.

Outside the dockyard, a huge crowd had gathered around the makeshift gallows, and Aitken was led there. By one estimate, twenty thousand people had gathered to watch him die.[46] This was a good turnout, especially as Portsmouth and its neighboring towns had a combined population of perhaps thirteen thousand permanent residents at the time.[47] The turnout was respectable even by the jaded standards of London, where attendance at public hangings depended on a felon's notoriety. A turnout of three to seven thousand was typical; notorious felons, by contrast, could expect crowds in the range of thirty to forty thousand.[48]

There is no record of how the crowd behaved that day, but it is likely to have greeted him with a chorus of hisses, shouts, and taunts. Thieves and highwaymen could expect a certain degree of sympathy in their final moments, but serious transgressors (murderers, sexual offenders, and the like) could not. When, for example, Theodore Gardelle was hanged for murder in 1761, he was greeted with hisses and shouts.[49]

The recalcitrance and exaltation that had characterized his behavior before and during his trial were gone. Only his courage remained, and if he was frightened, he did not show it. First he delivered a speech—this was standard—and he said exactly what Whitehall expected of him. There are three versions of what he actually said. Each version is abbreviated—one eyewitness account described the speech as a "long harangue"—and to that extent each is edited.[50] In the first two versions, Aitken delivers the standard dying speech. He confesses his guilt, expresses contrition, and acknowledges that his crimes are such that the state is right to take his life.[51] The first—and least varnished—version comes from Gambier, who may well have decided against attending the hanging and the protracted preliminaries on the scaffold. His account, written just after the hanging, gives no clue as to whether he was present or not:

> Just before he was turned off, he said he acknowledged the justice of his sentence and hop'd for forgiveness as he forgave all the world. And he wished success to his Majesty King George, his family and loyal subjects, and he hoped forgiveness for all the transactions he had been guilty of from the year 1772 since his apprenticeship and that the world would be satisfied about him for his life and be soon in print.[52]

The second version appears in *The Life of James Aitken*. The phrasing is stiff and unnatural, and contains a shameless plug for the book, but self-serving though it is, this version is more or less consistent with Gambier's:

> Good people, I am now going to suffer for a crime, the heinous-ness of which deserves a more severe punishment than what is going to be inflicted. My life has long been forfeited by the innu-merable felonies I have formerly committed; but I hope God, in his great mercy, will forgive me; and I hope the public, whom I have much injured, will carry their resentment no further, but for-give me, as I freely forgive all the world, and pray for me, that I may be forgiven above. I have made a faithful confession of every transaction of my life from my infancy to the present time, partic-ularly the malicious intention I had of destroying all the dock yards in this kingdom, which I have delivered to Mr. White, and desired him to have printed, for the satisfaction of the public. I die with no enmity in my heart to his Majesty and government, but wish the ministry success in all their undertakings; and I hope my untimely end will be a warning to all persons not to commit the like atrocious offence.[53]

The third version has Aitken departing from the time-honored formula. Far from expressing remorse or accepting his fate, he jus-tifies his actions and dies an unrepentant radical:

> When England...grew unnatural in her persecutions, I resolved to achieve some great mischief in revenge to her barbarity; and as she had brought fire, sword, rapine, murder, rapes, and ruin among her colonies, I determined, individually, to burn the docks of Plymouth and Portsmouth, for by crippling the fleet, I should prevent a further progress against America—such were

my determinations. In principle, I am a republican. I hate all kings of all nations and denominations.[54]

This is not to be believed. The source, a spoof called *John the Painter's Ghost*, hardly inspires confidence; nor does its author claim to have been present at Aitken's hanging. If Aitken had said anything inflammatory that day, someone among the thousands present would have reported it. None did.

But it was not Aitken who had the last word. It was John White. Even as Aitken was concluding his remarks, White stepped forward and delivered a speech of his own. He had a book to sell, and in the crowd were thousands of people who might want a souvenir of the occasion. Only one thing was missing—an account of Aitken's last day—but that would come soon enough. White was shameless. He said that he had "the confession just mentioned, and would take care to have it printed." He thanked the people present "for the great order and decency they had kept up." He thanked the mayor of Portsmouth "for his great civility and assistance in providing the borough constables, and attending himself in person." He again flattered his audience, telling them "that he was happy in hearing no reflections cast upon the prisoner in his last moments, who was sensible of the enormity of his crime, and going to suffer the law."[55]

White's little speech was oddly out of synch with the next step in the proceedings: Aitken's final devotions. Unlike the fictional Tom Clinch, who went to his death "without prayer-book or psalm," Aitken spent the last minutes of his life not in protest but in prayer. He is supposed to have kept at this for some time, and according to *The Hampshire Chronicle*, he gave every appearance of being earnest. He even prayed aloud for his king.[56]

Just before one o'clock, he concluded his prayers and dropped his handkerchief. This was the customary signal to the hangman to turn him off, but in Aitken's case the task fell to a team of men, probably riggers from the dockyard. Gambier says that Aitken was hanged at three minutes to one; the newspapers put the time at eight minutes to one.[57] The use of pulleys virtually guaranteed that he died not of a broken neck but rather of asphyxia. At the very least, he would have been conscious—and in excruciating pain—while being hoisted. Even with trapdoors, which were not widely used in England until 1783, death by hanging could take as long as ten minutes; during that time, moreover, the dying suffered horribly. Boswell, who evinced an unhealthy curiosity in the subject, once asked a professor of anatomy to explain exactly what happened. The answer he got was chilling: "The man who is hanged suffers a great deal" and "is not at once stupefied by the shock...a man is suffocated by hanging in a rope just as by having his respiration stopped by having a pillow pressed on the face....For some time after a man is thrown over he is sensible and is conscious that he is *hanging*."[58] Such sufferings were prolonged still further when a hangman failed to position or knot the noose in just the right way. He was left to hang for the customary time—one hour—and he was probably alive and perhaps even conscious for some of that time, although one account claims that he "did not struggle much" and that "the conflict was soon over."[59] This seems unlikely. In 1709, a man named John Smith had been left to hang for two hours, and even then he was not dead; in 1740, William Duell, a lad of seventeen, had been left to hang for half an hour, only to revive on the dissecting table.[60]

At the exact moment of death, Aitken would have soiled himself. He probably also had an erection—dying, in Defoe's sly words, "bravely, hard, like a cock."[61] The one thing that spectators did not see was his face as he died. He would have worn a sort of nightcap, and just before he was hanged this would have been pulled down over his face, thus sparing more sensitive souls the most obvious signs of his distress.

James Aitken died sometime between one and two in the afternoon, on 10 March 1777. He was not quite twenty-five years old.

CHAPTER TWELVE

His Fate and That of Many Others

JUST AFTER two that afternoon, Aitken's body was cut down and his cap was pulled back to reveal a face disfigured almost beyond recognition. The hangman was waiting. Custom allowed him the clothes worn by the condemned, no matter how shabby or soiled they might be. On rare occasions, convicts cheated the hangman by stripping just before they were hanged. A woman named Hannah Dagoe had done so back in 1763, removing her hat, cloak, and dress, and tossing them into the crowd before jumping off the tumbrel and to her death.[1] Not Aitken. He probably went to his death wearing all of the clothes that he owned—it was a cold day in March—and these would have included his famous brown coat.

The hangman quickly stripped Aitken's body of its clothes. They were damp with blood, slobber, and excrement. He may have sold everything on the spot as souvenirs (Aitken was a celebrity); if he did not, there were dozens of dealers in slops and used clothes close at hand, and each was more than willing to buy clothes and other items of questionable provenance.[2] At some point during these macabre proceedings, someone in a position of authority went through all of Aitken's clothes (it is unclear why this hadn't been done earlier). According to one account, a paper was found in one of Aitken's pockets. The newspapers reported that it implicated an important but unnamed individual.[3] The likeliest candidate is Bancroft.

The Gibbet *by Thomas Rowlandson (1756-1827). Two riders stop to gawk instead of hurrying on by. The corpse is in an advanced state of decay, held together only by the iron bands that ring it.* COURTESY OF THE YALE CENTER FOR BRITISH ART.

The men charged with gibbeting his corpse now began their grim work, tarring the body in an attempt to stave off decay as long as possible. It is likely that the pitching was done by one or more of the tar-heaters employed in the dockyard. These preparations always attracted huge crowds, as did the procession to the gibbet. Aitken's gibbet was located at Blockhouse Point, at the entrance to the harbor. There, according to one account, the body "was hung upon a new gibbet erected for this purpose, pursuant to his sentence, amidst a vast concourse of people...."[4]

Gibbeted bodies had an unfortunate habit of disappearing. The usual culprits were friends and family (of whom Aitken had none in Portsmouth), but souvenir-hunters were another source of mischief. The Crown fought back by using ever-higher posts—a height of thirty feet was not uncommon—and by studding these with thousands of nails.[5] In one case, dating from 1747, no fewer than twelve thousand nails were used, a number that brings home just how determined the Crown was to use felons' bodies to best effect.[6] For obvious reasons, popular interest in gibbeted bodies tended to peak early. In the early days, when the decay was especially dramatic, thousands of curiosity-seekers would gather, and with them, gin-sellers and other hawkers.[7] When, for example, the bodies of Peter Conway and Michael Richardson were put on display in 1770, as many as fifty thousand people visited the site within the first five days.[8]

Meanwhile, the Admiralty and the Navy Board were busily settling accounts. Two days after the hanging, they instructed a Mr. Seddon to pay out the rewards that they had offered—£1,050 in total.[9] We know that this amount was divided among several recipients, but we do not know who nor how many.[10] James Lowe and John Dalby are good candidates, as is John Baldwin. Additional payments, perhaps in lieu of a reward, were made to the various dockyard workers and other witnesses whose testimony had helped convict Aitken. John Courtney received the most: more than eight pounds for the expenses incurred by himself and his wife Anne over the course of the investigation.[11] In addition to transportation expenses, each witness was awarded a per diem allowance, capped at five shillings. The Navy Board was being uncharacteristically generous. The amount was more than twice the daily wage of the average dockyard worker, or enough to buy seventeen pints of beer.[12]

Two of the witnesses were not so lucky. Richard Voke and Richard Faithful were dismissed on 10 March, the same day that Aitken was hanged.[13] They were the only men to be punished for standing by and doing nothing. (Bancroft, who knew far more than either Voke or Faithful, kept his job, and later received a raise; Gambier, too, kept his job, and was promoted when he returned to active service.) Faithful, at least, was compensated for his travel expenses, but not for the time he had spent traveling to and from Odiham. It is hard to avoid the impression that the two workers were being scapegoated for a negligence that extended much higher up the ladder.

In the wake of the Portsmouth fire, the Navy Board implemented much needed reforms, starting with barring strangers from entering the dockyards unattended.[14] One outraged citizen went so far as to propose uniforms and identifying badges for all dockyard workers.[15] The plan, of course, had one glaring defect: with a little determination and money, anyone might procure a uniform and badge of his own.

It took several more weeks for the authorities to convince themselves that Deane was Aitken's only accomplice. One rumor had it that the French were in some way involved. This was not an unreasonable assumption. It was Vergennes, after all, who had signed Aitken's passport. This was sent to Germain two days after the execution, and the ministry, upon reviewing it, decided to let the matter drop.[16] The newspapers took the hint and urged their readers to do the same:

> Firing of dockyards, &c. is a crime so uncommonly atrocious, and so much of a public calamity, and which every power in Europe may be the object of, if once the success of it be tried, that it would be no wonder if the French, or any respectable Court in Europe, treated the perpetrators of such a crime as offenders against the law of honour and the law of nations, which are always regarded in the negotiations of European states.[17]

For a few weeks, there was talk of somehow arresting Deane and trying him for his part in the fires. Nobody, however, really believed that this would happen, and in any event, the French refused to extradite him.[18] The British did not press the point, presumably because they had no desire to goad the French into an open alliance with America. For their part, the French chose to laugh off the entire affair. According to one British spy, "the gravity given to the matter by the British court had afforded some laughter at Versailles."[19]

There was also a halfhearted attempt to implicate Franklin in the plot. The facts, however, stood in the way. Franklin had set sail for France in October of 1776, arriving in France only after Deane had met with Aitken.[20] If he knew anything, he knew it after the fact. This did not prevent *The Public Advertiser* from reporting that "a German, who is now abroad, and an American, who is a painter, and came over in the same ship with Dr. Franklin, were both made privy to the...diabolical transaction."[21]

Bancroft was another matter. In his case, there was evidence linking his name to Aitken's. It is clear that his involvement, peripheral though it was, came as a complete surprise to the ministry, for in February, just as Baldwin was being debriefed, a man was suddenly assigned to follow Bancroft and report on his movements.[22] In the end, it was agreed that Bancroft was too valuable to be punished or dismissed. Instead, he was sent to Paris. The plan had two advantages: it removed Bancroft from the scene just as uncomfortable questions were being asked about his role in the affair, and it put him in better position to spy on the American mission to Versailles. By the end of February, a deal had been struck. Bancroft would go to Paris at the earliest possible moment, and he would be awarded an annual pension of £200, backdated to Christmas 1776.[23]

Not everyone was keen on the plan. George III thoroughly mistrusted Bancroft. So did Mansfield.[24] According to Thomas

Hutchinson, the former royal governor of Massachusetts, Mansfield ruled that there was nothing improper in Bancroft's conduct. At the same time, Mansfield pointedly "said nothing in his favour."[25] Paul Wentworth, in the meantime, insisted that his old friend "had told twenty of his friends what John the Painter said to him," and that "he supposed him to be a spy employed by government." Nobody believed this, but still less did anyone care.

Bancroft did his part by writing a vindication of his conduct and publishing it, anonymously, in several newspapers. In it, he cast his meeting with Aitken in the best possible light. His version differed from Aitken's in two important respects. First, he denied that Aitken had told him anything specific, whether about Portsmouth or his next target.[26] And second, Bancroft claimed that "no secrecy was observed . . . respecting this extraordinary application, but, on the contrary, it was mentioned by him in detail to many reputable persons of different sides in the American controversy." If so, he had broken his promise to Aitken not to "inform against him."[27] Moreover, those "reputable persons" did not include Wentworth, who knew nothing of Bancroft's two meetings with Aitken until Baldwin mentioned them.

Just as Bancroft was setting off for Paris, he was arrested. It was a ploy to convince the American delegation in Paris of Bancroft's loyalty.[28] It worked. When Deane learned of the arrest, he saw in it further proof of Bancroft's sterling patriotism. "I feel more for Doctor Bancroft than I can express," he wrote. "He deserves much from us; consequently he will be pursued with the utmost rigour by them, though nothing capital, not even the correspondence, can be proved."[29] In any event, Bancroft was released almost immediately. By 26 March, he was on his way, calling on Wentworth just before leaving the country.[30]

By the time Bancroft arrived in Paris, Franklin was already there. Franklin wisely chose to say nothing of the affair, at least not in writing or in public. Aitken is mentioned in two of the letters that he is known to have received. The first, dated 7 March 1777, came from Patience Wright, one of Franklin's contacts in London. She merely reported what she had read in the newspapers: that there were plans to charge both Deane and Franklin with treason, and that Aitken was about to name prominent Americans in exchange for a royal pardon.[31] The information was wrong on both counts. The second letter, dated 29 March 1777, came from William Alexander, a banker in Dijon. Alexander warned Franklin of the British government's plans to extradite Deane. This time the information was correct, though nothing came of it.

When Franklin stepped down as ambassador, Jefferson took his place. With the job, he inherited the mess left by Deane. Matters came to a head in 1788. The war was over, and both Britain and America were trying to put the past behind them. Deane, unwelcome in his own country, had been allowed to settle in London. It was the worst possible time to release new information about his role in the John the Painter affair, and yet this is exactly what a shadowy French blackmailer proposed to do. His name was Foulloy, and he had Deane's letter-book for the year 1777, along with his ledgers for the years 1776 to 1780. It is unclear how these had fallen into Foulloy's hands. He claimed that he had taken them after Deane had reneged on a debt of 120 guineas. Foulloy's landlady in London told a different story. According to her, Foulloy "had run off, and carried away several things belonging to her, and that whilst Deane was in the house he had got possession of the keys of his trunks, opened them, examined his papers &c and taken out every thing which he thought proper without her knowledge and was gone to France."[32] This much is certain: Foulloy had stolen the books, and he realized that they could be used to blackmail the fledgling American government. With this in mind he approached Jefferson at his residence in the Hôtel de Lageac, and, showing him the two books, said that he was thinking of selling them to the ministry in London. Of course, the books contained passages that "might injure his own country," and so he was offering them to Jefferson first.[33]

Jefferson played a weak hand well. He asked to keep the two volumes for twenty-four hours, during which time he arranged to have the most important passages transcribed. One entry in particular caught his eye. It was dated 11 April 1777, and it was from Robert Morris, who is best remembered for his role in financing the American Revolution. In it, Morris referred to Deane's precipitous departure from France shortly after being implicated in the fires. "The affair of John the Painter who came nigh finishing the whole affair at one blow and his known attachment to America as well as correspondence with Dr. Franklin and myself obliges him [Deane] to fly and take refuge with me here."[34] The passage was damning not because it implicated Deane—his role in the plot was already public knowledge—but because it also seemingly implicated Franklin and Morris. Both men, it is true, knew something about the plot, but only after the fact. Even so, Jefferson was alarmed, so much so that he seriously considering paying Foulloy to have the sentence excised, seeing in it "evidence of a fact not proper to be committed to the hands of enemies."[35]

The day after Foulloy's first visit, Jefferson did as he had promised and returned the two volumes, but kept a copy of the more damning passages for himself. He promised to write to Congress and request the funds with which to buy them, but waited a month before actually writing to John Jay. (At the time, Jay was the new republic's Secretary for Foreign Affairs.) In his response, Jay took Jefferson to task for waiting so long, and instructed him to complete the purchase without delay, assuring him of congressional approval at some later date. "I have no doubt that Congress will be satisfied with it," he wrote. "To me it appears expedient, and the same opinion prevails among the members of Congress who have read your letter."[36] Jefferson, however, was still not to be rushed. Foulloy was left to wait for another three months, during which time he grew increasingly discouraged. In the end, his price went down from 120 guineas to just twenty. Foulloy turned over Deane's books and Jefferson destroyed them.

*　*　*

The *Arethusa* survived Aitken by only two years. After the hanging, workers from the dockyard reattached her mizzenmast and readied her for action. In 1778, with France and Britain again at war, she closed with the French frigate *Belle-Poule* and demanded her surrender, along with that of the *Coureur*. The French refused, and after an engagement lasting five hours the *Arethusa* withdrew, leaving the *Belle-Poule* to limp back to Brest. The engagement was at best a pyrrhic retreat, with the *Belle-Poule* losing more than half of her crew to death or injury, but it was reason enough for the French to celebrate, the women most of all. They wore tiny ships atop their hair, a coiffure that was dubbed the "Belle-Poule."[37] The *Arethusa* itself, along with her ill-fated mizzenmast, was wrecked off Ushant in 1779.[38]

John Baldwin still had one more thing he could sell: the story of the Bristol fires. This information had been suppressed during the trial, and in due course Baldwin sold it to the publisher of *Felix Farley's Bristol Journal*.[39] After that, Baldwin vanishes from sight.

Sir John Fielding survived Aitken by only three years, dying in 1780 at the age of fifty-nine. His house was targeted in the Gordon

Riots that year, and his personal papers, along with those of his half-brother Henry, were destroyed.

James Gambier outlived his nemesis by twelve years. The day before Aitken was hanged, Gambier wrote a long and not entirely coherent letter to Sandwich, defending his reputation and actions against the aspersions that had been cast on both. For weeks, he brooded over the trial, convinced that Davy had given him a black eye. "The style in which Sergeant Davy prefaced the cause must in the opinion of his Majesty and every person who read the trial...make my conduct, as commissioner of the dockyard, justly reprehensible for not in the least appearing to have taken any steps of enquiry...."[40] Too true. A few days after the trial, Gambier asked for a leave of absence, which he took as soon as Aitken was pronounced dead.[41]

The fire did no lasting damage to Gambier's career. Less than a year later, he was promoted to rear-admiral and dispatched to America, where he served directly under Lord Howe. For brief periods, when Howe was away, Gambier was put in charge of naval operations in North America. He must have done his job well enough, for in 1780, even as the war was going very badly, he was promoted to vice-admiral. He died not in action but in Bath, where he is buried in the abbey. Nearby, there is a simple plaque. It lists no achievements beyond his rank, saying only that James Gambier "departed this life January 28th 1789. Aged 61 years."

Silas Deane also died in 1789. He was just fifty-two years old. A year after Aitken was hanged, Deane was recalled to America in disgrace. The charges against him, however, had nothing to do with Aitken. Instead, Deane was accused of malfeasance and profiteering, and was dismissed from office. He was guilty as charged. But so, too, were most politicians on both sides of the Atlantic— which is to say that his offense was one of degree. In 1780, he returned to Paris, briefly staying with Franklin before moving on to Ghent. He was bitter and tired of the war, and he had come to see France and not Britain as the greater threat to his country. When British agents intercepted letters in which he said as much, they saw to it that they were published, making it all but impossible for him to return to America.[42] The British government, however, made no attempt to try him for treason, and after the war, Deane, with nowhere else to go, settled in London. There he let himself go. Unable to earn a living, he sank into debt and started drinking heavily. Bancroft visited him occasionally, but never for long. One of these visits, at Jefferson's request, was just after the Foulloy affair. Deane, he reported, had been living for the past two or three years with a prostitute who had somehow persuaded him to take out a lease on a house and sign it over to her. At one point, he was arrested for her debts, and when he suffered a stroke, she threatened to have him thrown out "at midnight and laid down in the middle of the street and there left to his fate." It was a sordid story, and Bancroft, who had a penchant for moralizing, took particular delight in telling it:

> She then made him give her his watch and other things to pawn to pay the arrears of rent due to the landlord of the house; and being thus stripped of almost every thing, his distress of mind, and the inebriety into which he plunged to escape reflection, brought on him a disorder, which soon produced a total loss of the powers of his body and mind, insomuch that he could not remember anything a single minute, nor use either his hands or feet.[43]

In Bancroft's estimation, Deane suffered from "dropsy, palsy, and idiotism." In any event, Deane made a partial recovery, and having, in Bancroft's words, "no means of subsistence in this country, nor any connection which could enable him to obtain it," he resolved to return to his native Connecticut.[44] This was not meant to be, and he died just as his ship was entering the English channel. His body was taken ashore and buried, without much ceremony, in Deal. It was perhaps a fitting end for a man who once scandalized a minister by telling him that he considered his own "soul to be no more than a blaze of a candle and his body a piece of manure that would produce grass and other vegetables, which asses, cows and horses would eat, and afterward, those beasts would be eaten by dogs, men, birds, and flies and ... he should pass from beast to beast, nine-hundred or a thousand years, and then nature would reproduce him into a form according to nature's Laws, wither into a philosopher, or a jackass."[45] So much for the man whom Aitken believed to be "the honestest man in the world."[46]

William Mansfield outlived Aitken by sixteen years. Like Sir John, his manuscripts were destroyed in the Gordon Riots of 1780. Mansfield's extreme conservatism, along with his tolerant attitudes toward Catholics, made him a natural target, and he barely escaped with his life. He did not recuse himself when given the chance to preside over the trial of the man who had given his name and blessing to the riots. In 1788, Mansfield retired; five years later, at the age of eighty-nine, he died "in a good old age, full of days, riches, and honour," and was buried in Westminister Abbey.[47]

Edmund Burke outlived Aitken by twenty years, dying in 1797 at the age of sixty-eight. He continued to disappoint his constituents in Bristol, so much that in 1780, when he was up for reelection to a second term, he withdrew from a race that he could not possibly have won.[48] A week after Aitken was hanged, Burke briefly bestirred himself on behalf of his constituents, introducing a bill "for more effectually securing his Majesty's ports, docks, dockyards, shipping, &c. from fire."[49] The bill was later subsumed under another, much to Burke's relief.[50]

He became more conservative with age. Aitken had provided Burke with an early example of what might happen when "the swinish multitude" read and acted on Reverend Richard Price's pamphlets. One of them, *Observations on the Nature of Civil Liberty*, had been found in Aitken's bundle, and it was one of Price's sermons, delivered in 1789, that prompted Burke to write his famous *Reflections on the Revolution in France*. As far as Burke was concerned, Price and his followers were as fleeting and inconsequential as grasshoppers, "little, shrivelled, meager, hopping, though loud and troublesome, insects of the hour." He might as well have been writing about Aitken. In many ways, Burke was right. Ordinary Britons, whom he likened in the most unflattering of terms to "thousands of great cattle, reposed beneath the shadow of the British oak," never warmed to the sort of radicalism that Aitken embraced without ever understanding.

Thomas Lawrence also died in 1797. One week after Aitken was hanged, he submitted a bill to Sandwich. He was paid ten pounds one shilling for the confession that he had managed to extract from Aitken.[51] He published a sequel of sorts, under the bland title of *A Narrative of Certain Facts*. It is thanks to this fulsome little book that we know about Aitken's final days. Lawrence's only real success in life was his son, the celebrated portrait painter of the same name. A few years after Aitken was hanged, Lawrence moved his family to Bath, having failed to make a go of the Black Bear Inn in Devizes. There he set up young Thomas in a studio, and the fashionable flocked to be sketched by the boy artist. The family lived off the proceeds. In 1786, the Lawrences moved to London, where Lawrence senior tried his hand at exhibiting a small collection of stuffed birds and other curiosities, along with some of his son's paintings. This, too, failed. At some point, he talked his son into giving him a yearly allowance, which he lived off until he died.

Edward Bancroft outlived them all, dying in 1821 at the age of seventy-five. In Paris, he found employment as Deane's secretary, giving him untrammeled access to all the delegation's correspondence. This he routinely forwarded to the British ambassador in Paris and the spy Paul Wentworth in London. Years later, when he was demanding still more money from the British government, he reminded his masters that he was the one who had kept them apprized of "every transaction of the American commissioners; of every step and vessel taken to supply the revolted colonies, with artillery, arms etc.; of every part of their intercourse with the French and other European courts; of the powers and instructions given by Congress to the commissioners, and of their correspondence with the secret committees etc."[52] While he was serving in Paris, the Americans raised his salary, as did the British. He made periodic trips back to Britain, each time supplying the Americans with useless information. In 1783, at the war's end, he returned to London, where he continued to thrive. He kept an eye on Deane, and in his own way felt sorry for him.[53] Among Americans, only his fellow commissioner Arthur Lee suspected him. Bancroft's duplicity went undetected for more than a hundred years, surfacing only when Benjamin Franklin Stevens took it upon himself to publish facsimiles of diplomatic documents from the time of the American Revolution.

Heriot's alone survives. Advances in medicine and public health presented its trustees with a problem—as more parents survived into old age, there were fewer orphans—and with time the school started admitting children whose parents were not only alive, but prosperous, too. In 1886, the hospital became a day school, admitting fee-paying boys, and in 1979, Heriot's again changed with the times, admitting girls for the first time. Where there were perhaps 140 boys in Aitken's day, there are now about 1,500 children.[54] Unlike the boys who attended it in Aitken's time, almost all its graduates now go to universities, most of these in Scotland. The original building still stands, and aside from the buildings that now surround it, it looks much the way it did when Aitken walked its corridors.

What then, of the sad hero of this story? For several years, his corpse hung above the entrance to Portsmouth harbor. For a short while, it attracted hordes of curiosity-seekers. It taunted Gambier, who wanted nothing more than to forget the episode, and it was there to greet his successor, Samuel Hood. A judge who visited Portsmouth in May of 1777 saw the body for himself. He was less horrified than amused, noting in his diary that "there are so many of those beacons struck about England, that they rather serve as Mercuries to point out roads to travellers than to warn against the like crimes."[55] George III, who visited the dockyard and fleet in 1778, could hardly have avoided seeing the corpse. By then, the body, stripped of flesh and organs, was more pathetic than frightening.

Over the years, bits and pieces of the body went missing. At some point, probably in the early nineteenth century, the remaining bones were taken down. The practice of gibbeting notorious felons came to an abrupt end in 1832 when the home secretary ordered the body of a man named James Cook cut down and given a decent burial.[56] It is not known whether some kind soul did the same for Aitken. One story, published in 1828, has it that "some sailors took the skeleton of this wretched man down some years after his execution, placed it in a sack, and left it in the chimney-corner of a public house in Gosport."[57] Another story, published in 1884, claimed that some men working at the site of the old gibbet uncovered Aitken's remains.[58] And yet another claimed that some-one cut off one of his fingers, and having somehow mummified it, used it as a tobacco stopper.[59] This last remnant of James Aitken was destroyed in an air raid during World War II.

The Germans succeeded where Aitken had failed, wreaking destruction beyond his most fervid imaginings. Ironically, most of the damage was accomplished using incendiary bombs. Portsmouth and Bristol's old towns were nearly destroyed. Old Portsmouth is gone, replaced, for the most part, by bleak housing estates, but the dockyard survived the war, and it still looks very much the way it did in Aitken's day. Bristol fared only somewhat better. The worst air raid occurred on 24 November 1940. For six hours, the city was targeted with incendiary bombs, and when the raid was at long last over, much of its old town lay in ruins.

* * *

For the briefest of moments, Aitken existed in legend, but in leg-end as in life he was destined to be short-lived. His trial was soon eclipsed by another—that of William Dodd, the king's chaplain, for forgery—and by the end of the year the British public had big-ger problems to worry about. News had come of the disaster at Saratoga, and with it, the first hints that the war might not be winnable. The first thing that was forgotten was Aitken's real name. It and his many aliases were discarded in favor of his prole-tarian sobriquet—John the Painter—and even this was discarded in favor of the more euphonic Jack the Painter.

His legend inspired only three literary efforts, each appearing shortly after his death. The first, *A Short Account of the Motives which Determined the Man, Called John the Painter*, got almost all the facts wrong, starting with the claim that Aitken was born in

America and was taught by "the master of a neighbouring country school."

The second, *John the Painter's Ghost*, was distinguished by its rants against Scotland and the king's favorites. Crude and often scabrous, the pamphlet contains lines that are strongly reminiscent of the anti-Scottish propaganda churned out by Wilkes and Charles Churchill in the mid-1760s, suggesting that the pamphlet's author may have been drawn from their inner circle:

> I rather look on James Aitken to have been an honour to his race, than a disgrace. He was a fellow of penetration, sense, and observation-prone to commit every violent deed to aggrandize his wealth, or sate his passions, a strong republican in principle, an enthusiast in religion, and a Quixote in romance. His robberies were committed on the nascent plan of clanism, which formerly taught every Scot to strip his neighbour for his convenience, if he was the strongest.[60]

The pamphlet's real interest lies in its premise. In eighteenth-century folklore, hanged felons often "come again" to harry the living, and this is exactly what John the Painter's ghost does, harrying Lord Temple (whose idea it had been to make use of Baldwin), the king, and even the queen and her ladies in waiting:

> At this the maids of honour scream'd,
> > The virtuous queen withdrew;
> And every lady of her train,
> > Was chill'd with deadly dew.[61]

And finally there was the play *Fire and Water!* It enjoyed the briefest of runs in London's Haymarket Theatre, probably in

1780. The characters—Commode the French milliner, Sulphur the arsonist, Firebrand his accomplice, Tremor the mayor of Portsmouth, and so on—are predictable. Sulphur, who has taken it upon himself to burn down the Portsmouth dockyard, is a great admirer of John the Painter: "A great man, Heaven knows! John was a pretty fellow: if he had not been so indiscreet as to commit a few burglaries, he would have merited canonization."[62]

Aitken is scarcely remembered in the two towns that he tried to burn down. In Bristol, local legend has it that a corbel from a ruined abbey bore an uncanny likeness of his face; it was still an attraction in 1789, when a light was installed for the benefit of the curious. It has since disappeared.[63]

So much for Aitken's afterlife in England. What about Scotland? Contrary to *John the Painter's Ghost,* the Scots did not "blush for the conduct of their countryman." The truth is that Aitken's exploits barely registered in his homeland. The Scots did not learn John the Painter's real identity until after he had been hanged. In local newspapers, the story unfolded the same way it had in London, the only difference being that Scotland got its news several days later. It was not until 14 March that *The Edinburgh Advertiser* revealed that John the Painter was in fact Scottish, having reported elsewhere in the same issue that "John the Painter is a native of Boston in New England."[64] In the next issue, which came out four days later, the publisher revealed Aitken's real name, along with his place of birth off the Cowgate.[65] He copied both facts straight from the London papers, and like them, he got the name of Aitken's father wrong, identifying him as David instead of George. The *Advertiser's* rival, the *Caledonian Mercury,* ran exactly the same story.[66] Only *The Edinburgh Evening Courant,* claiming a "tenderness for the place of his nativity and connections, &c. who feelingly would suffer," balked at printing

Aitken's name and place of birth.[67] Its publisher was being unduly sensitive. As far as everyone else in Scotland was concerned, the accident of Aitken's birth was just that.

That leaves America, Aitken's adoptive country. If anything, his efforts made even less of an impression in America than they did in Britain. Few Americans knew of his existence, and still fewer cared. This is not very surprising. Even in peacetime it took six or more weeks for a mail packet to cross the Atlantic; with the war, it took several more. News of the Portsmouth fire did not reach America until five months after the fact, by which time Aitken was long dead. *The Pennsylvania Evening Post* and *The Freeman's Journal* each gave the story just one paragraph, and neither newspaper gloated or even expressed approval.[68] Something approaching gloating can be detected in a story published in *The Independent Chronicle*, a newspaper published out of Boston. It put losses at one million pounds and claimed that the fire had raged out of control for three days.[69] What makes it interesting is that its source was French. A few weeks later, another installment of English newspapers arrived, and with them, news of the Bristol fires. These, too, failed to excite American editors.[70] Most Americans probably took an even dimmer view of setting fires in a city where so many of them had once done business.[71]

After this, there was no more news of Aitken until the end of May, when his execution was reported in several American newspapers.[72] This was an opportunity to say something kind about the young man who had given his life for America, but no one bothered.[73]

Things might have been different had Aitken actually succeeded in destroying not only Portsmouth, but Plymouth, Deptford, Chatham, and Woolwich. In that case, the ability of the Royal Navy to refit and fight would have been severely restricted, making it difficult to ship new regiments to America or resupply those already there. Of course, it is possible that the same sequence of events would have given Britain the political will not only to carry on the struggle for several more years, but also to pursue it with greater ruthlessness.

Either way, the result would have been the same. America would have won the war and Britain would have lost it, maybe sooner, maybe later. The basic flaw in Aitken's plan was the assumption that the war was Britain's to win. It was not. But if his actions had no effect on the war, that did not make him a failure in his own eyes. For the briefest of moments, he cheated obscurity and was the most famous man in England.

A NATION lost its footing. Reasonable people became unreasonably suspicious of the strangers in their midst. Conservative politicians exploited the crisis and attempted to prolong it, branding anyone who dared to oppose them as unpatriotic. The same events helped the ministry push through the American High Treason Bill, which allowed the Crown to hold American privateers without trial. Because they were deemed unlawful combatants, captured crews were held indefinitely, some in the prison hulk of the *Jersey*, others in Wallabout Bay off Brooklyn, and more in British prisons. There they languished, never knowing whether they would live or hang.

In the end, however, the fires that Aitken set had no lasting effect on how Britain viewed itself or the world. Moreover, he had a fair and open trial, if only by the limited standards of eighteenth-century justice. His crimes were deeply shocking, but they did not cause his contemporaries to discard their most cherished values, flawed and iniquitous though they were.

Their relative restraint becomes all the more remarkable when we consider that they had no police resources to speak of. The Bow Street Runners were the only thing that passed for a professional police force, and they were unable to catch Aitken. Sir John Fielding's contribution to solving the case was merely commonsensical: by urging the Lords of the Admiralty to offer a large reward, he acknowledged that Aitken would be caught by the ordinary people he met in the course of his wanderings. And it was ordinary people—apprentices, journeymen, landladies and the like—whose recollections and testimony sealed Aitken's fate.

The people who testified against him would never have been located without the help of John Baldwin. Of the many people who took advantage of Aitken and preyed on his loneliness, this man, this informer, was arguably the worst. But neither he nor the ministry that employed him was doing anything illegal. And that is precisely the point. When Aitken refused to answer Sir John's questions, he was not tortured or placed in isolation or subjected to sleep deprivation. He fell into the trap that had been set for him, but that was his choice. He did not *have* to unburden himself to Baldwin.

Ultimately, he was treated like any other felon. But he was not an ordinary felon, and because of this his contemporaries could not quite find the words to describe his crimes in Portsmouth and Bristol. Those with classical educations compared him to Herostratus, "who, to become immortal in history, set fire to the famous temple of Diana at Ephesus."[1] But to most Britons he was simply an "incendiary." It is a marvelous word, one that both describes his career as an arsonist and suggests a motive. In Johnson's *Dictionary of the English Language*, an *incendiary* is "one who sets houses or towns on fire in malice or for robbery." But an incendiary can also be "one who inflames factions, or promotes quarrels."[2]

Both definitions fall short of the mark. Aitken acted out of malice, but not as Johnson understood it. Nor does the word capture the larger and more sinister dimension of a plot that targeted not only dockyards and wharves, but also the civilians who lived and worked on their edges. His willingness to sacrifice noncombatants places his actions beyond the pale of mere sabotage.

It was here that words failed. The words *terrorism* and *terrorist* do not appear in Johnson's dictionary. Nor do they appear in a dictionary published three years after Aitken set his last fire.[3] The two words did not enter the language until the end of the century, during the Jacobin Reign of Terror, and in their first incarnation they meant something different from what they mean today. They referred to acts of terror committed on behalf of the state—not against it.

Contemporaries quickly forgot James Aitken and his attempts to harm them. They did not seriously believe that they or their descendants would be called upon to add such crimes to their understanding of the world. John Fielding, son of the novelist Henry Fielding and nephew of Sir John, spoke for his generation when he declared himself at a loss for words to describe "a crime of so atrocious and uncommon a nature." He found it "impossible to affix any epithet to the crime descriptive of its enormity," although he consoled himself with the thought that this was "the first instance of its existence, and I hope in God it will be the last."[4] Sadly, it was not.

THE SECONDARY literature is scant. Articles specifically about Aitken can be found in only three journals: the *Pennsylvania Magazine of History and Biography* (1939), the *Yale University Library Gazette* (1955), and *History Today* (1966). Each is useful up to a point, but none is comprehensive. Aitken also figures in three over-wrought articles by Julian Boyd. These appeared as a series in the *William and Mary Quarterly* in 1959. The research is first-rate, but the premise—that Bancroft poisoned Deane—is crank.

The best study by far is a pamphlet published by the Portsmouth City Council in 2001: "Burning the Dockyard: John the Painter and the American Revolution." Its author, Professor Neil York of Brigham Young University, has done an admirable job working through the convoluted and often contradictory sources for Aitken's life. My disagreements with his conclusions—a name here, a date there—are too few and trivial to itemize. A shorter and more readily obtainable version can be found in the new *Oxford Dictionary of National Biography*.

The primary sources are a bit of a minefield. The most common problem is plagiarism. This is especially true of newspaper accounts (a common enough practice in the eighteenth century), but it is also true of the various "confessions" published just after Aitken's death. (York catalogues these in full.) Each confession, moreover, reads suspiciously like any other criminal biography. As detailed in chapter 11, Aitken made two confessions, one right after the other. The first, published as *The Life of James Aitken*, was dictated to one of Sir John Fielding's clerks. The second, published in various newspapers, was dictated to Thomas Lawrence. It is much shorter, in large part because Aitken was by then tired and more than a little rattled. I have used the version printed in *The Hampshire Chronicle* on the twenty-fourth of March, 1777. It is dubbed, just a little too defensively, as "the GENUINE CONFESSION OF JOHN THE PAINTER." Most of the discrepancies between the two confessions are in fact quite innocent, and can be attributed to an understandable exhaustion on Aitken's part.

And finally, we have not one but two transcriptions of the trial. As with the confessions, one is much longer—and more comprehensive —than the other. This is the transcription taken by Joseph Gurney. It was published in 1777, very shortly after Aitken's death; it also appears in *A Complete Collection of State Trials and Proceedings for High Treason and Other Crimes and Misdemeanors*. The second transcription was taken by William Blanchard; as noted in chapter 10, it is the more colorful of the two, but its many gaps render it suspect.

ABBREVIATIONS

BRO	Bristol Record Office
Journal of a Lady	Andrews, Evangeline Walker, and Charles McLean Andrews, eds. *Journal of a Lady of Quality; Being the Narrative of a Journey from Scotland to the West Indies, North Carolina, and Portugal, in the Years 1774 and 1776.* New Haven: Yale University Press, 1934
Life of James Aitken	*The Life of James Aitken, Commonly Called John the Painter, an Incendiary, who Was Tried at the Castle of Winchester, on Thursday the 7th Day of March, 1777, and Convicted of Setting Fire to his Majesty's Dock-yard, at Portsmouth, Exhibiting a Detail of Facts of the Utmost Importance to Great Britain. The Whole Faithfully Taken down from the Convict's Own Mouth, on Friday, Saturday, and Sunday, Preceding his Execution.* Winchester: J. Wilkes, 1777

Narrative of Certain Facts	Lawrence, Thomas. *A Narrative of Certain Facts, Related by Mr Lawrence, of the Bear Inn, Devizes; Respecting his Several Conferences, at London and Winchester, with the Author of the Late Fires, at Portsmouth and Bristol.* London: T. Evans, 1777
NMM	National Maritime Museum
PMRS	Portsmouth Museum and Records Service
Portsmouth Guide	*The Portsmouth Guide; or, a Description of the Ancient and Present State of the Place; its Buildings, Charitable Foundations, Fairs, Markets, Play-house and Assembly-room; with the Times of Coming in and Going out of MACHINES, WAGONS, POSTS, &c. To which Is Added, Some Account of the ISLE OF WIGHT, a Description of SPITHEAD, the HARBOUR, the DOCK-YARD, GUN-WHARF, COMMON, GOSPORT, HASLAR HOSPITAL, Several of the Adjacent TOWNS, GENTLEMEN'S SEATS, &c. &c. Interspersed with many PARTICULARS, Useful, Curious, and Entertaining.* Portsmouth: Printed and sold by R. Carr, 1775
PRO	Public Record Office
State of the Prisons	Howard, John. *The State of the Prisons in England and Wales, with Preliminary Observations, and an Account of Some Foreign Prisons.* Warrington: William Eyres, 1777
"Trial of James Hill"	Gurney, Joseph. "The Trial of James Hill otherwise James Hinde, otherwise James Actzen or Aitken, (Known also by the Name of John the Painter) for Feloniously, Wilfully, and Maliciously Setting Fire to the Rope House in his Majesty's Dock-Yard, before the Hon. Sir William Henry Ashhurst, Knt. One of the Justices of his Majesty's Court of King's Bench, and the Hon. Sir Beaumont Hotham, Knt. One of the Barons of his Majesty's Court of Exchequer, March 6: 17 George III. A.D. 1777 [Taken in Short-Hand by Joseph Gurney; and Published by Permission of the Judges]." In *A Complete Collection of State Trials and Proceedings for High Treason and Other Crimes and Misdemeanors,* edited by T.B. Howell, 1317–68. London: Longman, Hurst, Rees, Orme, and Brown, 1816

PREFACE

1. Foreman, Amanda. *Georgiana. Duchess of Devonshire.* New York: Random House, 1998, pp. xiii–xiv.
2. *Life of James Aitken,* p. 14.
3. *The Public Advertiser,* 8 February 1777, p. 2.
4. *Life of James Aitken,* p. 22.

INTRODUCTION

1. Sylvia R. Frey, *The British Soldier in America: a Social History of Military Life* (Austin: University of Texas Press, 1981), p. 25; Robert W. Fogel et al., "Secular Changes in American and British Stature and Nutrition," in *Hunger and History. The Impact of Changing Food Production and Consumption Patterns on Society,* ed. Robert I. Rotberg and Theodore K. Rabb (Cambridge: Cambridge University Press, 1986), p. 265.
2. Charles Isham, ed., *Collections of the New-York Historical Society,* vol. 20 (New York: New-York Historical Society, 1888), p. 9.
3. NMM, *Navy Board Letters,* ADM/B/193, 1776.
4. Samuel Johnson, *A Dictionary of the English Language,* vol. 2 (London: J. Knapton; T. and T. Longman; C. Hitch and L. Hawes; A. Millar; and R. and J. Dodsley, 1755).
5. "Trial of James Hill," col. 1341.
6. *The General Evening Post,* 4–6 February 1777, p. 3; *The Public Advertiser,* 13 February 1777, p. 3; *The Hampshire Chronicle,* 3 February 1777, p. 3.
7. Rab A. Houston, "The Demographic Regime," in *People and Society in Scotland,* ed. Thomas M. Devine and Rosalind Mitchison (Edinburgh: John Donald Publishers Ltd, 1988), p. 14.
8. John Duffy, "The Passage to the Colonies," *Mississippi Valley Historical Review* 38 (1951), pp. 23–24.
9. *State of the Prisons,* p. 7.
10. NMM, Sandwich Papers, SAN F/10/40, 12 February 1777.
11. Charles Isham, ed., *Collections of the New-York Historical Society,* vol. 20 (New York: New-York Historical Society, 1888), p. 10.
12. NMM, *Portsmouth Dockyard Resident Commissioners' Reports to the Navy Board,* POR/F/16, 1775–1778.
13. *The General Evening Post,* 4–6 February 1777, p. 1; *The St. James's Chronicle,* 4–6 February 1777, p. 1.
14. NMM, *Navy Board Letters,* ADM/B/193, 1776.
15. Anne Buck, *Dress in Eighteenth-century England* (London: B.T. Batsford Ltd, 1979), p. 135; C. Willett Cunnington and Phillis Cunnington, *Handbook of English Costume in the Eighteenth Century* (London: Faber and Faber Limited, 1972), p. 241.
16. NMM, *Portsmouth Dockyard Resident Commissioners' Reports to the Navy Board,* POR/F/16, 1775–1778.
17. Charles Isham, ed., *Collections of the New-York Historical Society,* vol. 20 (New York: New-York Historical Society, 1888), p. 9.

18. Charles Royster, *A Revolutionary People at War. The Continental Army and American Character, 1775–1783* (Chapel Hill: University of North Carolina Press, 1979), p. 236.

19. Simon Schama, *Citizens. A Chronicle of the French Revolution* (New York: Vintage Books, 1989), p. 525.

20. C. Willett Cunnington and Phillis Cunnington, *Handbook of English Costume in the Eighteenth Century* (London: Faber and Faber Limited, 1972), p. 236.

21. NMM, *Navy Board Letters*, ADM/B/193, 1776.

22. "Trial of James Hill," col. 1341.

23. *The Hampshire Chronicle*, 3 February 1777, p. 3.

24. *The Hampshire Chronicle*, 3 February 1777, p. 1.

25. John M. Beattie, *Crime and the Courts in England 1660–1800* (Princeton: Princeton University Press, 1986), p. 139; Peter King, "Punishing Assault: the Transformation of Attitudes in the English Courts," *Journal of Interdisciplinary History* 27, no. 1 (1996), pp. 43–74.

26. "Trial of James Hill," col. 1338.

27. PMRS, S3/174/120, 16 October 1776.

28. Jessica F. Warner, "Historical Perspectives on the Shifting Boundaries around Youth and Alcohol. The Example of Preindustrial England, 1350–1750," *Addiction* 93, no. 5 (1998), pp. 641–657.

29. R.R. Palmer, *The Age of the Democratic Revolution. A Political History of Europe and America, 1760–1800*, 2 vols., vol. 1 (Princeton: Princeton University Press, 1959), pp. 248–253; Jonathan R. Dull, *A Diplomatic History of the American Revolution* (New Haven: Yale University Press, 1985), p. 66; Simon Schama, *Citizens. A Chronicle of the French Revolution* (New York: Vintage Books, 1989), pp. 25–27.

30. William B. Willcox, ed., *The Papers of Benjamin Franklin*, vol. 23 (New Haven: Yale University Press, 1983), p. 40.

31. Charles Royster, *A Revolutionary People at War. The Continental Army and American Character, 1775–1783* (Chapel Hill: University of North Carolina Press, 1979), pp. 377–378.

32. *Life of James Aitken*, pp. 13–14.

33. T.S. Ashton, *An Economic History of England: the 18th Century* (London: Methuen & Co., 1961), pp. 2–3. L. D. Schwarz, "The Standard of Living in the Long Run: London, 1700–1860," *Economic History Review* 38, no. 1 (1985), pp. 30–31.

34. Bruce P. Lenman, *Integration and Enlightenment. Scotland 1746–1832* (Edinburgh: Edinburgh University Press, 1992), p. 2; E. Anthony Wrigley and Roger S. Schofield, *The Population History of England, 1541–1871. A Reconstruction* (London: Edward Arnold, 1981), pp. 533–534.

35. Robert W. Malcolmson, *Life and Labour in England 1700–1780, Hutchinson Social History of England* (London: Hutchinson, 1981), pp. 144–146; W. Hamish Fraser, *Conflict and Class. Scottish Workers, 1700–1838, John Donald Publishers Ltd* (Edinburgh: 1988), p. 22.

36. Michael Sanderson, "Literacy and Social Mobility in the Industrial Revolution," *Past and Present* 56 (1972), pp. 75–104; Rab A. Houston, *Scottish Literacy and*

the Scottish Identity. Illiteracy and Society in Scotland and Northern England 1600–1800 (Cambridge: Cambridge University Press, 1985), p. 219.

CHAPTER ONE

1. New Register House, *Old Parish Reigster 685.1/27*, 4 October 1752.
2. Rab A. Houston, "The Demographic Regime," in *People and Society in Scotland,* ed. Thomas M. Devine and Rosalind Mitchison (Edinburgh: John Donald Publishers Ltd, 1988), pp. 13–14; Robert E. Tyson, "Demographic Change," in *Eighteenth Century Scotland: New Perspectives,* ed. Thomas M. Devine and J.R. Young (East Lothian: Tuckwell Press, 1999), pp. 202–203.
3. Hugo Arnot, *The History of Edinburgh* (Edinburgh: W. Creech, 1779), p. 337.
4. W. Hamish Fraser, *Conflict and Class. Scottish Workers, 1700–1838, John Donald Publishers Ltd* (Edinburgh: 1988), p. 21.
5. William Maitland, *The History of Edinburgh, from its Foundation to the Present Time* (Edinburgh: Hamilton, Balfour and Neill, 1753), pp. 299–300.
6. Rab A. Houston, *Social Change in the Age of Enlightenment: Edinburgh, 1660–1760* (Oxford: Clarendon Press, 1994), p. 239.
7. Joseph Collyer, *The Parent's and Guardian's Directory, and the Youth's Guide, in the Choice of a Profession or Trade* (London: R. Griffiths, 1761), p. 63.
8. Henry Paton, ed., *The Register of Marriages for the Parish of Edinburgh, 1701–1750* (Edinburgh: Scottish Record Society, 1908), p. 7.
9. Peter Laslett, *Family Life and Illicit Love in Earlier Generations. Essays in Historical Sociology* (Cambridge: Cambridge University Press, 1978), p. 203.
10. W. Hamish Fraser, *Conflict and Class. Scottish Workers, 1700–1838, John Donald Publishers Ltd* (Edinburgh: 1988), p. 164.
11. For an overview of the literature, see, among others, Jessica F. Warner and Robin Griller, "'My Pappa is out, and my Mamma is asleep.' Minors, their Routine Activities, and Interpersonal Violence in an Early Modern Town, 1653–1781," *Journal of Social History* 36, no. 3 (2003), p. 562.
12. *The Hampshire Chronicle,* 3 February 1777, p. 4.
13. Hugh Cunningham, *The Children of the Poor. Representations of Childhood since the Seventeenth Century,* ed. Peter Laslett and Michael Anderson, *Family, Sexuality and Social Relations in Past Times* (Oxford: Blackwell, 1991), p. 3 and *passim.*
14. Edward Topham, *Letters from Edinburgh; Written in the Years 1774 and 1775: Containing Some Observations on the Diversions, Customs, Manners, and Laws, of the Scotch Nation, During a Six Months Residence in Edinburgh,* 2 vols., vol. 1 (Dublin: W. Watson, 1780?), p. 42; Rab A. Houston, *Social Change in the Age of Enlightenment: Edinburgh, 1660–1760* (Oxford: Clarendon Press, 1994), p. 144. James Grant, *Cassell's Old and New Edinburgh: its History, its People, and its Places,* vol. 2 (London: Cassell, Petter, Galpin & Co., 1882), p. 238.
15. Walter Scott, *Guy Mannering,* ed. P.D. Garside (Edinburgh: Edinburgh University Press, 1999), chapter 37.
16. Robert Louis Stevenson, "Edinburgh: Picturesque Notes," in *The Works of Robert Louis Stevenson,* ed. Charles Curtis Bigelow (New York: The Davos Press, 1906), pp. 347–348.

17. Pat Rogers, ed., *Johnson and Boswell in Scotland. A Journey to the Hebrides* (New Haven: Yale University Press, 1993), p. 7.

18. Edward Topham, *Letters from Edinburgh; Written in the Years 1774 and 1775: Containing Some Observations on the Diversions, Customs, Manners, and Laws, of the Scotch Nation, During a Six Months Residence in Edinburgh*, 2 vols., vol. 1 (Dublin: W. Watson, 1780?), p. 100.

19. *The Scots Magazine*, September 1751, p. 453.

20. *The Scots Magazine*, August 1752, p. 378; A.J. Youngston, *The Making of Classical Edinburgh* (Edinburgh: University of Edinburgh Press, 1966), 3.

21. Rab A. Houston, *Social Change in the Age of Enlightenment: Edinburgh, 1660–1760* (Oxford: Clarendon Press, 1994), p. 8; David Allan, *Scotland in the Eighteenth Century. Union and Enlightenment* (London: Longman, 2002), p. 160.

22. Michael Flinn et al., *Scottish Population History from the 17th Century to the 1930s*, ed. Michael Flinn (Cambridge: Cambridge University Press, 1977), pp. 225–231; W. Hamish Fraser, *Conflict and Class. Scottish Workers, 1700–1838*, John Donald Publishers Ltd (Edinburgh: 1988), p. 12.

23. Christopher A. Whatley, "Royal Day, People's Day: the Monarch's Birthday in Scotland, c. 1660–1860," in *People and Power in Scotland*, ed. Roger Mason and Norman MacDougall (Edinburgh: John Donald Publishers Ltd, 1992), pp. 170–188; Christopher A. Whatley, "An Uninflammable People?," in *The Manufacture of Scottish History*, ed. Ian Donnachie and Christopher A. Whatley (Edinburgh: Polygon, 1992), p. 67.

24. William A. Speck, *The Butcher. The Duke of Cumberland and the Suppression of the 45* (Oxford: Basil Blackwell, 1981), pp. 183–185.

25. Linda Colley, *Britons: Forging the Nation 1707–1837* (New Haven: Yale University Press, 1992), pp. 124–127; Bruce P. Lenman, *Integration and Enlightenment. Scotland 1746–1832* (Edinburgh: Edinburgh University Press, 1992), p. 40; Ian D. White, "Urbanization in Eighteenth-century Scotland," in *Eighteenth Century Scotland: New Perspectives*, ed. Thomas M. Devine and J.R. Young (East Lothian: Tuckwell Press, 1999), p. 179; David Allan, *Scotland in the Eighteenth Century. Union and Enlightenment* (London: Longman, 2002), p. 81.

26. Vic A.C. Gatrell, *The Hanging Tree. Execution and the English People 1770–1868* (Oxford: Oxford University Press, 1994), p. 8.

27. Thomas Pennant, *A Tour in Scotland MDCCLXIX*, second ed. (London: B. White, 1772), p. 56.

28. William Maitland, *The History of Edinburgh, from its Foundation to the Present Time* (Edinburgh: Hamilton, Balfour and Neill, 1753), p. 446.

29. Olwen H. Hufton, "Women without Men: Widows and Spinsters in Britain and France in the Eighteenth Century," *Journal of Family History* 9, no. 4 (1984), p. 364; Bridget Hill, *Women, Work, and Sexual Politics in Eighteenth-century England* (New York: Basil Blackwell, 1989), p. 247.

30. Peter Laslett, *Family Life and Illicit Love in Earlier Generations. Essays in Historical Sociology* (Cambridge: Cambridge University Press, 1978), p. 208.

31. Francis J. Grant, ed., *The Register of Marriages of the City of Edinburgh, 1751–1800* (Edinburgh: Scottish Record Society, 1922), p. 610.

32. Michael Mitterauer, *A History of Youth*, ed. Peter Laslett and Michael Anderson, trans. Graeme Dunphy, *Family, Sexuality and Social Relations in Past Times* (Oxford: Blackwell, 1992), p. 94. Margaret Pelling, "Child Health as a Social Value in Early Modern England," *Social History of Medicine* 1, no. 2 (1988), pp. 146; 153; Pamela Sharpe, "Poor Children as Apprentices in Colyton, 1598–1830," *Continuity and Change* 6, no. 2 (1991), p. 254.

33. William Maitland, *The History of Edinburgh, from its Foundation to the Present Time* (Edinburgh: Hamilton, Balfour and Neill, 1753), p. 446.

34. William Steven, *History of George Heriot's Hospital, with a Memoir of the Founder, and an Account of the Heriot Foundation Schools*, ed. Frederick W. Bedford, third ed. (Edinburgh: Bell & Bradfute, 1872), p. 368.

35. George Heriot's School, *Record of Heriot Hospital*, 1744–1761, p. 457.

36. Alexander Law, *Education in Edinburgh in the Eighteenth Century* (London: University of London Press Ltd, 1965), pp. 135–136.

37. Maisie Steven, *Parish Life in Eighteenth-century Scotland. A Review of the Old Statistical Account* (Aberdeen: Scottish Cultural Press, 1995), pp. 20; 22.

38. Brian R.W. Lockhart, *Jinglin' Geordie's Legacy. A History of George Heriot's Hospital and School* (East Linton: Tuckwell Press, 2003), p. 75.

39. William Maitland, *The History of Edinburgh, from its Foundation to the Present Time* (Edinburgh: Hamilton, Balfour and Neill, 1753), p. 440.

40. Thomas Pennant, *A Tour in Scotland MDCCLXIX*, second ed. (London: B. White, 1772), pp. 54–55.

41. Alexander Law, *Education in Edinburgh in the Eighteenth Century* (London: University of London Press Ltd, 1965), pp. 138–139; George Heriot's School, *Record of Heriot Hospital*, 1761–1767, p. 44.

42. Alexander Law, *Education in Edinburgh in the Eighteenth Century* (London: University of London Press Ltd, 1965), p. 134.

43. William Maitland, *The History of Edinburgh, from its Foundation to the Present Time* (Edinburgh: Hamilton, Balfour and Neill, 1753), p. 441.

44. Rab A. Houston, *Social Change in the Age of Enlightenment: Edinburgh, 1660–1760* (Oxford: Clarendon Press, 1994), p. 263.

45. Callum G. Brown, *The Social History of Religion in Scotland since 1707* (Edinburgh: Edinburgh University Press, 1997), pp. 19–21; Nigel M. de S. Cameron et al., eds., *Dictionary of Scottish Church History and Theology* (Edinburgh: T & T Clark, 1993), pp. 300–301.

46. Walter Scott, *Guy Mannering*, ed. P.D. Garside (Edinburgh: Edinburgh University Press, 1999), vol. 2, chapter 16.

47. William Steven, *History of George Heriot's Hospital, with a Memoir of the Founder, and an Account of the Heriot Foundation Schools*, ed. Frederick W. Bedford, third ed. (Edinburgh: Bell & Bradfute, 1872), p. 122.

48. John Erskine, *The Education of Poor Children Recommended: a Sermon, Preached in Lady Glenorchy's Chapel, Edinburgh, May 18. 1774, Before the Managers of the Orphan-Hospital, and Published at their Desire* (Edinburgh: A. Murray & J. Cochran, 1774), p. 19.

49. John Macleod, *Scottish Theology in Relation to Church History since the Reformation* (Edinburgh: The Banner of Truth Trust, 1974), pp. 217–218; John Erskine,

The Signs of the Times Consider'd: or, the High PROBABILITY, that the Present APPEARANCES in New-England, and the West of Scotland, are a PRELUDE of the Glorious Things Promised to the CHURCH in the Latter Ages (Edinburgh: T. Lumisden and J. Robertson, 1742), p. 10.

50. John Erskine, *Shall I Go to War with my American Brethren? A Discourse from Judges the XXth and 28th* (London: G. Kearsly, 1769), p. 26.

51. John Erskine, *Reflections on the Rise, Progress, and Probable Consequences of the Present Contentions with the Colonies* (Edinburgh: 1776), p. 50.

52. Joseph Collyer, *The Parent's and Guardian's Directory, and the Youth's Guide, in the Choice of a Profession or Trade* (London: R. Griffiths, 1761), pp. 20–21.

53. Maisie Steven, *Parish Life in Eighteenth-century Scotland. A Review of the Old Statistical Account* (Aberdeen: Scottish Cultural Press, 1995), p. 50.

54. Alexander Somerville, *The Autobiography of a Working Man* (London: Macgibbon & Kee Ltd, 1967), p. 58.

55. George Heriot's School, *Record of Heriot Hospital*, 1761–1767, p. 292.

56. Andrew Hook, *Scotland and America. A Study of Cultural Relations 1750–1835* (Glasgow and London: Blackie, 1975), p. 11.

57. Geoffrey Alan Cranfield, *The Development of the Provincial Newspaper 1700–1760* (Oxford: Clarendon Press, 1962), p. v; Michael Harris and Alan J. Lee, "Introduction," in *The Press in English Society from the Seventeenth to the Nineteenth Centuries*, ed. Michael Harris and Alan J. Lee (London: Associated University Presses, 1986), p. 23; Michael Harris, *London Newspapers in the Age of Walpole. A Study of the Origins of the Modern English Press* (Toronto: Associated University Presses, 1987), p. 47; Marie Peters, "Historians and the Eighteenth-century Press: a Review of Possibilities and Problems," *Australian Journal of Politics and History* 34, no. 1 (1988), p. 38.

58. George Heriot's School, *Record of Heriot Hospital*, 1761–1767, p. 25.

59. *The Hampshire Chronicle*, 3 February 1777, p. 3.

60. *Justini historiæ philippicæ: cum versione anglica, ad verbum, quantum fieri potuit, facta. Or, the History of Justin; with an English Translation, as Literal as Possible*, trans. John Clarke, seventh ed. (London: L. Hawes, W. Clarke, and R. Collins, 1772).

61. Peter Gay, *The Enlightenment: an Interpretation. The Rise of Modern Paganism* (New York: W.W. Norton & Company, 1996), pp. 40; 43; 50.

62. *The General Evening Post*, 4–6 February 1777, p. 1; *The Hampshire Chronicle*, 3 February 1777, p. 1.

63. Voltaire, *Henriade. An Epick Poem. In Ten Canto's. Translated from the FRENCH into English Blank Verse* (London: C. Davis, 1732).

64. *Life of James Aitken*, p. 14.

65. National Archives of Scotland, *Catalogue of the Boys Admitted into Heriot's Hospital*, GD 421/10/7, 1659–1902.

66. Rab A. Houston, *Scottish Literacy and the Scottish Identity. Illiteracy and Society in Scotland and Northern England 1600–1800* (Cambridge: Cambridge University Press, 1985), pp. 241–243.

67. Alexander Somerville, *The Autobiography of a Working Man* (London: Macgibbon & Kee Ltd, 1967), pp. 36–37.

68. William Steven, *History of George Heriot's Hospital, with a Memoir of the Founder, and an Account of the Heriot Foundation Schools*, ed. Frederick W. Bedford, third ed. (Edinburgh: Bell & Bradfute, 1872), pp. 109–110; Alexander Law, *Education in Edinburgh in the Eighteenth* Century (London: University of London Press Ltd, 1965), pp. 139–140.

69. NMM, *Portsmouth Dockyard Resident Commissioners' Letters to the Admiralty*, POR/H/10, 1774–1778; NMM, *Portsmouth Dockyard Officers' Reports to the Navy Board*, POR/D/20, 1775–1777.

70. Michael Mitterauer, *A History of Youth*, ed. Peter Laslett and Michael Anderson, trans. Graeme Dunphy, *Family, Sexuality and Social Relations in Past Times* (Oxford: Blackwell, 1992), p. 4; Robert W. Fogel et al., "Secular Changes in American and British Stature and Nutrition," in *Hunger and History. The Impact of Changing Food Production and Consumption Patterns on Society*, ed. Robert I. Rotberg and Theodore K. Rabb (Cambridge: Cambridge University Press, 1986), p. 270.

71. Rab A. Houston, *Scottish Literacy and the Scottish Identity. Illiteracy and Society in Scotland and Northern England 1600–1800* (Cambridge: Cambridge University Press, 1985), p. 7; Robert A. Anderson, *Education and the Scottish People 1750–1918* (Oxford: Clarendon Press, 1995), p. 19.

72. George Heriot's School, *Record of Heriot Hospital*, 1761–1767, p. 329.

73. William Salmon, *Palladio Londinensis: or, the London Art of Building* (London: 1734), pp. 57–58.

74. Robert Campbell, *The London Tradesman. Being a Compendious View of All the Trades, Professions, Arts, Both Liberal and Mechanic, now Practised in the Cities of London and Westminster. Calculated for the Information of PARENTS, and Instruction of YOUTH in their Choice of Business* (New York: Augustus M. Kelley, Publishers, 1969), p. 104.

75. Joseph Collyer, *The Parent's and Guardian's Directory, and the Youth's Guide, in the Choice of a Profession or Trade* (London: R. Griffiths, 1761), p. 168.

76. John G. Rule, *The Experience of Labour in Eighteenth-century Industry* (London: Croon Helm, 1981), pp. 82–83; Robert W. Malcolmson, *Life and Labour in England 1700–1780, Hutchinson Social History of England* (London: Hutchinson, 1981), p. 77; Marcus Rediker, *Between the Devil and the Deep Blue Sea. Merchant Seamen, Pirates, and the Anglo-American Maritime World, 1700–1750* (Cambridge: Cambridge University Press, 1987), p. 93.

77. M. Dorothy George, *London Life in the Eighteenth Century*, second ed. (New York: Harper Torchbooks, 1964), p. 203.

78. Christian Warren, *Brush with Death. A Social History of Lead Poisoning* (Baltimore: The Johns Hopkins University Press, 2001), p. 14.

79. Robert Campbell, *The London Tradesman. Being a Compendious View of All the Trades, Professions, Arts, Both Liberal and Mechanic, now Practised in the Cities of London and Westminster. Calculated for the Information of PARENTS, and Instruction of YOUTH in their Choice of Business* (New York: Augustus M. Kelley, Publishers, 1969), p. 104.

80. Joseph Collyer, *The Parent's and Guardian's Directory, and the Youth's Guide, in the Choice of a Profession or Trade* (London: R. Griffiths, 1761), p. 168.

81. Francis J. Grant, ed., *The Register of Marriages of the City of Edinburgh, 1751–1800* (Edinburgh: Scottish Record Society, 1922), p. 68.

82. Edward Topham, *Letters from Edinburgh; Written in the Years 1774 and 1775: Containing Some Observations on the Diversions, Customs, Manners, and Laws, of the Scotch Nation, During a Six Months Residence in Edinburgh,* 2 vols., vol. 1 (Dublin: W. Watson, 1780?), pp. 45–46.

83. Joseph Collyer, *The Parent's and Guardian's Directory, and the Youth's Guide, in the Choice of a Profession or Trade* (London: R. Griffiths, 1761) p. 168.

84. *The Gentleman's Magazine,* March 1777, p. 123; NMM, Sandwich Papers, SAN F/10/40, 12 February 1777.

85. Alexander Law, *Education in Edinburgh in the Eighteenth Century* (London: University of London Press Ltd, 1965), p. 132.

86. Joseph Collyer, *The Parent's and Guardian's Directory, and the Youth's Guide, in the Choice of a Profession or Trade* (London: R. Griffiths, 1761), p. 168; R. Campbell, *The London Tradesman. Being a Compendious View of All the Trades, Professions, Arts, Both Liberal and Mechanic, now Practised in the Cities of London and Westminster. Calculated for the Information of PARENTS, and Instruction of YOUTH in their Choice of Business* (New York: Augustus M. Kelley, Publishers, 1969), p. 337.

87. W. Hamish Fraser, *Conflict and Class. Scottish Workers, 1700–1838, John Donald Publishers Ltd* (Edinburgh: 1988), p. 21; Bruce P. Lenman, *Integration and Enlightenment. Scotland 1746–1832* (Edinburgh: Edinburgh University Press, 1992), pp. 93–99.

88. Paul Griffiths, *Youth and Authority: Formative Experiences in England 1560–1640* (Oxford: Oxford University Press, 1996), pp. 399–400.

89. John G. Rule, *The Experience of Labour in Eighteenth-century Industry* (London: Croon Helm, 1981), p. 60; W. Hamish Fraser, *Conflict and Class. Scottish Workers, 1700–1838, John Donald Publishers Ltd* (Edinburgh: 1988), p. 34.

90. Linda Colley, *Britons: Forging the Nation 1707–1837* (New Haven: Yale University Press, 1992), p. 127.

91. *Scotch Modesty Displayed, in a Series of Conversations that Lately Passed between an Englishman and a Scotchman. Addressed to the Worthy PATRIOTS of England,* (London: John Bew, 1778), p. 19.

92. James Hayes, "Scottish Officers in the British Army, 1714–63," *Scottish Historical Review* 37, no. 1 (1958), p. 26; Linda Colley, "Whose Nation? Class and National Consciousness in Britain 1750–1830," *Past and Present* 113 (1986), p. 100.

93. J.A. Houlding, *Fit for Service. The Training of the British Army, 1715–1795* (Oxford: Clarendon Press, 1981), pp. 103–105.

94. T.S. Ashton, *Economic Fluctuations in England 1700–1800* (Oxford: Clarendon Press, 1959), p. 99; Michael Flinn et al., *Scottish Population History from the 17th Century to the 1930s,* ed. Michael Flinn (Cambridge: Cambridge University Press, 1977), p. 232; Bruce P. Lenman, *Integration and Enlightenment. Scotland 1746–1832* (Edinburgh: Edinburgh University Press, 1992), p. 53.

95. Ian Charles Cagrill Graham, *Colonists from Scotland: Emigration to North America, 1707–1783* (Ithaca: Cornell University Press, 1956), p. 28.

96. Keith Wrightson, *English Society 1580–1680, Hutchinson Social History of England* (London: Hutchinson, 1982), pp. 41–42.

97. Roger S. Schofield, "Age-specific Mobility in an 18th-century Rural English Parish," in *Migration and Society in Early Modern England,* ed. Peter Clark and David Souden (London: Hutchinson, 1987), p. 265.

98. Robert E. Tyson, "Demographic Change," in *Eighteenth Century Scotland: New Perspectives,* ed. Thomas M. Devine and J.R. Young (East Lothian: Tuckwell Press, 1999), pp. 195–196. T.C. Smout, N.C. Landsman, and T.M. Devine, "Scottish Emigration in the Seventeenth and Eighteenth Centuries," in *Europeans on the Move: Studies in European Migration, 1500–1800,* ed. Nicholas Canny (Oxford: Clarendon Press, 1994), pp. 76–112.

CHAPTER TWO

1. E. Anthony Wrigley, "A Simple Model of London's Importance in Changing English Society and Economy 1650–1750," in *Past and Present,* ed. Philip Abrams and E. Anthony Wrigley, *Past and Present Publications* (Cambridge: Cambridge University Press, 1978), p. 218.

2. Daniel Paterson, *A New and Accurate Description of the Direct and Principal Cross Roads in England and Wales, and Part of the Roads of Scotland,* 15 ed. (London: 1811), pp. 222–231.

3. Frederick A. Pottle, ed., *Boswell's London Journal 1762–1763* (New York: McGraw-Hill Book Company, Inc., 1950), pp. 42–43. Tobias George Smollett, *The Adventures of Roderick Random,* ed. Paul-Gabriel Boucé (Oxford: Oxford University Press, 1979), chapters 7–13.

4. Leon Radzinowicz, *A History of English Criminal Law and its Administration from 1750,* vol. 1 (London: Stevens & Sons Limited, 1948), p. 200.

5. Vic A.C. Gatrell, *The Hanging Tree. Execution and the English People 1770–1868* (Oxford: Oxford University Press, 1994), p. 248.

6. Edward Topham, *Letters from Edinburgh; Written in the Years 1774 and 1775: Containing Some Observations on the Diversions, Customs, Manners, and Laws, of the Scotch Nation, During a Six Months Residence in Edinburgh,* 2 vols., vol. 1 (Dublin: W. Watson, 1780?), pp. 47–48.

7. Frederick A. Pottle, ed., *Boswell's London Journal 1762–1763* (New York: McGraw-Hill Book Company, Inc., 1950), p. 44.

8. A.L. Beier and Roger Finlay, "Introduction: the Signficance of the Metropolis," in *London 1500–1700. The Making of the Metropolis,* ed. A.L. Beier and Roger Finlay (London: Longman, 1986), p. 20.

9. Penelope J. Corfield, *The Impact of English Towns 1700–1800* (Oxford: Oxford University Press, 1982), p. 68.

10. Tobias George Smollett, *The Adventures of Roderick Random,* ed. Paul-Gabriel Boucé (Oxford: Oxford University Press, 1979), chapter 13.

11. Frederick A. Pottle, ed., *Boswell's London Journal 1762–1763* (New York: McGraw-Hill Book Company, Inc., 1950), p. 72.

12. James Boswell, *The Life of Samuel Johnson* (Ware: Wordsworth Editions Limited, 1999), p. 200.

13. John Brewer, "The Misfortunes of Lord Bute: a Case-study in Eighteenth-century Political Argument and Public Opinion," *Historical Journal* 16, no. 1 (1973), pp. 3–43.

14. J.O. Bartley, "The Development of a Stock Character," *Modern Language Review* 38 (1943), pp. 283–284; Herbert M. Atherton, *Political Prints in the Age of Hogarth. A Study in the Ideographic Representation of Politics* (Oxford: Clarendon Press, 1974), pp. 211–213; Linda Colley, *Britons: Forging the Nation 1707–1837* (New Haven: Yale University Press, 1992), pp. 119–121.

15. *The Butiad, or Political Register; Being a Supplement to the British Antidote to Caledonian Poison. Containing Forty-three of the Most Humorous Political Prints; Interspersed with a Great Variety of Songs, Letters, Remarks, Extracts, Epigrams, &c. &c. &c.*, (London: E. Sumpter, 1763), from the prologue.

16. Charles Churchill, *A Prophecy of Famine: a Scots Pastoral. Part the Second* (London: E. Cabe, 1763), p. 13.

17. *The Public Advertiser*, 23 January 1777, p. 3.

18. Charles Isham, ed., *Collections of the New-York Historical Society*, vol. 20 (New York: New-York Historical Society, 1888), p. 9.

19. *The General Evening Post*, 8–11 February 1777, p. 4.

20. Linda Colley, *Britons: Forging the Nation 1707–1837* (New Haven: Yale University Press, 1992), p. 15.

21. William A. Speck, *The Butcher. The Duke of Cumberland and the Suppression of the 45* (Oxford: Basil Blackwell, 1981), p. 185.

22. Charles Churchill, *A Prophecy of Famine: a Scots Pastoral. Part the Second* (London: E. Cabe, 1763), p. 10.

23. Rab A. Houston, *Scottish Literacy and the Scottish Identity. Illiteracy and Society in Scotland and Northern England 1600–1800* (Cambridge: Cambridge University Press, 1985), pp. 16–21.

24. Paul H. Scott, "Boswell and the National Question," in *Boswell in Scotland and Beyond*, ed. Thomas Crawford (Glasgow: Association for Scottish Literary Studies, 1997), pp. 22–32.

25. *Narrative of Certain Facts*, p. 12.

26. *The London Magazine*, February 1777, p. 109.

27. *Life of James Aitken*, (Winchester: J. Wilkes, 1777), p. 21.

28. E. Anthony Wrigley and Roger S. Schofield, *The Population History of England, 1541–1871. A Reconstruction* (London: Edward Arnold, 1981), pp. 255; 424; David R. Weir, "Rather Never than Late: Celibacy and Age at Marriage in English Cohort Fertility, 1541–1871," *Journal of Family History* 9, no. 4 (1984), pp. 340–354.

29. Tony Henderson, *Disorderly Women in Eighteenth-century London: Prostitution and Control in the Metropolis 1730–1830*, ed. Patricia Skinner, Pamela Sharpe, and Penny Summerfield, *Women and Men in History* (London: Longman, 1999), p. 33.

30. Frederick A. Pottle, ed., *Boswell's London Journal 1762–1763* (New York: McGraw-Hill Book Company, Inc., 1950), pp. 49–50.

31. *Life of James Aitken*, p. 22.

32. Anna Clark, *Women's Silence, Men's Violence: Sexual Assault in England 1770–1845* (London: Pandora, 1987), p. 25.

33. *Life of James Aitken*, p. 15.
34. Penelope J. Corfield, *The Impact of English Towns 1700–1800* (Oxford: Oxford University Press, 1982), p. 105; L. D. Schwarz, *London in the Age of Industrialisation. Entrepreneurs, Labour Force and Living Conditions, 1700–1850*, ed. Peter Laslett, et al., vol. 19, *Cambridge Studies in Population, Economy and Society in Past Time* (Cambridge: Cambridge University Press, 1992), p. 120.
35. L. D. Schwarz, "The Standard of Living in the Long Run: London, 1700–1860," *Economic History Review* 38, no. 1 (1985), p. 25.
36. J.R. Kellett, "The Breakdown of Gild and Corporation Control over the Handicraft and Retail Trade in London," *Economic History Review* 10, no. 3 (1958), pp. 381–394.
37. L. D. Schwarz, *London in the Age of Industrialisation. Entrepreneurs, Labour Force and Living Conditions, 1700–1850*, ed. Peter Laslett, et al., vol. 19, *Cambridge Studies in Population, Economy and Society in Past Time* (Cambridge: Cambridge University Press, 1992), p. 49.
38. London Metropolitan Archives, MR/LV/6/57, 3 January 1736; London Metropolitan Archives, MR/LV/6/44, 3 January 1736.
39. PRO, PC 1/15/5, part 3, 3 April–7 June 1738.
40. John M. Beattie, *Policing and Punishment in London 1660–1750. Urban Crime and the Limits of Terror* (Oxford: Oxford University Press, 2001), p. 60.
41. *Life of James Aitken*, p. 15.
42. Nathaniel Crouch, *The Apprentices Companion* (London: Thomas Mercer, 1681), pp. 75–76.
43. Susan E. Klepp and Billy G. Smith, eds., *The Infortunate. The Voyage and Adventures of William Moraley, an Indentured Servant* (University Park, Pennsylvania: The Pennsylvania State University Press, 1992), p. 45.
44. "The History of the Remarkable Life of John Sheppard, Containing a Particular Account of his Many Robberies and Escapes." In *Drunks, Whores and Idle Apprentices. Criminal Biographies of the Eighteenth Century*, edited by Philip Rawlings, 37–75. London: Routledge, 1992, p. 42.
45. Jenny Uglow, *Hogarth. A Life and a World* (London: Faber and Faber, 1997), p. 438; John M. Beattie, *Policing and Punishment in London 1660–1750. Urban Crime and the Limits of Terror* (Oxford: Oxford University Press, 2001), p. 62.
46. John M. Beattie, *Crime and the Courts in England 1660–1800* (Princeton: Princeton University Press, 1986), p. 424.
47. Edward P. Thompson, *The Making of the English Working Class* (London: Victor Gollancz, 1964), p. 60.
48. Vic A.C. Gatrell, *The Hanging Tree. Execution and the English People 1770–1868* (Oxford: Oxford University Press, 1994), p. 7.
49. Joyce Lee Malcom, *To Keep and Bear Arms. The Origins of an Anglo-American Right* (Cambridge, Massachusetts: Harvard University Press, 1994), pp. 128–129.
50. Alexander Smith, *Memoirs of the Life and Times of the Famous Jonathan Wild, Together with the History and Lives, of Modern Rogues, Several of 'em his Acquaintance, that Have Been Executed before and since his Death, for the High-way, Pad, Shop-lifting, House-breaking, Picking of Pockets, and Impudent Robbing in the Streets, and Court* (New York: Garland Publishing, Inc., 1973), p. 33.

51. Gillian Spraggs, *Outlaws and Highwaymen: the Cult of the Robber in England from the Middle Ages to the Nineteenth Century* (London: Pimlico, 2001), pp. 181–183.

52. Peter Linebaugh, *The London Hanged. Crime and Civil Society in the Eighteenth Century* (London: Allen Lane, 1991), p. 189.

53. Van Muyden, ed. *A Foreign View of England in the Reigns of George I. and George II. The Letters of Monsieur César de Saussure to his Family* (London: John Murray, 1902), p. 128.

54. Alexander Smith, *Memoirs of the Life and Times of the Famous Jonathan Wild, Together with the History and Lives, of Modern Rogues, Several of 'em his Acquaintance, that Have Been Executed before and since his Death, for the High-way, Pad, Shop-lifting, House-breaking, Picking of Pockets, and Impudent Robbing in the Streets, and Court* (New York: Garland Publishing, Inc., 1973), p. 81.

55. "Trial of James Hill,", col. 1367.

56. *Life of James Aitken*, p. 15.

57. John Fielding, *A Plan for Preventing Robberies within Twenty Miles of London. With an Account of the Rise and Establishment of the Real Thieftakers. To which Is Added, Advice to Pawnbrokers, Stable-keepers, and Publicans* (London: A. Millar, 1755), p. 7.

58. R. Leslie-Melville, *The Life and Work of Sir John Fielding* (London: Lincoln Williams Ltd., 1934), p. 3.

59. John Fielding, *Sir John Fielding's Jests; or, New Fun for the Parlour and Kitchen: Being the Smartest, Wittiest, and Drollest Collection of Original Jests, Jokes, Repartees, &c. ever yet Published* (London: A. Millar, 1781), pp. 18–19.

60. R. Leslie-Melville, *The Life and Work of Sir John Fielding* (London: Lincoln Williams Ltd., 1934), p. 223.

61. Henry Fielding, *An Enquiry into the Causes of the Late Increase of Robbers*, ed. Malvin R. Zirker (Middletown: Wesleyan University Press, 1988); Henry Fielding, *Covent Garden Journal*, ed. Gerard Edward Jensen, vol. 1 (New Haven: Yale University Press, 1915), p. 241.

62. John Styles, "Sir John Fielding and the Problem of Criminal Investigation in Eighteenth-century England," *Transactions of the Royal Historical Society* 33 (1983), pp. 127–149.

63. *Life of James Aitken*, pp. 16–17.

64. Edward Miles Riley, ed., *The Journal of John Harrower: an Indentured Servant in the Colony of Virginia, 1773–1776* (New York: Holt, Rinehart and Winston, Inc., 1963), p. 17.

65. T.C. Smout, N.C. Landsman, and T.M. Devine, "Scottish Emigration in the Seventeenth and Eighteenth Centuries," in *Europeans on the Move: Studies in European Migration, 1500–1800*, ed. Nicholas Canny (Oxford: Clarendon Press, 1994), pp. 94–95; 98; Robert E. Tyson, "Demographic Change," in *Eighteenth Century Scotland: New Perspectives*, ed. Thomas M. Devine and J.R. Young (East Lothian: Tuckwell Press, 1999), p. 197.

66. Ian Charles Cagrill Graham, *Colonists from Scotland: Emigration to North America, 1707–1783* (Ithaca: Cornell University Press, 1956), pp. 24–27.

67. Bernard Bailyn, *Voyagers to the West. A Passage in the Peopling of America on the Eve of the Revolution* (New York: Alfred A. Knopf, 1986), p. 9.

68. E. Anthony Wrigley and Roger S. Schofield, *The Population History of England, 1541–1871. A Reconstruction* (London: Edward Arnold, 1981), p. 534.

69. Peter Wilson Coldham, ed., *Emigrants from England to the American Colonies 1773–1776* (Baltimore: Genealogical Publishing Co., Inc., 1988).

70. *The Gentleman's Magazine*, March 1777, p. 123.

71. Bernard Bailyn, *Voyagers to the West. A Passage in the Peopling of America on the Eve of the Revolution* (New York: Alfred A. Knopf, 1986), pp. 13–26; Bernard Bailyn, "Introduction: Europeans on the Move, 1500–1800," in *Europeans on the Move: Studies in European Migration, 1500–1800*, ed. Nicholas Canny (Oxford: Clarendon Press, 1994), p. 2.

72. *Life of James Aitken*, p. 17.

73. Abbot Emerson Smith, *Colonists in Bondage. White Servitude and Convict Labor in America 1607–1776* (Gloucester, Massachusetts: Peter Smith, 1965), p. 17. David Dobson, *Scottish Emigration to Colonial America, 1607–1785* (Athens, Georgia: The University of Georgia Press, 1994), from the inside cover.

74. *Life of James Aitken*, p. 17.

75. Susan E. Klepp and Billy G. Smith, eds., *The Infortunate. The Voyage and Adventures of William Moraley, an Indentured Servant* (University Park, Pennsylvania: The Pennsylvania State University Press, 1992), p. 53.

76. Edward Miles Riley, ed., *The Journal of John Harrower: an Indentured Servant in the Colony of Virginia, 1773–1776* (New York: Holt, Rinehart and Winston, Inc., 1963), p. 19.

77. Susan E. Klepp and Billy G. Smith, eds., *The Infortunate. The Voyage and Adventures of William Moraley, an Indentured Servant* (University Park, Pennsylvania: The Pennsylvania State University Press, 1992), pp. 50; 54.

78. Edward Miles Riley, ed., *The Journal of John Harrower: an Indentured Servant in the Colony of Virginia, 1773–1776* (New York: Holt, Rinehart and Winston, Inc., 1963), p. 30.

79. John Duffy, "The Passage to the Colonies," *Mississippi Valley Historical Review* 38 (1951), p. 21; Abbot Emerson Smith, *Colonists in Bondage. White Servitude and Convict Labor in America 1607–1776* (Gloucester, Massachusetts: Peter Smith, 1965), p. 207.

80. Susan E. Klepp and Billy G. Smith, eds., *The Infortunate. The Voyage and Adventures of William Moraley, an Indentured Servant* (University Park, Pennsylvania: The Pennsylvania State University Press, 1992), p. 59.

81. Edward Miles Riley, ed., *The Journal of John Harrower: an Indentured Servant in the Colony of Virginia, 1773–1776* (New York: Holt, Rinehart and Winston, Inc., 1963), p. 29.

82. *Journal of a Lady of Quality*, pp. 48–49.

83. John Duffy, "The Passage to the Colonies," *Mississippi Valley Historical Review* 38 (1951), p. 23.

CHAPTER THREE

1. "Trial of James Hill," col. 1334.

2. "Mr. Potter's Journall from Virginia to N. England," in *Travels in the American Colonies*, ed. Newton D. Mereness (New York: The Macmillan Company, 1916), pp. 4–10.

3. "Trial of James Hill," col. 1334.

4. Abbot Emerson Smith, *Colonists in Bondage. White Servitude and Convict Labor in America 1607–1776* (Gloucester, Massachusetts: Peter Smith, 1965), p. 19.

5. John M. Jennings, "The Poor Unhappy Transported Felon's Sorrowful Account of his Fourteen Years Transportation at Virginia in America," *Virginia Magazine of History and Biography* 56 (1948), pp. 189–190.

6. "The Life, Travels, Exploits, Frauds and Robberies, of Charles Speckman, alias Brown, who Was Executed at TYBURN, on Wednesday the 23d of November, 1763," in *Drunks, Whores and Idle Apprentices. Criminal Biographies of the Eighteenth Century*, ed. Philip Rawlings (London: Routledge, 1992), p. 193.

7. Abbot Emerson Smith, *Colonists in Bondage. White Servitude and Convict Labor in America 1607–1776* (Gloucester, Massachusetts: Peter Smith, 1965), p. 35.

8. John M. Jennings, "The Poor Unhappy Transported Felon's Sorrowful Account of his Fourteen Years Transportation at Virginia in America," *Virginia Magazine of History and Biography* 56 (1948), p. 191.

9. Peter F. Copeland, *Working Dress in Colonial and Revolutionary America* (Westport, Connecticut: Greenwood Press, 1977), pp. 174; 204.

10. Susan E. Klepp and Billy G. Smith, eds., *The Infortunate. The Voyage and Adventures of William Moraley, an Indentured Servant* (University Park, Pennsylvania: The Pennsylvania State University Press, 1992), p. 71.

11. *The Virginia Gazette*, 7 January 1773, p. 3.

12. Abbot Emerson Smith, *Colonists in Bondage. White Servitude and Convict Labor in America 1607–1776* (Gloucester, Massachusetts: Peter Smith, 1965), p. 233.

13. M. Dorothy George, *London Life in the Eighteenth Century*, second ed. (New York: Harper Torchbooks, 1964), p. 134; Michael Parker Banton, *The Coloured Quarter: Negro Immigrants in an English City* (London: Jonathan Cape, 1955), p. 23.

14. Edmund S. Morgan, *American Slavery, American Freedom. The Ordeal of Colonial Virginia* (New York: Norton, 1975), p. 5.

15. John M. Jennings, "The Poor Unhappy Transported Felon's Sorrowful Account of his Fourteen Years Transportation at Virginia in America," *Virginia Magazine of History and Biography* 56 (1948), p. 191.

16. William Eddis, *Letters from America Historical and Descriptive Comprising Occurrences from 1769 to 1777 Inclusive*, ed. Aubrey C. Land (Cambridge, Massachusetts: Harvard University Press, 1969), p. 38.

17. Carl Bridenbaugh, *The Colonial Craftsman* (New York: New York University Press, 1950), pp. 138–141.

18. David W. Galeonson, *White Servitude in Colonial America. An Economic Analysis* (Cambridge: Cambridge University Press, 1981), p. 129.

19. Abbot Emerson Smith, *Colonists in Bondage. White Servitude and Convict Labor in America 1607–1776* (Gloucester, Massachusetts: Peter Smith, 1965), pp. 256–257.

20. "The Life, Travels, Exploits, Frauds and Robberies, of Charles Speckman, alias Brown, who Was Executed at TYBURN, on Wednesday the 23d of November, 1763," in *Drunks, Whores and Idle Apprentices. Criminal Biographies of the Eighteenth Century*, ed. Philip Rawlings (London: Routledge, 1992), p. 194.

21. Susan E. Klepp and Billy G. Smith, eds., *The Infortunate. The Voyage and Adventures of William Moraley, an Indentured Servant* (University Park, Pennsylvania: The Pennsylvania State University Press, 1992), p. 109.

22. "The Life and Actions of James Dalton, (the Noted Street-robber)," in *Drunks, Whores and Idle Apprentices. Criminal Biographies of the Eighteenth Century*, ed. Philip Rawlings (London: Routledge, 1992), p. 97.

23. *Journal of a Lady of Quality*, p. 159.

24. Samuel Thronley, ed., *The Journal of Nicholas Cresswell 1774–1777* (London: Jonathan Cape, Ltd., 1925), pp. 47–48.

25. Susan E. Klepp and Billy G. Smith, eds., *The Infortunate. The Voyage and Adventures of William Moraley, an Indentured Servant* (University Park, Pennsylvania: The Pennsylvania State University Press, 1992), p. 112.

26. Gordon S. Wood, *The Radicalism of the American Revolution* (New York: Vintage Books, 1993) pp. 57–77.

27. Carl Bridenbaugh, ed., *A Tour through Part of the North Provinces of America: Being, a Series of LETTERS Wrote on the Spot, in the Years 1774, & 1775. To which Are Annex'd, TABLES, Shewing the Roads, the Value of Coins, Rates of Stages, &c.* (New York: The New York Times & Arno Press, 1968), p. ix.

28. Adolph B. Benson, ed., *The America of 1750: Peter Kalm's Travels in North America. The English Version of 1770*, 2 vols., vol. 1 (New York: Wilson-Erickson Inc., 1937), p. 17.

29. Bernard Bailyn, *The Peopling of British North America: an Introduction* (New York: Alfred A. Knopf, 1986), p. 11.

30. John Duffy, *Epidemics in Colonial America* (Baton Rouge: Louisiana State University Press, 1953), pp. 15; 218.

31. Adolph B. Benson, ed., *The America of 1750: Peter Kalm's Travels in North America. The English Version of 1770*, 2 vols., vol. 1 (New York: Wilson-Erickson Inc., 1937), p. 192.

32. Samuel Thronley, ed., *The Journal of Nicholas Cresswell 1774–1777* (London: Jonathan Cape, Ltd., 1925), p. 18.

33. Susan E. Klepp and Billy G. Smith, eds., *The Infortunate. The Voyage and Adventures of William Moraley, an Indentured Servant* (University Park, Pennsylvania: The Pennsylvania State University Press, 1992), p. 107.

34. Samuel Thronley, ed., *The Journal of Nicholas Cresswell 1774–1777* (London: Jonathan Cape, Ltd., 1925), p. 22.

35. Evangeline Walker Andrews and Charles McLean Andrews, eds., *Journal of a Lady* (New Haven: Yale University Press, 1934), p. 183.

36. *The Hampshire Chronicle*, 24 March 1777, p. 4.

37. *Life of James Aitken*, p. 18.

38. William Eddis, *Letters from America Historical and Descriptive Comprising Occurrences from 1769 to 1777 Inclusive*, ed. Aubrey C. Land (Cambridge, Massachusetts: Harvard University Press, 1969), p. 38. Susan E. Klepp and

Billy G. Smith, eds., *The Infortunate. The Voyage and Adventures of William Moraley, an Indentured Servant* (University Park, Pennsylvania: The Pennsylvania State University Press, 1992), p. 96.

39. Gordon S. Wood, *The Radicalism of the American Revolution* (New York: Vintage Books, 1993), pp. 53; 60.

40. William Eddis, *Letters from America Historical and Descriptive Comprising Occurrences from 1769 to 1777 Inclusive,* ed. Aubrey C. Land (Cambridge, Massachusetts: Harvard University Press, 1969), p. 38.

41. "The Life, Travels, Exploits, Frauds and Robberies, of Charles Speckman, alias Brown, who Was Executed at TYBURN, on Wednesday the 23d of November, 1763," in *Drunks, Whores and Idle Apprentices. Criminal Biographies of the Eighteenth Century,* ed. Philip Rawlings (London: Routledge, 1992), p. 194.

42. F.W. Clonts, "Travel and Transportaion in Colonial North Carolina," *North Carolina Historical Review* 3, no. 1 (1926), p. 24.

43. *Journal of a Lady of Quality,* pp. 146–147.

44. Ferdinand-M. Bayard, *Travels of a Frenchman in Maryland and Virginia with a Description of Philadelphia and Baltimore in 1791 or Travels in the Interior of the United States, to Bath, Winchester, in the Valley of the Shenandoah, etc., etc., during the Summer of 1791,* trans. Ben C. McCary (Williamsburg, Virginia: self-published, 1950), p. 27.

45. Susan E. Klepp and Billy G. Smith, eds., *The Infortunate. The Voyage and Adventures of William Moraley, an Indentured Servant* (University Park, Pennsylvania: The Pennsylvania State University Press, 1992), p. 112.

46. "The Life and Actions of James Dalton, (the Noted Street-robber)," in *Drunks, Whores and Idle Apprentices. Criminal Biographies of the Eighteenth Century,* ed. Philip Rawlings (London: Routledge, 1992), p. 97.

47. *The Virginia Gazette,* 7 January 1773, p. 3.

48. *The Virginia Gazette,* 25 August 1774, p. 3.

49. *Life of James Aitken,* p. 21.

50. Susan E. Klepp and Billy G. Smith, eds., *The Infortunate. The Voyage and Adventures of William Moraley, an Indentured Servant* (University Park, Pennsylvania: The Pennsylvania State University Press, 1992), pp. 96–97.

51. Charles Isham, ed., *Collections of the New-York Historical Society,* vol. 19 (New York: New-York Historical Society, 1887), p. 10.

52. *The Virginia Gazette,* 7 January 1773, p. 2.

53. *The Virginia Gazette,* 7 January 1775, p. 4.

54. Adam Gordon, "Journal of an Officer who Travelled in America and the West Indies in 1764 and 1765," in *Travels in the American Colonies,* ed. Newton D. Mereness (New York: The Macmillan Company, 1916), p. 411.

55. William Eddis, *Letters from America Historical and Descriptive Comprising Occurrences from 1769 to 1777 Inclusive,* ed. Aubrey C. Land (Cambridge, Massachusetts: Harvard University Press, 1969), p. 33.

56. Billy G. Smith, *The "Lower Sort": Philadelphia's Laboring People, 1750–1800* (Ithaca: Cornell University Press, 1990), p. 84.

57. Carl Bridenbaugh, ed., *A Tour through Part of the North Provinces of America: Being, a Series of LETTERS Wrote on the Spot, in the Years 1774, & 1775. To which Are*

Annex'd, TABLES, Shewing the Roads, the Value of Coins, Rates of Stages, &c. (New York: The New York Times & Arno Press, 1968), p. 9.

58. Sharon V. Salinger, *"To serve well and faithfully": Labor and Indentured Servants in Pennsylvania, 1682–1800* (Cambridge: Cambridge University Press, 1987), pp. 156–157; Tina H. Sheller, "Freemen, Servants, and Slaves: Artisans and the Craft Structure of Revolutionary Baltimore Town," in *American Artisans. Crafting Social Identity, 1750–1850*, ed. Howard B. Rock, Paul A. Gilje, and Robert Asher (Baltimore: The Johns Hopkins University Press, 1995), p. 27.

59. Susan E. Klepp and Billy G. Smith, eds., *The Infortunate. The Voyage and Adventures of William Moraley, an Indentured Servant* (University Park, Pennsylvania: The Pennsylvania State University Press, 1992), p. 64.

60. Adolph B. Benson, ed., *The America of 1750: Peter Kalm's Travels in North America. The English Version of 1770*, 2 vols., vol. 1 (New York: Wilson-Erickson Inc., 1937), p. 33.

61. Adam Gordon, "Journal of an Officer who Travelled in America and the West Indies in 1764 and 1765," in *Travels in the American Colonies*, ed. Newton D. Mereness (New York: The Macmillan Company, 1916), p. 411.

62. Samuel Thronley, ed., *The Journal of Nicholas Cresswell 1774–1777* (London: Jonathan Cape, Ltd., 1925), p. 156.

63. Sharon V. Salinger, *"To serve well and faithfully": Labor and Indentured Servants in Pennsylvania, 1682–1800* (Cambridge: Cambridge University Press, 1987), p. 3; Billy G. Smith, *The "Lower Sort": Philadelphia's Laboring People, 1750–1800* (Ithaca: Cornell University Press, 1990), p. 42.

64. Billy G. Smith, *The "Lower Sort": Philadelphia's Laboring People, 1750–1800* (Ithaca: Cornell University Press, 1990), pp. 160–164.

65. Adam Gordon, "Journal of an Officer who Travelled in America and the West Indies in 1764 and 1765," in *Travels in the American Colonies*, ed. Newton D. Mereness (New York: The Macmillan Company, 1916), p. 414.

66. Carl Bridenbaugh, ed., *A Tour through Part of the North Provinces of America: Being, a Series of LETTERS Wrote on the Spot, in the Years 1774, & 1775. To which Are Annex'd, TABLES, Shewing the Roads, the Value of Coins, Rates of Stages, &c.* (New York: The New York Times & Arno Press, 1968), p. 34.

67. Samuel Thronley, ed., *The Journal of Nicholas Cresswell 1774–1777* (London: Jonathan Cape, Ltd., 1925), p. 158.

68. *Life of James Aitken*, p. 18.

69. Benjamin Woods Labaree, *The Boston Tea Party* (New York: Oxford University Press, 1964), pp. 142–143.

70. Andrew Hook, *Scotland and America. A Study of Cultural Relations 1750–1835* (Glasgow and London: Blackie, 1975), p. 50. David Allan, *Scotland in the Eighteenth Century. Union and Enlightenment* (London: Longman, 2002), p. 174; Margaret Wheeler Willard, ed., *Letters on the American Revolution 1774–1776* (Boston: Houghton Mifflin Company, 1925), pp. 16–17.

71. Isaac S. Harrell, "North Carolina Loyalists," *North Carolina Historical Review* 3, no. 3 (1926), p. 575.

72. Alan L. Karras, *Sojourners in the Sun. Scottish Migrants in Jamaica and the Chesapeake 1740–1800* (Ithaca: Cornell University Press, 1992), pp. 3–5;

Michael Fry, "A Commercial Empire: Scotland and British Expansion in the Eighteenth Century," in *Eighteenth Century Scotland: New Perspectives*, ed. Thomas M. Devine and J.R. Young (East Lothian: Tuckwell Press, 1999), p. 62.

73. Ian Charles Cagrill Graham, *Colonists from Scotland: Emigration to North America, 1707–1783* (Ithaca: Cornell University Press, 1956), p. 167; Alan L. Karras, *Sojourners in the Sun. Scottish Migrants in Jamaica and the Chesapeake 1740–1800* (Ithaca: Cornell University Press, 1992), p. 191.

74. *Journal of a Lady of Quality*, p. 196.

75. Carl Bridenbaugh, ed., *A Tour through Part of the North Provinces of America: Being, a Series of LETTERS Wrote on the Spot, in the Years 1774, & 1775. To which Are Annex'd, TABLES, Shewing the Roads, the Value of Coins, Rates of Stages, &c.* (New York: The New York Times & Arno Press, 1968), p. 40.

76. Ian Charles Cagrill Graham, *Colonists from Scotland: Emigration to North America, 1707–1783* (Ithaca: Cornell University Press, 1956), p. 168.

77. Alan L. Karras, *Sojourners in the Sun. Scottish Migrants in Jamaica and the Chesapeake 1740–1800* (Ithaca: Cornell University Press, 1992), p. 193.

78. Andrew Hook, *Scotland and America. A Study of Cultural Relations 1750–1835* (Glasgow and London: Blackie, 1975), p. 49.

79. Franklin Bowditch Dexter, ed., *The Literary Diary of Ezra Stiles, D.D., LL.D.*, vol. 2 (New York: Charles Scribner's Sons, 1901), p. 185.

80. R.R. Palmer, *The Age of the Democratic Revolution. A Political History of Europe and America, 1760–1800*, 2 vols., vol. 1 (Princeton: Princeton University Press, 1959), p. 170; Andrew Hook, *Scotland and America. A Study of Cultural Relations 1750–1835* (Glasgow and London: Blackie, 1975), p. 62; Colin Bonwick, *English Radicals and the American Revolution* (Chapel Hill: University of North Carolina Press, 1977), p. 31.

81. NMM, Sandwich Papers, SAN F/10/40, 12 February 1777; *Life of James Aitken*, pp. 18–19.

82. Marcus Rediker, *Between the Devil and the Deep Blue Sea. Merchant Seamen, Pirates, and the Anglo-American Maritime World, 1700–1750* (Cambridge: Cambridge University Press, 1987), p. 136.

83. Susan E. Klepp and Billy G. Smith, eds., *The Infortunate. The Voyage and Adventures of William Moraley, an Indentured Servant* (University Park, Pennsylvania: The Pennsylvania State University Press, 1992), p. 124.

84. Simon Schama, *Citizens. A Chronicle of the French Revolution* (New York: Vintage Books, 1989), pp. 26–29.

85. Charles Isham, ed., *Collections of the New-York Historical Society*, vol. 20 (New York: New-York Historical Society, 1888), p. 11.

86. Mrs. Paget Toynbee, ed., *The Letters of Horace Walpole, Fourth Earl of Orford*, 16 vols., vol. 10 (Oxford: Clarendon Press, 1904), p. 6.

87. Robert McCluer Calhoon, *The Loyalists in Revolutionary America 1760–1781* (New York: Harcourt Brace Jovanovich, Inc., 1973), pp. 462–463.

CHAPTER FOUR

1. *The Hampshire Chronicle*, 17 February 1777, p. 4; NMM, Sandwich Papers, SAN F/10/40, 12 February 1777.

2. *Life of James Aitken*, p. 19.

3. Samuel Thronley, ed., *The Journal of Nicholas Cresswell 1774–1777* (London: Jonathan Cape, Ltd., 1925), p. 276.

4. Susan E. Klepp and Billy G. Smith, eds., *The Infortunate. The Voyage and Adventures of William Moraley, an Indentured Servant* (University Park, Pennsylvania: The Pennsylvania State University Press, 1992), p. 133.

5. Bernard Bailyn, "Introduction: Europeans on the Move, 1500–1800," in *Europeans on the Move: Studies in European Migration, 1500–1800*, ed. Nicholas Canny (Oxford: Clarendon Press, 1994), p. 4.

6. Sylvia R. Frey, *The British Soldier in America: a Social History of Military Life* (Austin: University of Texas Press, 1981), pp. 6–7; 25.

7. S.R. Conway, "The Recruitment of Criminals into the British Army, 1775–81," *Bulletin of the Institute of Historical Research* 58, no. 137 (1985), p. 46.

8. J.A. Houlding, *Fit for Service. The Training of the British Army, 1715–1795* (Oxford: Clarendon Press, 1981), p. 118.

9. John Fortescue, ed., *The Correspondence of King George the Third*, 6 vols., vol. 3 (London: Macmillan and Co., Limited, 1928), p. 423.

10. "Trial of James Hill," col. 1367.

11. *Life of James Aitken*, pp. 20; 22.

12. *The St. James's Chronicle*, 11–13 February 1777, p. 3.

13. J.A. Lowe, ed., *Records of the Portsmouth Division of Marines 1764–1800*, vol. 7, *Portsmouth Record Series* (Portsmouth: Published by the City of Portsmouth, 1990), p. xlvii.

14. *The Gentleman's Magazine*, March 1777, p. 122.

15. *The London Magazine*, February 1777, p. 108.

16. Lincoln B. Faller, *Turned to Account. The Forms and Functions of Criminal Biography in Late Seventeenth- and Early Eighteenth-century England* (Cambridge: Cambridge University Press, 1987), p. 1.

17. NMM, *Portsmouth Dockyard Officers' Reports to the Navy Board*, POR/D/20, 1775–1777.

18. Susan E. Klepp and Billy G. Smith, eds., *The Infortunate. The Voyage and Adventures of William Moraley, an Indentured Servant* (University Park, Pennsylvania: The Pennsylvania State University Press, 1992), pp. 139; 140.

19. *The General Evening Post*, 11–13 February 1777, p. 3; *The Public Advertiser*, 13 February 1777, p. 3; *The Hampshire Chronicle*, 17 February 1777p. 3.

20. *Life of James Aitken*, pp. 21; 22.

21. *The Hampshire Chronicle*, 17 February 1777, p. 4.

22. NMM, *Portsmouth Dockyard Resident Commissioners' Reports to the Navy Board*, POR/F/16, 1775–1778.

23. N.A.M. Rodger, *The Wooden World. An Anatomy of the Georgian Navy* (London: Collins, 1986), pp. 170–178.

24. "Trial of James Hill," col. 1333.

25. NMM, *Navy Board Letters*, ADM/B/193, 1776.

26. *The Hampshire Chronicle*, 17 February 1777, p. 3.

27. *The Hampshire Chronicle*, 17 February 1777, p. 4.

28. John Harold Plumb, *England in the Eighteenth Century* (Baltimore: Penguin Books, 1960), pp. 38–40; Eveline Cruickshanks, "The Political Management of Sir Robert Walpole, 1720–42," in *Britain in the Age of Walpole*, ed. Jeremy Black, *Problems in Focus* (London: Macmillan, 1984), p. 12.

29. John Brewer, "The Wilkites and the Law 1763–1774: a Study of Radical Notions of Governance," in *An Ungovernable People. The English and their Law in the Seventeenth and Eighteenth Centuries*, ed. John Brewer and John Styles (New Brunswick, New Jersey: Rutgers University Press, 1980), pp. 170–171.

30. Colin Bonwick, *English Radicals and the American Revolution* (Chapel Hill: University of North Carolina Press, 1977), pp. 11–12.

31. Edward P. Thompson, *The Making of the English Working Class* (London: Victor Gollancz, 1964), pp. 58–59.

32. R.R. Palmer, *The Age of the Democratic Revolution. A Political History of Europe and America, 1760–1800*, 2 vols., vol. 1 (Princeton: Princeton University Press, 1959), p. 239.

33. Thomas Paine, *Rights of Man, Common Sense, and Other Political Writings*, ed. Mark Philp (Oxford: Oxford University Press, 1995), pp. 20; 53.

34. Colin Bonwick, *English Radicals and the American Revolution* (Chapel Hill: University of North Carolina Press, 1977), p. 40.

35. Edward P. Thompson, *The Making of the English Working Class* (London: Victor Gollancz, 1964), p. 27.

36. Jack Fruchtman, *Thomas Paine. Apostle of Freedom* (New York: Four Walls Eight Windows, 1994), p. 209.

37. Richard Price, *Observations on the Nature of Civil Liberty, the Principles of Government, and the Justice and Policy of the War with America*, eighth ed. (London: T. Cadell, 1778), p. 56.

38. Jack Fruchtman, "The Apocalyptic Politics of Richard Price and Joseph Priestley: a Study in Late Eighteenth-century English Republican Radicalism," *Transations of the American Philosophical Society* 73, no. 4 (1983), p. 104.

39. Linda Colley, *Britons: Forging the Nation 1707–1837* (New Haven: Yale University Press, 1992), p. 140.

40. Dalphy I. Fogerstrom, "Scottish Opinion and the American Revolution," *William and Mary Quarterly* 9, no. April (1954), p. 256.

41. *Life of James Aitken*, pp. 22–23.

42. Once, for example, he was observed "grinding charcoal on a painter's colour-stone, quite fine, and breaking gunpowder with a knife, as painters do vermillion, to mix the two in clear water till it came to the consistency of new milk." See *The Hampshire Chronicle*, 17 February 1777, p. 3.

43. NMM, *Portsmouth Dockyard Officers' Reports to the Navy Board*, POR/D/20, 1775–1777; NMM, *Portsmouth Dockyard Resident Commissioners' Reports to the Navy Board*, POR/F/16, 1775–1778; *Life of James Aitken*, p. 24.

44. NMM, *Navy Board Letters*, ADM/B/193, 1776.

45. "Trial of James Hill," col. 1343.

46. Brian Lavery, ed., *Shipboard Life and Organisation, 1731–1815*, vol. 138,

Publications of the Navy Record Society (Aldershot: Ashgate Publishing Limited, 1998), p. 451.

47. *Portsmouth Guide*, p. 25. "The Voyage of Don Manoel Gonzales (Late Merchant) of the City of Lisbon in Portugal, to Great Britain," in *A General Collection of the Best and Most Interesting Voyages and Travels in All Parts of the World; Many of which Are Now First Translated into English*, ed. J.H. Pinkerton (Philadelphia: Kimber and Contrad, 1810), p. 30.

48. Daniel Defoe, *Tour thro' the Whole Island of Great Britain. Divided into Circuits or Journies*, 4 vols., vol. 1 (London: D. Browne... 1762), p. 202.

49. NMM, Sandwich Papers, SAN F/45c/16, 13 August 1773.

50. Henry Kitson, "The Early History of Portsmouth Dockyard, 1496–1800, IV," *Mariner's Mirror* 34 (1948), p. 273; Roger Morriss, *The Royal Dockyards during the Revolutionary and Napoleonic Wars* (Leicester: Leicester University Press, 1983), p. 45.

51. Philip MacDougall, *Royal Dockyards* (London: David & Charles, 1982), pp. 119–120.

52. *The London Evening-Post*, 3–5 July 1760, p. 2–3.

53. Philip MacDougall, *Royal Dockyards* (London: David & Charles, 1982), p. 120.

54. *The Gazetteer and New Daily Advertiser*, 30 July 1770, p. 2.

55. *The Gazetteer and New Daily Advertiser*, 31 July 1770, p. 2.

56. *The Gazetteer and New Daily Advertiser*, 2 August 1770, p. 2.

57. *The Gazetteer and New Daily Advertiser*, 3 August 1770, p. 4.

58. *The Gazetteer and New Daily Advertiser*, 14 August 1770, p. 2.

59. *The Gazetteer and New Daily Advertiser*, 11 August 1770, p. 4.

60. *The Gazetteer and New Daily Advertiser*, 8 August 1770, p. 1.

61. *The London Evening-Post*, 27–29 August 1770, p. 3.

62. *The London Evening-Post*, 17–19 September 1770, p. 3.

63. Philip MacDougall, *Royal Dockyards* (London: David & Charles, 1982), p. 121.

64. *Life of James Aitken*, p. 59.

65. Philip MacDougall, *Royal Dockyards* (London: David & Charles, 1982), p. 87; B.H. Patterson, *A Military Heritage. A History of Portsmouth and Portsea Town Fortifications* (Portsmouth: Acme Printing Co. Ltd., 1987), p. 23.

66. J.A. Lowe, ed., *Records of the Portsmouth Division of Marines 1764–1800*, vol. 7, *Portsmouth Record Series* (Portsmouth: Published by the City of Portsmouth, 1990), pp. xxx–xxxi.

67. Margaret J. Hoad, *Portsmouth—as Others Have Seen it. Part I 1540–1790*, vol. 15, *Portsmouth Papers* (Portsmouth: Portsmouth City Council, 1972), p. 18.

68. James M. Haas, "The Royal Dockyards: the Earliest Visitations and Reform 1749–1778," *Historical Journal* 13, no. 2 (1970), pp. 206–207; Philip MacDougall, *Royal Dockyards* (London: David & Charles, 1982), p. 100; R.J.B. Knight, ed., *Portsmouth Dockyard Papers 1774–1783: the American War. A Calendar*, vol. 6, *Portsmouth Record Series* (Portsmouth: Published by the City of Portsmouth, 1987), pp. 47–48.

69. Daniel Defoe, *Tour thro' the Whole Island of Great Britain. Divided into Circuits or Journies*, 4 vols., vol. 1 (London: D. Browne... 1762), pp. 205–206.

70. Roger Morriss, *The Royal Dockyards during the Revolutionary and Napoleonic Wars* (Leicester: Leicester University Press, 1983), p. 104.

71. *Life of James Aitken*, p. 24.

72. *The Hampshire Chronicle*, 17 February 1777, p. 3.

73. NMM, *Navy Board Letters*, ADM/B/193, 1776.

CHAPTER FIVE

1. *Life of James Aitken*, pp. 25–26.

2. Lloyd Kramer, *Lafayette in Two Worlds. Public Cultures and Personal Identities in an Age of Revolution* (Chapel Hill: The University of North Carolina Press, 1996), p. 18.

3. Charles Royster, *A Revolutionary People at War. The Continental Army and American Character, 1775–1783* (Chapel Hill: University of North Carolina Press, 1979), p. 18.

4. William B. Willcox, ed., *The Papers of Benjamin Franklin*, vol. 23 (New Haven: Yale University Press, 1983), p. 173.

5. PMRS, S3/173/98, 23 March 1776; S3/174/6, 2 May 1776; S3/175/18, 31 December 1776.

6. Charles Royster, *A Revolutionary People at War. The Continental Army and American Character, 1775–1783* (Chapel Hill: University of North Carolina Press, 1979), p. 90.

7. *Life of James Aitken*, p. 26.

8. Adam Gopnik, ed. 2004. *Americans in Paris. A Literary Anthology*. (New York: The Library of America, 2004), p. 2.

9. *Life of James Aitken*, p. 26.

10. Alexander Law, *Education in Edinburgh in the Eighteenth Century*, (London: University of London Press Ltd, 1965), p. 211.

11. Frederick A. Pottle, ed., *Boswell on the Grand Tour: Germany and Switzerland 1764* (London: William Heinemann Ltd, 1953), p. 213.

12. Thomas P. Abernethy, "Commercial Activities of Silas Deane in France," *American Historical Review* 39, no. 3 (1934), pp. 477–485; Kalman Goldstein, "Silas Deane: Preparations for Rascality," *Historian* 43, no. 1 (1980), pp. 75–97.

13. Julian P. Boyd, "Silas Deane: Death by a Kindly Teacher of Treason? Part I," *William and Mary Quarterly* 16, no. 2 (1959), p. 166.

14. Orville T. Murphy, "The View from Versailles. Charles Gravier Comte de Vergennes's Perceptions of the American Revolution," in *Diplomacy and Revolution. The Franco-American Alliance of 1778*, ed. Ronald Hoffman and Peter J. Albert (Charlottesville: University Press of Virginia, 1981), pp. 112–114.

15. Edward Bancroft, *A Narrative of the Objects and Proceedings of Silas Deane, as Commissioner of the United Colonies to France; Made to the British Government in 1776*, ed. Paul Leicester Ford (Brooklyn: Historical Printing Club, 1891), pp. 26–27. Orville T. Murphy. *Charles Gravier, Comte de Vergennes: French Diplomacy in the Age of Revolution, 1719–1787* (Albany: State University of New York Press, 1982), p. 240.

16. William B. Willcox, ed., *The Papers of Benjamin Franklin*, vol. 23 (New Haven: Yale University Press, 1983), p. 211.

17. Deane's version of their encounter, complete with the quotes that appear here, can be found in Charles Isham, ed. *Collections of the New-York Historical Society*, vol. 20 (New York: New-York Historical Society, 1888), pp. 6–11.

18. Charles Isham, ed., *Collections of the New-York Historical Society*, vol. 20 (New York: New-York Historical Society, 1888), pp. 8–11.

19. *Life of James Aitken*, pp. 27–30.

20. *The Hampshire Chronicle*, 17 March 1777, p. 3.

21. Charles Isham, ed., *Collections of the New-York Historical Society*, vol. 20 (New York: New-York Historical Society, 1888), pp. 6–7.

22. "Trial of James Hill," col. 1366; *The London Magazine*, March 1777, p. 116.

23. "Trial of James Hill," col.s 1346–1347.

24. Julian P. Boyd, "Silas Deane: Death by a Kindly Teacher of Treason? Part II," *William and Mary Quarterly* 16, no. 3 (1959), p. 342.

CHAPTER SIX

1. *Life of James Aitken*, p. 36.

2. NMM, *Letters from the Navy Board*, POR/G/1, 1773–1803.

3. "Trial of James Hill," col. 1330.

4. *The Public Advertiser*, 22 January 1777, p. 3.

5. "Trial of James Hill," col. 1342.

6. "Trial of James Hill," col. 1345.

7. "Trial of James Hill," col.s 1341–1342.

8. *Life of James Aitken*, p. 37.

9. *Life of James Aitken*, p. 37.

10. NMM, *Navy Board Warrants*, POR/A/27, 1775–1777. NMM, *Portsmouth Dockyard Resident Commissioners' Letters to the Admiralty*, POR/H/10, 1774–1778.

11. "Trial of James Hill," col. 1331.

12. Philip MacDougall, *Royal Dockyards* (London: David & Charles, 1982), p. 14.

13. *Life of James Aitken*, p. 38.

14. NMM, *Portsmouth Dockyard Officers' Reports to the Navy Board*, POR/D/20, 1775–1777.

15. "Trial of James Hill," col. 1324.

16. *Life of James Aitken*, p. 40.

17. "Trial of James Hill," col. 1343.

18. NMM, *Navy Board Letters*, ADM/B/193, 1776. PMRS, *Index to the Twelfth Rate of 1775 for Portsmouth Common in the Parish of Portsea, as Compiled by E. Edwards in 1982*, 1775.

19. *Life of James Aitken*, p. 41.

20. NMM, *Navy Board Warrants*, POR/A/27, 1775–1777.

21. *Life of James Aitken*, p. 31.

22. PMRS, S3/179/43, 26 August 1779; S3/177/48, 24 December 1777.

23. Jessica F. Warner, *Craze. Gin and Debauchery in an Age of Reason*, hardcover ed. (New York: Four Walls Eight Windows, 2002), p. 29.

24. PMRS, *Index to the Twelfth Rate of 1775 for Portsmouth Common in the Parish of Portsea, as Compiled by E. Edwards in 1982*, 1775.
25. NMM, *Navy Board Letters*, ADM/B/193, 1776.
26. *Life of James Aitken*, p. 42.
27. "Trial of James Hill," col. 1333.
28. *The Hampshire Chronicle*, 17 March 1777, p. 3.
29. "Trial of James Hill," col. 1344.
30. NMM, *Portsmouth Dockyard Resident Commissioners' Reports to the Navy Board*, POR/F/16, 1775–1778.
31. NMM, *Navy Board Letters*, ADM/B/193, 1776; "Trial of James Hill, col. 1342.
32. PMRS, S3/41/95, 9 July 1703.
33. *Life of James Aitken*, pp. 42–43.
34. NMM, *Navy Board Letters*, ADM/B/193, 1776.
35. NMM, *Navy Board Letters*, ADM/B/193, 1776.

CHAPTER SEVEN
1. *Life of James Aitken*, p. 43.
2. "Trial of James Hill," col.s 1343–1344.
3. *Life of James Aitken*, pp. 43–44.
4. *Portsmouth Guide*, pp. 74–76.
5. *Life of James Aitken*, p. 44.
6. *Life of James Aitken*, pp. 44–45.
7. Julian P. Boyd, "Silas Deane: Death by a Kindly Teacher of Treason? Part I," *William and Mary Quarterly* 16, no. 2 (1959), pp. 165–187.
8. Edward Bancroft, *An Essay on the Natural History of Guiana* (London: T. Becket and P.A. DeHondt, 1769).
9. Samuel Flagg Bemis, "British Secret Service and the French-American Alliance," *American Historical Review* 29, no. 3 (1924), pp. 474–475.
10. Edward Bancroft, *Remarks on the Review of the Controversy between Great Britain and her Colonies. In which the Errors of its Author are Exposed, and the Claims of the Colonies Vindicated, upon the Evidence of Historical Facts and Authentic Records* (London: T. Becket and P.A. De Hondt, 1769).
11. Edward Bancroft, *The History of Charles Wentworth, Esq. In a Series of Letters. Interspersed with a Variety of Important Reflections Calculated to Improve Morality, and Promote the Oeconomy of Human Life*, vol. 1 (London: T. Becket, 1770).
12. Edward Bancroft, *A Narrative of the Objects and Proceedings of Silas Deane, as Commissioner of the United Colonies to France; Made to the British Government in 1776*, ed. Paul Leicester Ford (Brooklyn: Historical Printing Club, 1891); Samuel Flagg Bemis, "British Secret Service and the French-American Alliance," *American Historical Review* 29, no. 3 (1924), pp. 474–495.
13. *Life of James Aitken*, p. 47.
14. Bryant Lillywhite, *London Coffee-houses. A Reference Book of Coffee Houses of the Seventeenth, Eighteenth and Nineteenth Centuries* (London: George Allen and Unwin Ltd, 1963), pp. 510–511.
15. *The General Evening Post*, 11–13 March 1777, p. 1.

16. *Life of James Aitken*, p. 46.
17. NMM, *Navy Board Letters*, ADM/B/193, 1776.
18. Daniel A. Baugh, *British Naval Administration in the Age of Walpole* (Princeton: Princeton University Press, 1965), p. 295. PMRS, *Index to the Twelfth Rate of 1775 for Portsmouth Common in the Parish of Portsea, as Compiled by E. Edwards in 1982*, 1775.
19. *The Gazetteer and New Daily Advertiser*, 30 July 1770, p. 2.
20. NMM, Sandwich Papers, SAN F/10/51, 9 March 1777.
21. *The General Evening Post*, 7–10 December 1776, p. 3.
22. *The Morning Chronicle, and London Advertiser*, 10 December 1776, p. 2.
23. Daniel A. Baugh, ed., *Naval Administration 1715–1750*, vol. 120, *Publications of the Navy Record Society* (London: The Navy Records Society, 1977), p. 310.
24. *The Scots Magazine*, December 1776, p. 673.
25. NMM, *Navy Board Letters*, ADM/B/193, 1776.
26. NMM, *Navy Board Letters*, ADM/B/194, 1777.
27. NMM, Sandwich Papers, SAN F/45c/63, 8 December 1776. NMM, Sandwich Papers, SAN F/45c/63, 8 December 1776.
28. *The Public Advertiser*, 16 December 1776, p. 2.
29. *The General Evening Post*, 7–10 December 1776, p. 4.
30. NMM, *Portsmouth Dockyard Resident Commissioners' Reports to the Navy Board*, POR/F/16, 1775–1778.
31. NMM, *Portsmouth Dockyard Officers' Reports to the Navy Board*, POR/D/20, 1775–1777.
32. NMM, *Letters from the Navy Board*, POR/G/1, 1773–1803.
33. *The St. James's Chronicle*, 4–6 February 1777, p. 4.
34. NMM, *Portsmouth Dockyard Officers' Reports to the Navy Board*, POR/D/20, 1775–1777.
35. NMM, *Letters from the Navy Board*, POR/G/1, 1773–1803.
36. *The Hampshire Chronicle*, 16 December 1776, p. 3.
37. *The St. James's Chronicle*, 7–10 December 1776, p. 3.
38. *The General Evening Post*, 7–10 December 1776, p. 3.
39. *The General Evening Post*, 7–10 December 1776, p. 3.
40. NMM, Sandwich Papers, SAN F/45c/63, 8 December 1776.
41. NMM, *Navy Board Letters*, ADM/B/193, 1776.
42. *The General Evening Post*, 7–10 December 1776, p. 1.

CHAPTER EIGHT
1. PRO, *Navy Board Minute Book*, ADM 106/2594, 1776.
2. NMM, *Navy Board Letters*, ADM/B/193, 1776.
3. NMM, *Portsmouth Dockyard Officers' Reports to the Navy Board*, POR/D/20, 1775–1777.
4. PRO, *Navy Board Minute Book*, ADM 106/2594, 1776.
5. National Maritime Museum, *Portsmouth Dockyard Resident Commissioners' Reports to the Navy Board*, POR/F/16, 1775–1778.

6. NMM, *Portsmouth Dockyard Resident Commissioners' Reports to the Navy Board*, POR/F/16, 1775–1778.

7. NMM, Sandwich Papers, SAN F/10/16, 15 January 1777.

8. NMM, Sandwich Papers, SAN F/10/23, 23 January 1777.

9. NMM, *Navy Board Letters*, ADM/B/193, 1776.

10. NMM, *Portsmouth Dockyard Resident Commissioners' Reports to the Navy Board*, POR/F/16, 1775–1778.

11. NMM, *Portsmouth Dockyard Officers' Reports to the Navy Board*, POR/D/20, 1775–1777.

12. NMM, *Navy Board Letters*, ADM/B/193, 1776.

13. *The Hampshire Chronicle*, 27 January 1777, p. 3; "Trial of James Hill," col. 1339.

14. *The General Evening Post*, 16–18 January 1777, p. 3.

15. E. Shiercliff, *The Bristol & Hotwell Guide* (Bristol: Mills, and Co., 1809), p. 17; R.I. James, "Bristol Society in the Eighteenth Century," in *Bristol and its Adjoining Counties*, ed. C.M. MacInnes and W.F. Whittard (Bristol: University of Bristol, 1955), p. 232.

16. *Felix Farley's Bristol Journal*, 25 January 1777, p. 3.

17. R.I. James, "Bristol Society in the Eighteenth Century," in *Bristol and its Adjoining Counties*, ed. C.M. MacInnes and W.F. Whittard (Bristol: University of Bristol, 1955), p. 233; Elizabeth Ralph, *The Streets of Bristol* (Bristol: The Bristol Branch of the Historical Association, 2001), pp. 16–18.

18. W.E. Minchinton, ed., *Politics and the Port of Bristol in the Eighteenth Century. The Petitions of the Society of Merchant Venturers 1698–1803*, vol. 23, *Bristol Record Society's Publications* (Bristol: Bristol Record Society, 1963), p. 137.

19. *Life of James Aitken*, p. 54.

20. "Trial of James Hill," col. 1340

21. *The General Evening Post*, 16–18 January 1777, p. 3.

22. *Felix Farley's Bristol Journal*, 25 January 1777, p. 3.

23. *Life of James Aitken*, pp. 48–49.

24. *Felix Farley's Bristol Journal*, 25 January 1777, p. 3.

25. *Life of James Aitken*, p. 53.

26. "Trial of James Hill," col. 1346.

27. *The General Evening Post*, 16–18 January 1777, p. 3.

28. *Life of James Aitken*, p. 53.

29. *The Hampshire Chronicle*, 27 January 1777, p. 5.

30. *Life of James Aitken*, p. 57.

31. PRO, *Hanoverian State Papers Domestic 1714–1782*, SP 37/12, 5 February 1777.

32. *The Hampshire Chronicle*, 27 January 1777, p. 4.

33. *The London Gazette*, 14–18 January 1777, p. 1.

34. *Felix Farley's Bristol Journal*, 25 January 1777, p. 3.

35. *Life of James Aitken*, p. 57.

36. *Felix Farley's Bristol Journal*, 25 January 1777, p. 3.

37. PRO, *Hanoverian State Papers Domestic 1714–1782*, SP 37/12, 21 January 1777.

38. George H. Guttridge, ed., *The Correspondence of Edmund Burke*, vol. 3 (Chicago: University of Chicago Press, 1961), p. 325.

39. *Felix Farley's Bristol Journal,* 25 January 1777, p. 3.
40. *The Public Advertiser,* 22 January 1777, p. 2.
41. BRO, *Town Clerk's Letter Boxes,* box 119, 1777.
42. PRO, *Hanoverian State Papers Domestic 1714–1782,* SP 37/12, 18 January 1777.
43. PRO, *Hanoverian State Papers Domestic 1714–1782,* SP 37/12, 19 January 1777.
44. PRO, *Hanoverian State Papers Domestic 1714–1782,* SP 37/12, 21 January 1777.
45. *The Hampshire Chronicle,* 27 January 1777, p. 4.
46. *The Hampshire Chronicle,* 27 January 1777, p. 4.
47. *The St. James's Chronicle,* 16–18 January 1777, p. 1.
48. *The General Evening Post,* 16–18 January 1777, p. 1.
49. PRO, *Hanoverian State Papers Domestic 1714–1782,* SP 37/12, 21 January 1777; *The Public Advertiser,* 22 January 1777, p. 2.
50. *The St. James's Chronicle,* 16–18 January 1777, p. 1.
51. *The Public Advertiser,* 22 January 1777, p. 2.
52. *The General Evening Post,* 16–18 January 1777, p. 3.
53. *The General Evening Post,* 16–18 January 1777, p. 1.
54. P.T. Underdown, *Bristol and Burke,* ed. Patrick McGrath (Bristol: The Bristol Branch of the Historical Association, 1961), p. 9.
55. George H. Guttridge, ed., *The Correspondence of Edmund Burke,* vol. 3 (Chicago: University of Chicago Press, 1961), pp. 320–321.
56. *Felix Farley's Bristol Journal,* 25 January 1777, p. 2.
57. George H. Guttridge, ed., *The Correspondence of Edmund Burke,* vol. 3 (Chicago: University of Chicago Press, 1961), p. 321.
58. *The St. James's Chronicle,* 16–18 January 1777, p. 3; *The General Evening Post,* 16–18 January 1777, p. 1.
59. George H. Guttridge, ed., *The Correspondence of Edmund Burke,* vol. 3 (Chicago: University of Chicago Press, 1961), pp. 325–326.
60. PRO, *Hanoverian State Papers Domestic 1714–1782,* SP 37/12, 5 February 1777.
61. *Felix Farley's Bristol Journal,* 25 January 1777, p. 3.
62. *The St. James's Chronicle,* 16–18 January 1777, p. 2.
63. *The St. James's Chronicle,*16–18 January 1777, p. 1.
64. *The London Magazine,* February 1777, p. 110.
65. *The General Evening Post,* 16–18 January 1777, p. 1.
66. *The Public Advertiser,* 22 January 1777, p. 3.
67. *The General Evening Post,* 16–18 January 1777, p. 4.
68. Major had enemies. One, writing under the pseudonym of "Justice," even accused him of planting the canister in an attempt to secure a promotion; the same correspondent hoped to see Major "fall before his accusers like dragon before the ark, guilty, guilty." See NMM, *Navy Board Letters,* ADM/B/194, 1777.
69. NMM, *Portsmouth Dockyard Officers' Reports to the Navy Board,* POR/D/20, 1775–1777.
70. NMM, *Navy Board Letters,* ADM/B/194, 1777; John Fortescue, ed., *The Correspondence of King George the Third,* 6 vols., vol. 3 (London: Macmillan and Co., Limited, 1928), pp. 416–417.
71. *The General Evening Post,* 16–18 January 1777, p. 1.

72. NMM, Sandwich Papers, SAN F/9/143, no date 1777?.

73. *The St. James's Chronicle*, 16–18 January 1777, p. 4.

74. *The General Evening Post*, 16–18 January 1777, p. 4.

75. *The General Evening Post*, 16–18 January 1777, p. 4.

76. *The St. James's Chronicle*, 16–18 January 1777, p. 2.

77. NMM, Sandwich Papers, SAN F/10/23, 23 January 1777; PRO, *Hanoverian State Papers Domestic 1714–1782*, SP 37/12, 23 January 1777.

78. *The Hampshire Chronicle*, 27 January 1777, p. 3.

79. *The General Evening Post*, 16–18 January 1777, p. 4.

80. *The St. James's Chronicle*, 16–18 January 1777, p. 1.

81. *The Public Advertiser*, 22 January 1777, p. 3.

82. *The Hampshire Chronicle*, 27 January 1777, p. 1.

83. *The Hampshire Chronicle*, 27 January 1777, p. 2.

84. *The St. James's Chronicle*, 16–18 January 1777, p. 4; *The Public Advertiser*, 22 January 1777, p. 2.

85. *The Public Advertiser*, 22 January 1777, p. 2.

86. *The Hampshire Chronicle*, 27 January 1777, p. 2.

87. *The General Evening Post*, 16–18 January 1777, p. 4.

88. *Felix Farley's Bristol Journal*, 25 January 1777, p. 4.

89. *The Public Advertiser*, 22 January 1777, p. 2.

90. Charles Isham, ed., *Collections of the New-York Historical Society*, vol. 19 (New York: New-York Historical Society, 1887), pp. 484–485.

91. William Cobbett, ed., *The Parliamentary History of England, from the Earliest Period to the Year 1803*, vol. 19 (London: T.C. Hansard, 1814), col. 5.

92. NMM, *Letters from the Navy Board*, POR/G/1, 1773–1803.

93. NMM, *Portsmouth Dockyard Resident Commissioners' Letters to the Admiralty*, POR/H/10, 1774–1778.

94. *The Newcastle Courant*, 1 February 1777, p. 1.

95. PRO, *Navy Board Minute Book*, ADM 106/2595, 1777.

96. NMM, *Portsmouth Dockyard Resident Commissioners' Letters to the Admiralty*, POR/H/10, 1774–1778; NMM, *Portsmouth Dockyard Officers' Reports to the Navy Board*, POR/D/20, 1775–1777.

97. *The St. James's Chronicle*, 16–18 January 1777, p. 5.

98. *The General Evening Post*, 16–18 January 1777, p. 3.

CHAPTER NINE

1. *The General Evening Post*, 21–23 January 1777, p. 3.

2. Daniel A. Baugh, *British Naval Administration in the Age of Walpole* (Princeton: Princeton University Press, 1965), p. 295.

3. PRO, *Out-letters, Secretary of the Admiralty*, ADM 2/736, 1776–1777, pp. 118–119.

4. Michael Harris, "Print and Politics in the Age of Walpole," in *Britain in the Age of Walpole*, ed. Jeremy Black, *Problems in Focus* (London: Macmillan, 1984), p. 190; John Styles, "Sir John Fielding and the Problem of Criminal Investigation in Eighteenth-century England," *Transactions of the Royal Historical Society* 33 (1983), p. 137.

5. *Life of James Aitken*, p. 58.

6. *Life of James Aitken*, p. 59.

7. John Fortescue, ed., *The Correspondence of King George the Third*, 6 vols., vol. 3 (London: Macmillan and Co., Limited, 1928), p. 426.

8. *Life of James Aitken*, pp. 59–60; NMM, *Letters from the Navy Board*, POR/G/1, 1773–1803.

9. *The London Magazine*, February 1777, p. 109; "Trial of James Hill," col. 1345.

10. John Motherhill, *The Case of John Motherhill, the Brightelmstone Taylor Who Was Tried at East Grinstead for a Rape* (London: Printed for R. Randall, 1786), p. 10.

11. *State of the Prisons*, p. 27. The best biography of Howard remains Dereck Lionel Howard, *John Howard: Prison Reformer* (New York: Archer House Inc., 1963).

12. *State of the Prisons*, pp. 7; 9; 12.

13. BRO, *Town Clerk's Letter Boxes*, box 119, 1777.

14. NMM, *Portsmouth Dockyard Resident Commissioners' Reports to the Navy Board*, POR/F/16, 1775–1778.

15. Charles Isham, ed., *Collections of the New-York Historical Society*, vol. 19 (New York: New-York Historical Society, 1887), p. 484.

16. *The Hampshire Chronicle*, 3 February 1777, p. 1.

17. *The St. James's Chronicle*, 1–4 February 1777, p. 1; NMM, *Portsmouth Dockyard Resident Commissioners' Letters to the Admiralty*, POR/H/10, 1774–1778.

18. PRO, *Hanoverian State Papers Domestic 1714–1782*, SP 37/12, 3 February 1777.

19. *The St. James's Chronicle*, 1–4 February 1777, p. 3.

20. Daniel Paterson, *A New and Accurate Description of the Direct and Principal Cross Roads in England and Wales, and Part of the Roads of Scotland*, 15 ed. (London: 1811), p. 45; Thomas de Quincy, *The English Mail Coach* (London: Blackie & Son Limited, 1913), p. 86.

21. *The General Evening Post*, 21–23 January 1777, p. 4.

22. *Narrative of Certain Facts*, p. 10.

23. *The General Evening Post*, 21–23 January 1777, p. 4.

24. PRO, *Hanoverian State Papers Domestic 1714–1782*, SP 37/12, 3 February 1777.

25. *The General Evening Post*, 21–23 January 1777 p. 1.

26. *The General Evening Post*, 21–23 January 1777, p. 3; *The London Magazine*, February 1777, pp. 109–110.

27. *The Public Advertiser*, 10 February 1777, p. 2.

28. *The General Evening Post*, 21–23 January 1777, p. 3; *The St. James's Chronicle*, 1–4 February 1777, p. 3.

29. *Felix Farley's Bristol Journal*, 8 February 1777, p. 3.

30. *The London Magazine*, February 1777, p. 122.

31. *The Westminster Magazine*, March 1777, p. 131.

32. "Trial of James Hill," col.1332.

33. Charles Isham, ed., *Collections of the New-York Historical Society*, vol. 20 (New York: New-York Historical Society, 1888), p. 3.

34. *The Westminster Magazine*, March 1777, p. 132.

35. *The Public Advertiser*, 10 February 1777, p. 3.

36. Charles Isham, ed., *Collections of the New-York Historical Society*, vol. 19 (New York: New-York Historical Society, 1887), p. 495.

37. *The Hampshire Chronicle*, 3 February 1777, p. 3.

38. *The St. James's Chronicle*, 1–4 February 1777, p. 1.

39. *The St. James's Chronicle*, 1–4 February 1777, p. 3; *The General Evening Post*, 21–23 January 1777, p. 3; *The Public Advertiser*, 10 February 1777, p. 3.

40. NMM, Sandwich Papers, SAN F/10/40, 12 February 1777.

41. *The St. James's Chronicle*, 1–4 February 1777, p. 1; *The General Evening Post*, 21–23 January 1777, p. 1.

42. *The Public Advertiser*, 10 February 1777, p. 3.

43. *The St. James's Chronicle*, 1–4 February 1777, p. 1; *The Public Advertiser*, 10 February 1777, p. 1.

44. *The Hampshire Chronicle*, 3 February 1777.

45. Vic A.C. Gatrell, *The Hanging Tree. Execution and the English People 1770–1868* (Oxford: Oxford University Press, 1994), p. 298.

46. Sylvia R. Frey, *The British Soldier in America: a Social History of Military Life* (Austin: University of Texas Press, 1981), p. 4.

47. Charles Isham, ed., *Collections of the New-York Historical Society*, vol. 19 (New York: New-York Historical Society, 1887), p. 484.

48. Michael Harris, "Trials and Criminal Biographies: a Case Study in Distribution," in *Sale and Distribution of Books from 1700*, ed. Robin Myers and Michael Harris (Oxford: Oxford Polytehnic Press, 1982), pp. 1–36; Andrea K. McKenzie, "Making Crime Pay: Motives, Marketing Strategies, and the Printed Literature of Crime in England, 1670–1770," in *Criminal Justice in the Old World and the New*, ed. Greg T. Smith, Allyson N. May, and Simon Devereaux (Toronto: University of Toronto, 1998), pp. 235–269.

49. John M. Beattie, *Crime and the Courts in England 1660–1800* (Princeton: Princeton University Press, 1986), p. 345. Vic A.C. Gatrell, *The Hanging Tree. Execution and the English People 1770–1868* (Oxford: Oxford University Press, 1994), p. 7; John M. Beattie, *Policing and Punishment in London 1660–1750. Urban Crime and the Limits of Terror* (Oxford: Oxford University Press, 2001), pp. 472–473.

50. *Narrative of Certain Facts*, pp. 4–6.

CHAPTER TEN

1. *The Public Advertiser*, 3 March 1777, p. 3.

2. *Narrative of Certain Facts*, p. 11.

3. John M. Beattie, *Crime and the Courts in England 1660–1800* (Princeton: Princeton University Press, 1986), p. 350; *Policing and Punishment in London 1660–1750. Urban Crime and the Limits of Terror* (Oxford: Oxford University Press, 2001), p. 261.

4. *The Hampshire Chronicle*, 3 March 1777, p. 3.

5. *The Public Advertiser*, 3 March 1777, p. 3.

6. *The Public Advertiser*, 3 March 1777, p. 3.

7. Martin Madan, *Thoughts on Executive Justice, with Respect to our Criminal Laws, Particularly on the Circuits* (London: J. Dodsley, 1785), p. 24; Douglas Hay, "Property, Authority, and the Criminal Law," in *Albion's Fatal Tree. Crime and*

Society in Eighteenth-century England (London: Allen Lane, 1975), p. 27. *Felix Farley's Bristol Journal*, 8 March 1777, p. 3; *The Hampshire Chronicle*, 3 March 1777, p. 3.

8. *The Edinburgh Advertiser*, 11–14 March 1777, 165; *The Caledonian Mercury*, 15 March 1777.

9. *The Hampshire Chronicle*, 3 March 1777, p. 3.

10. *The Public Advertiser*, 3 March 1777, p. 2.

11. *The Public Advertiser*, 3 March 1777, p. 3. *The London Chronicle*, 4 March 1777, p. 216.

12. *The General Evening Post*, 1–4 March 1777, p. 3.

13. *The Edinburgh Advertiser*, 11–14 March 1777, 165; *The Caledonian Mercury*, 15 March 1777.

14. PRO, *Gaol Book for the Western Circuit*, ASSI 23/8, part 1, 1774–1798.

15. John M. Beattie, *Crime and the Courts in England 1660–1800* (Princeton: Princeton University Press, 1986), p. 350.

16. "Trial of James Hill," col. 1332.

17. *The Trial of James Hill...Taken in Short-hand by a Gentleman at the Trial*, (London: E. Foresight, 1777), p. 3.

18. *The Hampshire Chronicle*, 3 March 1777, p. 3.

19. *Narrative of Certain Facts*, pp. 39–40.

20. "Trial of James Hill," col. 1330.

21. *The London Magazine*, March 1777, p. 118.

22. Peter Linebaugh, *The London Hanged. Crime and Civil Society in the Eighteenth Century* (London: Allen Lane, 1991), pp. 78; 85.

23. Douglas Hay, "Property, Authority, and the Criminal Law," in *Albion's Fatal Tree. Crime and Society in Eighteenth-century England* (London: Allen Lane, 1975), p. 27.

24. Edward Wynne, *Strictures on the Lives and Characters of the Most Eminent Lawyers of the Present Day* (London: G. Kearsley, 1790), p. 121.

25. Edward Wynne, *Strictures on the Lives and Characters of the Most Eminent Lawyers of the Present Day* (London: G. Kearsley, 1790), pp. 171–172.

26. Vic A.C. Gatrell, *The Hanging Tree. Execution and the English People 1770–1868* (Oxford: Oxford University Press, 1994), p. 512.

27. Donna T. Andrew and Randall McGowen, *The Perreaus and Mrs. Rudd: Forgery and Betrayal in Eighteenth-century London* (Berkeley: University of California Press, 2001), p. 225.

28. Peter Linebaugh, *The London Hanged. Crime and Civil Society in the Eighteenth Century* (London: Allen Lane, 1991), p. 360.

29. William K. Wimsatt and Frederick A. Pottle, eds., *Boswell for the Defence 1769–1774* (New York: McGraw-Hill Book Company, Inc., 1959), p. 176.

30. Henry Roscoe, *Lives of Eminent British Lawyers* (London: Longman, Rees, Orme, Brown, & Green, 1830), p. 191.

31. Romney Sedgwick, ed., *The History of Parliament. The House of Commons 1715–1745*, 2 vols., vol. 2 (New York: Oxford University Press, 1970), pp. 260–261; N.W. Surry and James H. Thomas, eds., *Book of Original Entries 1731–1751* (Portsmouth: Published by the City of Portsmouth, 1976), p. 105.

32. NMM, *Portsmouth Dockyard Officers' Reports to the Navy Board*, POR/D/20,

1775–1777; *Portsmouth Dockyard Resident Commissioners' Reports to the Navy Board*, POR/F/16, 1775–1778.

33. *The Westminster Magazine*, March 1777, p. 130.
34. Joseph Gurney, *The Trial (at Large) of James Hill* (London: J. Wenman, 1777).
35. "Trial of James Hill," col. 1328.
36. *Felix Farley's Bristol Journal*, 8 March 1777, p. 3; *The Public Advertiser*, 3 March 1777, p. 2.
37. *The Public Advertiser*, 3 March 1777, p. 2; *The Hampshire Chronicle*, 3 March 1777, p. 3.
38. "Trial of James Hill," col. 1333.
39. "Trial of James Hill," col. 1335.
40. *The Public Advertiser*, 3 March 1777, p. 2.
41. "Trial of James Hill," col. 1363.
42. *The Public Advertiser*, 3 March 1777, p. 2; Peter Orlando Hutchinson, ed., *The Diary and Letters of His Excellency Thomas Hutchinson*, vol. 2 (London: Sampson Low, Marston, Searle & Rivington, 1886), p. 141.
43. John M. Beattie, *Policing and Punishment in London 1660–1750. Urban Crime and the Limits of Terror* (Oxford: Oxford University Press, 2001), pp. 272–273.
44. *Felix Farley's Bristol Journal*, 8 March 1777, p. 3; *Felix Farley's Bristol Journal*, 8 March 1777, p. 4; "Trial of James Hill," col. 1363.
45. *The Hampshire Chronicle*, 3 March 1777, p. 3. *The London Magazine*, March 1777, p. 119.
46. *Narrative of Certain Facts*, p. 16.
47. "Trial of James Hill," col. 1364; *The Gentleman's Magazine*, March 1777, p. 123; *The London Magazine*, March 1777, p. 119.
48. *The General Evening Post*, 1–4 March 1777, p. 4.
49. *The General Evening Post*, 1–4 March 1777, p. 4; *The Hampshire Chronicle*, 3 March 1777, p. 3.
50. *The Public Advertiser*, 3 March 1777, p. 2.
51. "Trial of James Hill," col. 1363.
52. Vic A.C. Gatrell, *The Hanging Tree. Execution and the English People 1770–1868* (Oxford: Oxford University Press, 1994), p. 536; John M. Beattie, *Policing and Punishment in London 1660–1750. Urban Crime and the Limits of Terror* (Oxford: Oxford University Press, 2001), pp. 259–260.
53. *The Hampshire Chronicle*, 3 March 1777, p. 3.
54. PRO, *Gaol Book for the Western Circuit*, ASSI 23/8, part 1, 1774–1798; *The St. James's Chronicle*, 8–11 March 1777, p. 3.

CHAPTER ELEVEN

1. Van Muyden, ed. *A Foreign View of England in the Reigns of George I. and George II. The Letters of Monsieur César de Saussure to his Family* (London: John Murray), p. 123.
2. *The Hampshire Chronicle*, 17 March 1777, p. 3.
3. Leon Radzinowicz, *A History of English Criminal Law and its Administration from 1750*, vol. 1 (London: Stevens & Sons Limited, 1948), p. 168.

4. Daniel Defoe, *Street Robberies, Consider'd: the Reason of their Being so Frequent, with Probable Means to Prevent 'em* (London: J. Roberts, 1728), pp. 52–53.

5. *Narrative of Certain Facts*, pp. 14–15.

6. *Narrative of Certain Facts*, p. 23.

7. John Fortescue, ed., *The Correspondence of King George the Third*, 6 vols., vol. 3 (London: Macmillan and Co., Limited, 1928), pp. 423–427.

8. *The Hampshire Chronicle*, 17 March 1777, p. 4; *Felix Farley's Bristol Journal*, 15 March 1777, p. 3.

9. From *The Affecting Case of the Unfortunate Thomas Daniels, who Was Tried at the Sessions Held at the Old Bailey, September, 1761, for the Supposed Murder of his Wife*, as quoted by Philip Rawlings, *Drunks, Whores and Idle Apprentices. Criminal Biographies of the Eighteenth Century* (London: Routledge, 1992), pp. 8–9.

10. *The Hampshire Chronicle*, 17 March 1777, p. 4.

11. *Narrative of Certain Facts*, p. 38.

12. *The General Evening Post*, 6–8 March 1777, p. 5.

13. *The St. James's Chronicle*, 6–8 March 1777, p. 4.

14. *The Public Advertiser*, 4 March 1777, p. 2.

15. *State of the Prisons*, p. 353.

16. *Narrative of Certain Facts*, p. 30.

17. Daniel Defoe, *Street Robberies, Consider'd: the Reason of their Being so Frequent, with Probable Means to Prevent 'em* (London: J. Roberts, 1728), p. 53.

18. Bernard Mandeville, *An Enquiry into the Causes of the Frequent Executions at Tyburn* (London: J. Roberts, 1725), p. 17.

19. *State of the Prisons*, p. 357.

20. Jessica F. Warner, *Craze. Gin and Debauchery in an Age of Reason*, hardcover ed. (New York: Four Walls Eight Windows, 2002), pp. 46–47; Michael Ignatieff, *A Just Measure of Pain. the Penitentiary in the Industrial Revolution, 1750–1850* (New York: Pantheon Books, 1978), p. 37; John M. Beattie, *Crime and the Courts in England 1660–1800* (Princeton: Princeton University Press, 1986), p. 290.

21. Corporation of London Records Office, Miscellaneous MSS. 184.6, 6 February 1787.

22. *The Caledonian Mercury*, 15 March 1777; *The Edinburgh Advertiser*, 11–14 March 1777, p. 165.

23. *The Public Advertiser*, 4 March 1777, p. 2.

24. Alexander Smith, *Memoirs of the Life and Times of the Famous Jonathan Wild, Together with the History and Lives, of Modern Rogues, Several of 'em his Acquaintance, that Have Been Executed before and since his Death, for the High-way, Pad, Shop-lifting, House-breaking, Picking of Pockets, and Impudent Robbing in the Streets, and Court* (New York: Garland Publishing, Inc., 1973), pp. 217–218.

25. Peter Linebaugh, "The Tyburn Riot against the Surgeons," in *Albion's Fatal Tree. Crime and Society in Eighteenth-century England* (London: Allen Lane, 1975), pp. 82–83.

26. Leon Radzinowicz, *A History of English Criminal Law and its Administration from 1750*, vol. 1 (London: Stevens & Sons Limited, 1948), p. 179; Michael Harris,

"Trials and Criminal Biographies: a Case Study in Distribution," in *Sale and Distribution of Books from 1700*, ed. Robin Myers and Michael Harris (Oxford: Oxford Polytehnic Press, 1982), pp. 1–36.

27. "The Life, Travels, Exploits, Frauds and Robberies, of Charles Speckman, alias Brown, who Was Executed at TYBURN, on Wednesday the 23d of November, 1763," in *Drunks, Whores and Idle Apprentices. Criminal Biographies of the Eighteenth Century*, ed. Philip Rawlings (London: Routledge, 1992), p. 211.

28. NMM, Sandwich Papers, SAN F/10/54, 11 March 1777.

29. Leon Radzinowicz, *A History of English Criminal Law and its Administration from 1750*, vol. 1 (London: Stevens & Sons Limited, 1948), p. 169.

30. Daniel Defoe, *Street Robberies, Consider'd: the Reason of their Being so Frequent, with Probable Means to Prevent 'em* (London: J. Roberts, 1728), p. 52.

31. Peter Linebaugh, "The Tyburn Riot against the Surgeons," in *Albion's Fatal Tree. Crime and Society in Eighteenth-century England* (London: Allen Lane, 1975), p. 112.

32. "Clever Tom Clinch, Going to Be Hanged," in *The Poetical Works of Jonathan Swift* (London: Bell and Daldy, 1833), pp. 202–203.

33. Peter Linebaugh, "The Tyburn Riot against the Surgeons," in *Albion's Fatal Tree. Crime and Society in Eighteenth-century England* (London: Allen Lane, 1975), p. 111.

34. *The Hampshire Chronicle*, 17 March 1777, p. 3.

35. Peter Linebaugh, "The Tyburn Riot against the Surgeons," in *Albion's Fatal Tree. Crime and Society in Eighteenth-century England* (London: Allen Lane, 1975), p. 67. John Howard, *The State of the Prisons in England and Wales, with Preliminary Observations, and an Account of Some Foreign Prisons* (Warington: William Eyres, 1777), p. 359.

36. NMM, Sandwich Papers, SAN F/10/52, 10 March 1777; *The St. James's Chronicle*, 6–8 March 1777, p. 1.

37. Edward Topham, *Letters from Edinburgh; Written in the Years 1774 and 1775: Containing Some Observations on the Diversions, Customs, Manners, and Laws, of the Scotch Nation, During a Six Months Residence in Edinburgh*, 2 vols., vol. 1 (Dublin: W. Watson, 1780?), p. 77.

38. Leon Radzinowicz, *A History of English Criminal Law and its Administration from 1750*, vol. 1 (London: Stevens & Sons Limited, 1948), p. 171.

39. *The Hampshire Chronicle*, 17 March 1777, p. 3; *The St. James's Chronicle; or, British Evening-Post*, 6–8 March 1777, p. 3.

40. *Life of James Aitken*, pp. 61–62.

41. NMM, Sandwich Papers, SAN F/10/52, 10 March 1777.

42. *The St. James's Chronicle; or, British Evening-Post*, 6–8 March 1777, p. 3; *The Public Advertiser*, 4 March 1777, p. 2.

43. David Lyon, *The Sailing Navy List: All the Ships of the Royal Navy Built, Purchased and Captured 1688–1860, SNR Occasional Publications 5* (London: Conway Maritime Press, 1993), p. 205.

44. *The Pennsylvania Evening Post*, 25 February 1777, p. 104; PRO, *Out-letters from the Lords of the Admiralty*, ADM 2/245, 1776–1777.

45. *The Public Advertiser*, 4 March 1777, p. 2.

46. *The St. James's Chronicle; or, British Evening-Post*, 6–8 March 1777, p. 3.; *The Hampshire Chronicle*, 17 March 1777, p. 3.

47. Peter Stuart Christie, "Occupations in Portsmouth 1550–1851" (M.Phil., Portsmouth Polytechnic, 1976), p. 182.

48. Vic A.C. Gatrell, *The Hanging Tree. Execution and the English People 1770–1868* (Oxford: Oxford University Press, 1994), p. 7.

49. G.T. Crook, ed., *The Complete Newgate Calendar*, vol. 3 (London: Privately Printed for the Navarre Society, 1925), p. 316.

50. *The St. James's Chronicle*, 6–8 March 1777, p. 3.

51. J.A. Sharpe, "'Last Dying Speeches': Religion, Ideology and Public Execution in Seventeenth-century England," *Past and Present* 107 (1985), pp. 144–167.

52. NMM, Sandwich Papers, SAN F/10/52, 10 March 1777.

53. *Life of James Aitken*, pp. 62–63.

54. *John the Painter's Ghost: how he Appeared on the Night of his Execution to Lord Temple; and how his Lordship Did Communicate the Same at Full Court, to the Astonishment of All Present: Now Partially, and Circumstantially Related*, (London: J. Williams, 1777), pp. 2–3.

55. *Life of James Aitken*, pp. 63–64.

56. *The Hampshire Chronicle*, 17 March 1777, p. 3.

57. NMM, Sandwich Papers, SAN F/10/52, 10 March 1777.

58. William K. Wimsatt and Frederick A. Pottle, eds., *Boswell for the Defence 1769–1774* (New York: McGraw-Hill Book Company, Inc., 1959), p. 304.

59. *The Gentleman's Magazine*, March 1777, p. 123. Joseph Gurney, *The Trial (at Large) of James Hill; Otherwise James Hind; Otherwise, James Actzen* (London: G. Kearsly, 1777), p. 40.

60. Peter Linebaugh, "The Tyburn Riot against the Surgeons," in *Albion's Fatal Tree. Crime and Society in Eighteenth-century England* (London: Allen Lane, 1975), p. 104.

61. Daniel Defoe, *Street Robberies, Consider'd: the Reason of their Being so Frequent, with Probable Means to Prevent 'em* (London: J. Roberts, 1728), p. 52.

CHAPTER TWELVE

1. G.T. Crook, ed., *The Complete Newgate Calendar*, vol. 4 (London: Privately Printed for the Navarre Society, 1926), p. 17.

2. Warner, Jessica F. "Violence against and amongst Jews in an Early Modern Town. Tolerance and its Limits in Portsmouth, 1718–1781." *Albion* 35, no. 3 (2004), pp. 428–452.

3. *The Caledonian Mercury*, 15 March 1777.

4. *The Public Advertiser*, 8 March 1777, p. 2.

5. Vic A.C. Gatrell, *The Hanging Tree. Execution and the English People 1770–1868* (Oxford: Oxford University Press, 1994), p. 87.

6. Leon Radzinowicz, *A History of English Criminal Law and its Administration from 1750*, vol. 1 (London: Stevens & Sons Limited, 1948), p. 216.

7. Jessica F. Warner, *Craze. Gin and Debauchery in an Age of Reason*, paperback ed. (New York: Random House Trade Paperbacks, 2003), pp. 48–49.

8. G.T. Crook, ed., *The Complete Newgate Calendar*, vol. 4 (London: Privately Printed for the Navarre Society, 1926), p. 68.

9. PRO, *Out-letters from the Lords of the Admiralty*, ADM 2/245, 1776–1777, p. 261.

10. PRO, *Admiralty Out-letters*, ADM 2/1059, 1776–1779, pp. 79–80.

11. NMM, *Navy Board Warrants*, POR/A/27, 1775–1777.

12. Daniel A. Baugh, *British Naval Administration in the Age of Walpole* (Princeton: Princeton University Press, 1965), p. 309; T.S. Ashton, *Economic Fluctuations in England 1700–1800* (Oxford: Clarendon Press, 1959), p. 37.

13. NMM, *Navy Board Warrants*, POR/A/27, 1775–1777; NMM, *Letters from the Navy Board*, POR/G/1, 1773–1803.

14. PRO, *Out-letters from the Lords of the Admiralty*, ADM 2/245, 1776–1777, pp. 263–264.

15. *The General Evening Post*, 6–8 March 1777, pp. 3–4.

16. PRO, *Letters from the Lords of the Admiralty to the Secretaries of State*, ADM 2/373, 1776–1782, p. 29.

17. *The General Evening Post*, 6–8 March 1777, p. 5; *The Public Advertiser*, 8 March 1777, p. 2.

18. William B. Willcox, ed., *The Papers of Benjamin Franklin*, vol. 23 (New Haven: Yale University Press, 1983), pp. 531–532.

19. British Library, Auckland Papers, Additional MS. 34,413, 1776–1777; Benjamin Franklin Stevens, ed., *Facsimiles of Manuscripts Relating to America, 1773–1783*, 25 vols., vol. 2 (London: 1889), manuscript 145.

20. William B. Willcox, ed., *The Papers of Benjamin Franklin*, vol. 23 (New Haven: Yale University Press, 1983), p. lviii.

21. *The Public Advertiser*, 8 March 1777, p. 2.

22. Benjamin Franklin Stevens, ed., *Facsimiles of Manuscripts in European Archives Relating to America, 1773–1783*, 25 vols., vol. 1 (London: 1889), manuscripts 33; 35; 40; 43; 45.

23. Samuel Flagg Bemis, "British Secret Service and the French-American Alliance," *American Historical Review* 29, no. 3 (1924), pp. 493–494.

24. Jonathan R. Dull, *A Diplomatic History of the American Revolution* (New Haven: Yale University Press, 1985), p. 64.

25. Peter Orlando Hutchinson, ed., *The Diary and Letters of His Excellency Thomas Hutchinson*, vol. 2 (London: Sampson Low, Marston, Searle & Rivington, 1886), pp. 142; 144.

26. *The St. James's Chronicle*, 11–13 March 1777, p. 1.

27. *The Hampshire Chronicle*, 24 March 1777, p. 4.

28. Lewis Einstein, *Divided Loyalties: Americans in England during the War of Independence* (London: Cobden-Sanderson, 1933), p. 14; Julian P. Boyd, "Silas Deane: Death by a Kindly Teacher of Treason? Part II," *William and Mary Quarterly* 16, no. 3 (1959), pp. 339–340.

29. Charles Isham, ed., *Collections of the New-York Historical Society*, vol. 20 (New York: New-York Historical Society, 1888), p. 24.

30. Benjamin Franklin Stevens, ed., *Facsimiles of Manuscripts Relating to America, 1773–1783*, 25 vols., vol. 2 (London: 1889), manuscript 145.

31. William B. Willcox, ed., *The Papers of Benjamin Franklin*, vol. 23 (New Haven: Yale University Press, 1983), pp. 447–448.

32. Julian P. Boyd, William H. Gaines, and Joseph H. Harrison, eds., *The Papers of Thomas Jefferson*, vol. 14 (Princeton: Princeton University Press, 1958), p. 631.

33. Julian P. Boyd and Mina R. Bryan, eds., *The Papers of Thomas Jefferson*, vol. 13 (Princeton: Princeton University Press, 1956), p. 316.

34. Julian P. Boyd and Mina R. Bryan, eds., *The Papers of Thomas Jefferson*, vol. 13 (Princeton: Princeton University Press, 1956), pp. 468–469.

35. Julian P. Boyd and Mina R. Bryan, eds., *The Papers of Thomas Jefferson*, vol. 13 (Princeton: Princeton University Press, 1956), p. 466.

36. Julian P. Boyd, William H. Gaines, and Joseph H. Harrison, eds., *The Papers of Thomas Jefferson*, vol. 14 (Princeton: Princeton University Press, 1958), p. 287.

37. Simon Schama, *Citizens. A Chronicle of the French Revolution* (New York: Vintage Books, 1989), p. 39.

38. David Lyon, *The Sailing Navy List: All the Ships of the Royal Navy Built, Purchased and Captured 1688–1860, SNR Occasional Publications 5* (London: Conway Maritime Press, 1993), p. 205.

39. *Felix Farley's Bristol Journal*, 15 March 1777, p. 3.

40. NMM, Sandwich Papers, SAN F/10/51, 9 March 1777.

41. NMM, *Navy Board Warrants*, POR/A/27, 1775–1777.

42. William C. Stinchcombe, "A Note on Silas Deane's Death," *William and Mary Quarterly* 32, no. 4 (1975), p. 619.

43. Julian P. Boyd, William H. Gaines, and Joseph H. Harrison, eds., *The Papers of Thomas Jefferson*, vol. 14 (Princeton: Princeton University Press, 1958), pp. 630–631.

44. Julian P. Boyd and William H. Gaines, eds., *The Papers of Thomas Jefferson*, vol. 15 (Princeton: Princeton University Press, 1958), p. 353.

45. Sheldon S. Cohen, "Samuel Peters Comments on the Death of Silas Deane," *New England Quarterly* 40, no. 3 (1967), p. 427.

46. "Trial of James Hill," col. 1328.

47. John Campbell, *The Lives of the Chief Justices of England*, 3 vols., vol. 2 (London: John Murray, 1849), p. 561.

48. P.T. Underdown, *Bristol and Burke*, ed. Patrick McGrath (Bristol: The Bristol Branch of the Historical Association, 1961), p. 17.

49. *The Edinburgh Advertiser*, 11–14 March 1777, p. 172.

50. Paul Langford et al., eds., *The Writings and Speeches of Edmund Burke*, vol. 3 (Oxford: Clarendon Press, 1996), p. 338.

51. PRO, *Admiralty Out-letters*, ADM 2/1059, 1776–1779, p. 80.

52. Samuel Flagg Bemis, "British Secret Service and the French-American Alliance," *American Historical Review* 29, no. 3 (1924), pp. 493–494.

53. William C. Stinchcombe, "A Note on Silas Deane's Death," *William and Mary Quarterly* 32, no. 4 (1975), p. 620.

54. Alexander Law, *Education in Edinburgh in the Eighteenth Century, University of London Press Ltd* (London: 1965), p. 109.

55. Peter Orlando Hutchinson, ed., *The Diary and Letters of His Excellency Thomas Hutchinson*, vol. 2 (London: Sampson Low, Marston, Searle & Rivington, 1886), p. 142.

56. Vic A.C. Gatrell, *The Hanging Tree. Execution and the English People 1770–1868* (Oxford: Oxford University Press, 1994), p. 269.

57. Henry Slight and Julian Slight, *Chronicles of Portsmouth* (London: Lupton Relfe, 1828), p. 137.

58. *Hampshire Chronicle*, 22 November 1884, p. 7.

59. Neil L. York, *Burning the Dockyard: John the Painter and the American Revolution*, vol. 71, *The Portsmouth Papers* (Portsmouth: Portsmouth City Council, 2001), p. 19.

60. *John the Painter's Ghost: how he Appeared on the Night of his Execution to Lord Temple; and how his Lordship Did Communicate the Same at Full Court, to the Astonishment of All Present: Now Partially, and Circumstantially Related*, (London: J. Williams, 1777), p. 2.

61. Peter Linebaugh, "The Tyburn Riot against the Surgeons," in *Albion's Fatal Tree. Crime and Society in Eighteenth-century England* (London: Allen Lane, 1975), p. 106.

62. Miles Peter Andrews, *Fire and Water! A Comic Opera: in Two Acts. Performed at the Theatre-Royal in the Hay-Market* (Dublin: James and Richard Byrn, 1780), p. 17.

63. John Latimer, *The Annals of Bristol in the Eighteenth Century*, 3 vols., vol. 2 (Bristol: George's, 1970), p. 428.

64. *The Edinburgh Advertiser*, 11–14 March 1777, pp. 163; 164.

65. *The Edinburgh Advertiser*, 11–14 March 1777, p. 173.

66. *The Caledonian Mercury*, 15 March 1777.

67. *The Edinburgh Evening Courant*, 22 March 1777.

68. *The Pennsylvania Evening Post*, 5 April 1777, p. 186; *Freeman's Journal or New-Hampshire Gazette*, 31 May 1777.

69. *The Independent Chronicle*, 10 April 1777.

70. *The Pennsylvania Evening Post*, 5 April 1777, p. 210.

71. Kenneth Morgan, *Bristol and the Atlantic Trade in the Eighteenth Century* (Cambridge: Cambridge University Press, 1993), pp. 10–11.

72. *Freeman's Journal or New-Hampshire Gazette*, 31 May 1777; *The Norwich Packet; and the Connecticut, Massachusetts, New Hampshire & Rhode-Island Weekly Advertiser*, 26 May–2 June 1777.

73. More than two hundred years would pass before Aitken was recognized for his questionable part in the American Revolution. That recognition is to be found in the unlikeliest of spots: a website maintained by the Central Intelligence Agency. His name appears under the dubious rubric of "wartime special operations," where the plan that he presented to Deane is described as "sabotage," and not as terrorism.

EPILOGUE

1. *The London Magazine*, March 1777, p. 115.

2. Samuel Johnson, *A Dictionary of the English Language*, vol. 1 (London: J. Knapton; T. and T. Longman; C. Hitch and L. Hawes; A. Millar; and R. and J. Dodsley, 1755).

3. Thomas Sheridan, *A General Dictionary of the English Language*, vol. 1 (London: J. Dodsley; C. Dilly; J. Wilkie, 1780).

4. "Trial of James Hill," col. 1319.

JESSICA WARNER is the author of *Craze: Gin and Debauchery in an Age of Reason*. Born and raised in Washington, D.C., she is a graduate of Princeton and Yale. She works as a research scientist at the Centre for Addiction and Mental Health and as an assistant professor in the Department of Psychiatry at the University of Toronto.